Communications in Computer and Information Science 1658

T0207324

More information about this series at https://link.springer.com/bookseries/7899

Rafael Valencia-García ·
Martha Bucaram-Leverone ·
Javier Del Cioppo-Morstadt · Néstor Vera-Lucio ·
Emma Jácome-Murillo (Eds.)

Technologies and Innovation

8th International Conference, CITI 2022
Guayaquil, Ecuador, November 14–17, 2022
Proceedings

Editors
Rafael Valencia-García ⓘ
Universidad de Murcia
Murcia, Spain

Martha Bucaram-Leverone ⓘ
Universidad Agraria del Ecuador
Guayaquil, Ecuador

Javier Del Cioppo-Morstadt ⓘ
Universidad Agraria del Ecuador
Guayaquil, Ecuador

Néstor Vera-Lucio ⓘ
Universidad Agraria del Ecuador
Guayaquil, Ecuador

Emma Jácome-Murillo ⓘ
Universidad Agraria del Ecuador
Guayaquil, Ecuador

ISSN 1865-0929   ISSN 1865-0937 (electronic)
Communications in Computer and Information Science
ISBN 978-3-031-19960-8   ISBN 978-3-031-19961-5 (eBook)
https://doi.org/10.1007/978-3-031-19961-5

This Springer imprint is published by the registered company Springer Nature Switzerland AG
The registered company address is: Gewerbestrasse 11, 6330 Cham, Switzerland

Preface

The 8th International Conference on Technologies and Innovation (CITI 2022) was held during November 14–17, 2022, in Guayaquil, Ecuador. The CITI series of conferences aims to become an international framework and meeting point for professionals who are mainly devoted to research, development, innovation, and university teaching within the field of computer science and technology applied to any important field of innovation. CITI 2022 was organized as a knowledge-exchange conference consisting of several contributions about current innovative technology. These proposals deal with the most important aspects and future prospects from an academic, innovative, and scientific perspective. The goal of the conference to investigate the feasibility of advanced and innovative methods and techniques and their application in different domains in the field of computer science and information systems, which represents innovation in current society.

We would like to express our gratitude to all the authors who submitted papers to CITI 2022, and our congratulations to those whose papers were accepted. There were 48 submissions this year. Each submission was reviewed by at least three Program-Committee (PC) members. Only the papers with an average score of ≥ 1.0 were considered for final inclusion, and almost all accepted papers had positive reviews. Finally, the PC decided to accept 19 full papers.

We would also like to thank the Program Committee members, who agreed to review the manuscripts in a timely manner and provided valuable feedback to the authors.

November 2022

Rafael Valencia-García
Martha Bucaram-Leverone
Javier Del Cioppo-Morstadt
Néstor Vera-Lucio
Emma Jácome-Murillo

Organization

Honorary Committee

Martha Bucaram-Leverone	Universidad Agraria del Ecuador, Ecuador
Javier Del Cioppo-Morstadt	Universidad Agraria del Ecuador, Ecuador
Emma Jácome-Murillo	Universidad Agraria del Ecuador, Ecuador
Teresa Samaniego Cobo	Universidad Agraria del Ecuador, Ecuador

Program Chairs

Rafael Valencia-García	Universidad de Murcia, Spain
Martha Bucaram-Leverone	Universidad Agraria del Ecuador, Ecuador
Javier Del Cioppo-Morstadt	Universidad Agraria del Ecuador, Ecuador
Néstor Vera-Lucio	Universidad Agraria del Ecuador, Ecuador
Emma Jácome-Murillo	Universidad Agraria del Ecuador, Ecuador

Program Committee

Jacobo Bucaram Ortiz	Universidad Agraria del Ecuador, Ecuador
Martha Bucaram-Leverone	Universidad Agraria del Ecuador, Ecuador
Rina Bucaram Leverone	Universidad Agraria del Ecuador, Ecuador
Rafael Valencia-García	Universidad de Murcia, Spain
Ricardo Colomo-Palacios	Ostfold University College, Norway
Ghassan Beydoun	University of Technology Sydney, Australia
Antonio A. López-Lorca	University of Melbourne, Australia
Chunguo Wu	Jillin University, China
Siti Hajar Othman	Universiti Teknologi Malaysia, Malaysia
Anatoly Gladun	V.M.Glushkov Institute of Cybernetics, National Academy Sciences of Ukraine, Ukraine
Aarón Ayllón-Benítez	Université de Bordeaux, France
Giner Alor-Hernández	Instituto Tecnológico de Orizaba, Mexico
José Luis Ochoa	Universidad de Sonora, México
Ana Muñoz	Universidad Técnica Federico Santa María, Chile
Miguel Ángel Rodríguez-García	Universidad Rey Juan Carlos, Spain
Lucía Serrano-Luján	Universidad Rey Juan Carlos, Spain
Eugenio Martínez-Cámara	Universidad de Granada, Spain
José Antonio García-Díaz	Universidad de Murcia, Spain
José Antonio Miñarro-Giménez	Universidad de Murcia, Spain

Ángel García Pedrero	Universidad Politécnica de Madrid, Spain
Miguel Vargas-Lombardo	Universidad Tecnologica de Panama, Panama
Denis Cedeño Moreno	Universidad Tecnologica de Panama, Panama
Viviana Yarel Rosales Morales	Instituto Tecnologico de Orizaba, Mexico
Claudia Victoria Isaza Narvaez	Universidad de Antioquia, Colombia
Raquel Vasquez Ramirez	Instituto Tecnologico de Orizaba, Mexico
Janio Jadán Guerrero	Universidad Indoamérica, Ecuador
Yordani Cruz Segura	Universidad de las Ciencias Informáticas. Cuba
Freddy Tapia León	Universidad de las Fuerzas Armadas ESPE, Ecuador
Nemury Silega Martínez	Universidad de las Ciencias Informáticas, Cuba
Astrid Duque Ramos	Universidad de Antioquia, Colombia
Nelson Becerra Correa	Universidad Distrital Francisco José de Caldas, Colombia
Alireza khackpour	Ostfold University College, Norway
Mary Sánchez-Gordon	Ostfold University College, Norway
María José Marín Pérez	Universidad de Murcia, Spain
Ángela Almela	Universidad de Murcia, Spain

Local Organizing Committee

Katty Lagos-Ortiz	Universidad Agraria del Ecuador, Ecuador
Teresa Samaniego-Cobo	Universidad Agraria del Ecuador, Ecuador
Néstor Vera-Lucio	Universidad Agraria del Ecuador, Ecuador

Sponsoring Institutions

http://www.uagraria.edu.ec/

Contents

Apps and User Interfaces

Machine Learning

A Machine Learning Study About the Vulnerability Level of Poverty in Perú

Henry A. Silva Marchan[1]([⊠]) [iD], Oscar J. M. Peña Cáceres[2] [iD],
Dania M. Ricalde Moran[1] [iD], Teresa Samaniego-Cobo[3] [iD],
and Charles M. Perez-Espinoza[3] [iD]

[1] Universidad Nacional de Tumbes, Tumbes, Peru
{hsilvam,dmricaldem}@untumbes.edu.pe
[2] Universidad Nacional de Piura, Piura, Peru
openaca@unp.edu.pe
[3] Universidad Agraria del Ecuador, Guayaquil, Ecuador
{tsamaniego,cperez}@uagraria.edu.ec

Abstract. In recent years, people have been requiring new livelihoods that allow them to have enough economical resources for the development of their daily activities, considering the problematic that COVID-19 has brought to their lives. The objective of this research was to analyze machine learning algorithms such as Decision Tree, Random Forest, Naive Bayes, Logistic Regression and Vector Support Machine, in order to identify the risk level to fall into poverty for a person in Perú, basing the analysis on the National Household Survey (NHS) that the National Institute of Statistics and Informatics (NISI) provided on 2020. The methodology was presented in four stages, organization and structuring of the database, analysis and identification of the variables, application of the learning algorithms and evaluation of the performance of the aforementioned algorithms. Python programming language and the STATA software allowed the exploration of 91,315 registers and 33 variables. Results showed that the Decision Tree algorithm has an accuracy of 98%, while other algorithms are below the indicated range, so dynamism is expected in the application of this algorithm for socioeconomic areas that can be materialized through a permanent evaluation and analysis platform that helps to focus strategies and proposals for the benefit of the population with economic limitations.

Keywords: Poverty · COVID-19 · Machine learning · Algorithms

1 Introduction

Initial stages of life, such as childhood and puberty, are stages of special vulnerability. Being poor in these stages can affect the opportunities of children and teenagers to develop in the future, and it is highly likely that they will affect them throughout their lives. In 2020, poverty impacted this specific population at a high rate, in the case of children under 5 years by 43.2%, poverty affected 41.9% of children in the range of 5 to

R. Valencia-García et al. (Eds.): CITI 2022, CCIS 1658, pp. 3–14, 2022.
https://doi.org/10.1007/978-3-031-19961-5_1

9 years, and in the case of teenagers, 34.7% were impacted by poverty. This high rates also reach the young adult population from 30 to 44 years of age [1].

In this context, it is necessary to mention that information technologies have evolved in an exorbitant way, which has given rise to the use of automatic learning techniques able to generate estimations, calculate probabilities, and predictions. This research aims to analyze machine learning algorithms such as Decision Tree, Random Forest, Naive Bayes, Logistic Regression and Vector Support Machine, to identify the level of risk of poverty of a person in Perú, based on the National Household Survey (NHS) that the National Institute of Statistics and Informatics (NISI) applied during the year 2020.

Presence of the SARS-COV-2 virus in Perú, which caused COVID-19, was officially reported on March 6, 2020 and on the 25th of the same month, the Supreme decree #94 was officialized, through which social isolation measures aimed at a new social coexistence were arranged. These measures revealed the limitations and deficiencies of the current health system, but also what role should assume the industry and society while dealing with COVID-19 [2].

This research aims to determine which classification model allows identifying how prone an individual is to the risk of being poor in Perú, considering the economic impact generated by COVID-19.

2 Related Work

The economy sector in Perú and in the rest of the world, has begun to promote the application of automatic learning algorithms in order to demonstrate the existing optimization opportunity related to diagnoses and scenarios that involve vulnerable population. This activity is aiming to determine the levels of poverty that may exist in the geographic area of a community, taking into account socioeconomic factors that may affect.

Mahsa et al. determined the household benefits and subsidies through the use of data mining approaches, by which the authors point out that poverty is known as a widespread economic and political challenge, especially in times of crisis, such as COVID-19. This study gathers the visions of data mining and machine learning, tracing a uniform path for the development of current proposals. For this purpose, it was necessary to adopt the social criterion based on parameters such as income and expenses from a data set of 18,885 surveys applied in households, essential elements that were considered to measure the poverty rate of the population and determine to what extent the households are poor or rich [3].

Ochoa et al. revealed in their study, an automatic learning approach for the estimation of multidimensional poverty, that data analysis techniques and social sciences to evaluate the socioeconomic behavior of the population is a potential means that contributes to strengthening the decision making. On the other hand, machine learning algorithms would help reduce the gap on the main problems of the social sciences, such as the shortage of data [4].

The aforementioned investigations showed the need and usefulness of these computational means and that they could be considered as priority elements in order to reduce paths and develop new social policies.

3 Vulnerability of Poverty in Perú

Perú is one of the countries in Latin America with the highest economic growth since the 1990s, through wise macroeconomic policies and structural reforms. Perú went from being a country with triple-digit inflation rates and low growth, to being one of the fastest growing economies in Latin America and the Caribbean, with average growth figures of 5.95% between 2002 and 2013 [2]. It is worth mentioning that since 2002, the Central Reserve Bank of Perú adopted the policy of Explicit Inflation Targets, which allows better management of inflation problems and, therefore, to enjoy macroeconomic stability. Despite having faced an international financial crisis, Perú has always maintained and sought its economic growth. In 2004, the monetary poverty level at the country was 58.7%, and in 2013 it achieved a significant reduction of 34.8% [3]. It is important to point out that the deployment of the Peruvian economy towards growth paths has reduced the incidence of poverty, still, it has not contributed to reduce the vulnerability of falling into it.

Since 2014, Peruvian economy began a slowdown process caused mainly by a reduction in the production of the fishing, mining, and manufacturing sectors, poverty continued to decline, perhaps not at the same rate generated by the years of expansion.

In 2019 poverty was reduced to 20.2% but in the first quarter of 2020, economic growth began to feel its first effects caused by the COVID-19 health crisis, when exports were affected because of measures applied. Measures like restricting the border with China and the United States, situation that is severely affecting the Peruvian economy.

Nevertheless, the situation would worsen in March 2020 with the measures adopted by the Peruvian state, when the first case of COVID-19 was registered. Restrictions were strictly enforced, in which the productive activities of the economy were limited, and companies dedicated to producing essential goods and services were authorized to operate. Overtime, the situation worsened for Peruvian families, especially for those whose livelihood comes from the informal sector and who must generate daily income to survive, this added to the food shortage generated by a collective hysteria against restrictions, the increased price of medicine and personal care products needed to control COVID-19 contagious.

Increase in confirmed cases of the virus and the high number of infections that put to test an obsolete health system, whose investment with respect to GDP was limited, completely destabilized the economy, is so, according to data from the Fund of the United Nations for Children [5] maintains that monetary poverty in Perú in 2020 was 30.3%, which would represent an increase of 10.1% points compared to 2019, showing that all the progress made over 10 years to reduce poverty levels had not caused the desired effect. If absolute values are analyzed, according to INEI [1], poverty affected 9 million 820 thousand people who had a level of expenditure lower than the cost of the basic consumption basket.

Main causes attributed for this setback is the substantial increase in unemployment, caused by the restrictions imposed by the government, in order to reduce capacity in work centers and public and private spaces, to this is added the suspension of working hours which granted employers the power to temporarily paralyze workers payment but without termination of the labor relationship. Measures which generated informal employment increase, [6] as there is no employment, there is no income and, therefore, consumption, affecting the country's production. Informal employment rate in Perú is very high and represents a problem in the labor market, it is expected that it will fluctuate between 70% and 80% for the next twelve years. Regarding this context, labor activities by citizens focused and took refuge in informality, considering that a large percentage of the population had to leave their jobs, a situation that came to be represented in 1.5 million lost jobs [7].

Informality continues to be a pending issue in the policies adopted by the powers of the State, due to the existence of high costs of entering the formal sector, the lack of access to credit and the high tax burden. These results suggest that the reduction of informality could be achieved through policies aimed at strengthening institutions and compliance with laws, in such a way that the pandemic has showed the society the "need" of formal jobs.

Consequently, unemployment has been generating a reduction in purchasing power in families, and therefore in its members, who, because of being unemployed are vulnerable to returning to the level of poverty; considering that family income is one of the most sensitive variables that affect people's vulnerability, since a person who cannot cover the basic family basket in a sustained manner is more susceptible to falling into poverty; it is important to clarify that only formal employment statistics are reported, which does not reflect the true reality in a country where the INEI in 2018 indicated that 72.5% of the economically active population work in informal jobs [8].

Other variable that affects the level of poverty is education, according to INEI, a family whose head of household has a high educational level is less vulnerable to falling into poverty, this is because people who have a greater level of studies can reach higher levels of income, therefore, they can cover at least the basic family basket.

Geographical location is undoubtedly an important variable in Perú to measure poverty, thus in 2020 poverty affected 45.7% of the population in rural areas and 26.0% in urban areas; increasing by 4.9% points and 11.4% points, respectively; when compared to the year 2019 [1].

Therefore, it is necessary to analyze poverty according to the life cycle of the human being and reflect on the rate of extreme poverty that the population in Perú has in recent years, particularly from 2012 to 2021, as shown in Fig. 1.

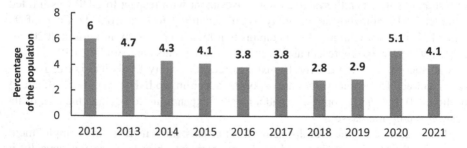

Fig. 1. Extreme poverty in Perú: 2012–2021

4 Review of Classification Algorithms

In recent years there has been a slight increase in studies mainly focused on the application of Machine Learning (ML) through Artificial Intelligence where the aim is to optimize the usage of the growing volume of digital data. The application of these forecasting tools specifically in financial services can derive into significant benefits, as it also helps to reduce the exposure to risks considering that it is a volatile and ambiguous system for society [9]. Among the various Latin American countries, Chile has deployed ML and Big Data activities in order to forecast the general and underlying inflation of the Consumer Price Index, and some of the conclusions reveal that ML methods are not the best in projecting inflation over simple linear and univariate competitors [10].

Forecast of formal employment in several cities of the world has become a necessity but also an obligation, particularly in Colombia, the need to examine the occupational rate in 62 cities reflect the increase of formal employment rates, therefore, some of the applied alternatives were oriented on the Ordinary Least Squares algorithms of ML, with results showing that the participation of active population in formal employment would increase between 13 and 32 points [11].

Perú has been affected by similar events, studies related to the prediction of credit risks through ML have presented favorable results for the financial system and the Peruvian state, due to the fact that the activity of microcredits granting was dynamized through the application of technologies such as ML and establish a continuous improvement to the predominance of the identified variables [12].

The process of choosing an appropriate classification algorithm for a particular task requires some experience and practice, considering that each algorithm has its own characteristics and is defined based on different assumptions according to the context in which we find ourselves.

Eventually, the performance of a classification algorithm, both in terms of computational performance and predictive power, will depend on the data available for the learning process. The five main steps involved in training a machine learning algorithm can be summarized as: select features, choose a performance measure, choose a classification algorithm, evaluate model performance and finally, tune the algorithm [13].

4.1 Decision Tree Model

Decision trees are versatile Machine Learning algorithms that can perform both classification and regression tasks, even multi-output tasks, because they are considered powerful algorithms capable of fitting complex data sets [14].

The classification tree and regression algorithm procedure is based on non-parametric analysis and facilitates work with independent, dependent, continuous and categorical variables, which offers an advantage over other algorithms such as automated chi-square interaction detection which performs the classification function on the basis of independent categorical variables [15].

4.2 Random Forest Model

A random forest model is an assembly of decision trees, usually trained using the bagging method, usually with max_samples sets which size are in proportion to the training set. The random forest algorithm introduces extra randomness when it grows trees; instead of looking for the best feature, when you split a node, it looks for the best feature in a random subset of features [16].

It is a predictive model based on the combinations of multiple and diverse decision trees. Among its advantages there is the reduction of the generalization error while using a greater number of trees to build the model. [17].

4.3 Naïve Bayes Model

Bayes' theorem is an equation that describes the relation of conditional probabilities of statistical quantities [8]. In Bayesian classification we are interested in finding the probability of a class occurring, given some observed characteristics of the data. Bayes' theorem shows how we can express it in terms of quantities that can be calculated directly.

The Naïve-Bayes Classifier (NBC) algorithm is a simple probabilistic classifier with a strong independence assumption. Although the assumption of attribute independence is generally a poor assumption and is often uncertain for true data sets, it usually provides better classification accuracy on real-time datasets than any other classifier [18].

4.4 Logistic Regression Model

It is one of the most widely used algorithms for classification in the industry, similar to the perceptron and Adeline, the logistic regression model is also a binary classification model that can be extended to multiclass classification [13].

In logistic regression, the dependent variable can be dichotomous, it means that it can apply for two categories, nominal polynomial, fitting in three or more categories with a non-natural order, or ordinal polynomial, which is based on three or more categories with a natural order[19].

From a set of input data, the output will be discrete and not continuous by using the Logistic Regression algorithm [20]. Logistic Regression is a supervised algorithm and is used for classification. In this case, it was classified into output values, where the value of 1 indicates that the person is in a state of poverty and 2 in a state of non-poverty.

4.5 Support Vector Machine Model

A Support Vector Machine (SVM) is a versatile and powerful machine learning model, capable of performing linear or non-linear classifications, regressions and even outlier detection [21]. It is one of the most popular machine learning models and anyone interested in the subject should include it in their toolbox. SVMs work especially well for classifying small to medium sized complex data sets.

The SVM is a method that achieves high degrees of correct classification in several types of applications. It is a supervised learning algorithm, which works as a linear classifier that separates the data into two classes. Basically, the algorithm finds among the various hyperplanes that separate these two classes, the ideal hyperplane that maximizes the margin between the support vectors [19].

5 Data Extraction

After emphasizing the various models framed in automatic learning algorithms, it was defined the data to be used, data presented by the national household survey and applied by the Institute of Statistics and Informatics of Perú during 2020. This survey is made up of 29 modules, of which it was necessary to use the data corresponding to modules 2, 3 and 5, because they provided the characteristics of household members, education, jobs and income, respectively. In addition to this, it was necessary to use the STATA tool to obtain the data and to know the composition of each of the variables described in Table 1.

Data source[1] has 91,315 records, where 80% was used for training activities and 20% for the test set.

Table 1. Extracted variables from the national household survey

Variable	Module	Description
Conglomerate	Module 2	Cluster number
Housing		Housing selection number
Home		Household sequential number
Codperso		Person order number
Ubigeo		Geographic location
Domain		Geographic domain
Stratum		Geographic stratum
p203		Relationship to the head of the household
p207		Sex
p208a		Age in completed years
p209		marital or marital status
facpob07		Annual expansion factor
p301a	Module 3	Last grade of studies passed
p301b		Final year of studies
p301c		Last degree of studies
p301d		Study center
i541a		Total income in your secondary occupation

Figure 2 shows how the databases were merged horizontally, to proceed with the generation of variables, such as the total number of hours worked, monthly salary, weekly salary and weekly hourly salary.

Google Collaboratory, widely known as Google Colab, is an open-source service provided by Google to anyone with a Gmail account, this tool is mainly helpful while dealing with a large database and no specialized resources. Google Colab makes GPU for research available to people who don't have enough resources or can't afford one [22].

---

[1] https://github.com/OSCARPC/Un-estudio-de-aprendizaje-automatico-para-el-nivel-de-vulner abilidad-de-la-pobreza-en-el-Peru.git.

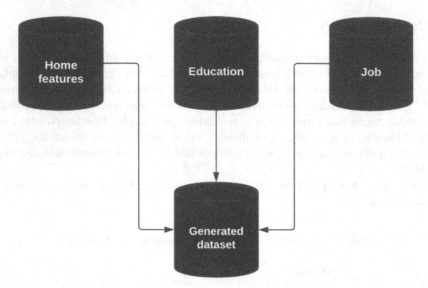

Fig. 2. Horizontal merge of the data extracted from the modules

Google services were used and at the beginnings it was necessary to have a Gmail email account in order to host the dataset in the Google Drive environment, and later link it to the work platform, Google Colab. Google Colab service provides 12.72 GB of RAM and 358.27 GB of hard drive space at runtime. Each runtime lasts for 12 h, after which the runtime restarts and the user has to establish a connection again. Google Colab allows to generate programming code, in this research it allowed to program the classification algorithms in the Python programming language.

Python is a simple, fast and lightweight programming language and is ideal for learning, experimenting, practicing and working on the topics of machine learning, neural networks and deep learning [23], is available for the main operating systems such as Linux, Windows, macOS, without any limit for the development of proposals that help make decisions efficiently and safely for the benefit of the population, particularly.

The classification process was developed in two stages, the first of learning and the second of classification. In the learning phase, the classification algorithm analyzes the training data while in the classification phase, the test data is used to estimate the accuracy of the classification rules. If the precision is acceptable, the rules can be applied to the new data tuples [24].

6 Treatment of Missing Data

It is common to find data sources in which information is not available for some variables in certain records, giving rise to what is known as missing values or missing data, at that can be generated by different causes. For example, non-response to certain questions in a survey such as: age, income, etc. In addition to errors while recording data, errors in the manual entry of data in the database or errors in the measurement instruments.

The simplest and most appropriate technique for the treatment of missing data consist in eliminating the database records that contain missing values, which is known as elimination by list, this method can only be applied when the number of instances with missing values is small, keeping in mind that it can introduce significant bias in the data. That is why, when instances with missing data are not eliminated, we assume values for them, a process known as imputation. This process can be done manually, although it is a slow procedure that requires expert knowledge and is an alternative to using automatic imputation techniques.

The automatic imputation techniques are structured in two groups, 1) univariate imputation techniques, focused on assigning values to a single variable, without taking into account the rest of the elements of the database and 2) techniques of multivariate imputation, where the complete database is used for the assignation of the values.

In these cases, reference is made to multivariate data, where there is a set of n individuals, in which p variables have been observed, as indicated in Eqs. (1) and (2).

$$X_1, X_2, ..., X_p \tag{1}$$

$$x_{jk} = \text{value of the kth variable in the jth register } j = 1, \ldots, n \, k = 1, \ldots, p \tag{2}$$

Considering that the univariate imputation technique was used in the study, where the substitution method was applied, which uses a measure of centralization, also known as the arithmetic mean, median for quantitative variables or mode for qualitative variables, which is calculated on the available values of the variable, to replace the missing values.

7   Discussion of Results

The confusion matrix is one of the most widely used and useful means of evaluating the quality of classification models based on machine learning. In particular, when one class is confused with another, it can be clearly displayed, allowing us to handle different types of errors separately.

The accuracy of the model is basically the total number of correct predictions divided by the total number of predictions, it refers to how close the measurement re-sult is to the true value, in statistical terms [25]. In a practical way, the accuracy is the number of positive predictions that were correct, in this case 80% of the data was framed in the training section and 20% in the test section.

According to the National Institute of Statistics and Informatics, a person is considered vulnerable to poverty when their monthly income is less than three hundred soles (S/. 344.00) and when facing a binary classification problem, the output variable whose value is 1, for those poor people and 2 for a non-poor person.

The result of the classification algorithms indicated in Sect. 2, are reflected in Table 2, the same ones that reveal which is more efficient, both in the training and testing stage. In addition to this, it is important to specify that a cross-validation was carried out, an aspect that revealed the false positives and false negatives within the training set.

The precision in the training and test criteria expressed in Table 2 indicate that the Decision Tree and Random Forest algorithms are the most convenient to use for this type

Table 2. Accuracy comparison of classification models

Algorithm - Model	Training	Test
Decision tree	0.99	0.98
Random forest	0.99	0.98
Naïve bayes	0.80	0.80
Logistic regression	0.77	0.78
Support vector machine	0.85	0.79

of study, considering that the data set represents a good volume to exploit and obtain results closer to reality. However, to this, the Support Vector Machine, Naive Bayes and Logistic Regression algorithms have represented close results, the same ones that could be considered for very particular studies and on a different scale.

8 Conclusion

It has been established that access to open data is one of the means that contributes to the development of studies framed in machine learning. However, it is important to mention that the data available in the ENAHO must go through a pre-processing stage and thus have an integrated and transparent structure that reflects as little noise as possible. Programming techniques contributed to this work, through the Python programming language, which showed to have the capacity, versatility and dynamism at the time of data ordering.

One of the limitations of the study was to identify and characterize the variables, due to the fact that a data dictionary was not available, so it is essential that institutions promote a digital government through an open access portal with the purpose that researchers, organizations and private companies carry out studies without gaps that discourage the good intentions of contributing to society.

Given the lack of technological infrastructure, the Google Colab platform contributed to the development of this study, where the Decision Tree, Random Forest, Naive Bayes, Logistic Regression and Support Vector Machine algorithms were coded and executed. The training and test results were evaluated through a confusion matrix, identifying that the Decision Tree and Random Forest have represented an accuracy of 98%, however, the tests carried out determine that the Decision Tree algorithm expresses a better prediction about a person being poor or not.

It is important to point out that the study is fragmented in a period of time, corresponding to the year 2020, whose rate of job opportunities was very low, however, it is the best reference to develop proposals and alternatives of a strategic nature to boost employability in geographic sectors with greater exposure and reduce the number of gaps that do not contribute to develop a better quality of life for human beings.

To exploit the 29 data modules offered by the ENAHO, it is proposed to experiment with the application of tools such as Hadoop and Apache Spark, as they are linked to Big Data methods and techniques for the analysis of large data sources that allow to reveal new behavior patterns between the modules of Education, Health, Transportation and Communications, which could contribute to the development of time lines and also the state can adopt new employability policies, which help reduce this poverty gap in the Peruvian population.

It is recommended that future research in this area of study make use of a set of historical data from 2004 to 2021, in order to improve the quality of results and an evaluation of the post-pandemic scenario, also to know if the conditions about facing poverty in Perú have improved or in which state they are.

References

1. National Institute of Statistics and Informatics, Peru: Evolution of Monetary Poverty 2009, 2020 (2021)
2. Vargas, C.M.: Reflections on COVID-19 infection, Medical College of Perú and the public health. Acta Med. Perú **37**, 8–10 (2020). https://doi.org/10.35663/amp.2020.371.929
3. Mahsa Alavi, S., Omid Mahdi Ebadati, A.E., Masoud Alavi, S.A., Firoozan Sarnaghi, T.: Determination of households benefits from subsidies by using data mining approaches. J. Inform. Technol. Polit. 1 (2022). https://doi.org/10.1080/19331681.2022.2097974
4. Guaraca, M.E.O., Castro, R., Pallaroso, A.A., Machado, A., Sucozhañay, D.: Machine learning approach for multidimensional poverty estimation. Revista Tecnológica - ESPOL **33**(2), 205–225 (2021). https://doi.org/10.37815/rte.v33n2.853
5. United Nations Children's Fund: COVID-19: Impact on poverty and inequality in children and adolescents in Perú. Estimations 2020–2021. UNICEF (2020)
6. Manayay, D.T.: El empleo informal en el Perú: Una breve caracterización 2007–2018. Pensamiento Crítico **25**(1), 51–75 (2020). https://doi.org/10.15381/pc.v25i1.18477
7. Gamero, J., Pérez, J.: Perú > Impact of COVID-19 on employment and labor income. Organización Internacional de Trabajo 1 (2020). https://www.ilo.org/wcmsp5/groups/public/---ame ricas/---ro-lima/documents/publication/wcms_756474.pdf
8. Barreto, I.B., Sánchez, R.M.S., Marchan, H.A.S.: Consecuencias económicas y sociales de la inamovilidad humana bajo Covid – 19 caso de estudio Perú. Lecturas de Economía **94**, 285–303 (2021). https://doi.org/10.17533/udea.le.n94a344397
9. Fernández, A.: I Artificial intelligence in financial services. Analytical articles. Econ. Bull. Scielo. **5**, 10 (2019)
10. Leal, F., Molina, C., Zilberman, E.: Projection of Inflation in Chile with Machine Learning Methods. Chile Central Bank (2020)
11. Lora, E.: Forecasting formal employment in cities. Econ. Bull. Rosario. **24**, 1–38 (2021). https://doi.org/10.12804/revistas.urosario.edu.co/economia/a.10029
12. Aceituno Rojo, M.R.: Predictive model of credit risk analysis using Machine Learning in an entity of the microfinance sector. UNA-Puno, vol. 102 (2019)
13. Raschka, S., Mirjalili, V.: A tour of machine learning classifiers with scikit-learn. In: Python Machine Learning, pp. 73–127. Spain (2019)
14. Géron, A.: Decision tree. In: Learn Machine Learning with Scikit-Learn, Keras and TensorFlow, p. 197 (2019)
15. Ávila-Toscano, J.H., Pérez, I.R., Guajardo, E.S., Marenco-Escuderos, A.: Influencia de la producción de nuevo conocimiento y tesis de postgrado en la categorización de los grupos de investigación en Ciencias Sociales: árbol de decisiones aplicado al modelo científico colombiano. Revista española de Documentación Científica **41**(4), 218 (2018). https://doi.org/10. 3989/redc.2018.4.1547

16. Géron, A.: Random forest. In: Learn Machine Learning wih Scikit-Learn, Keras and TensorFlow, p. 216 (2019)
17. Quintana-Zaez, I.J.C., Velarde-Bedregal, H.R., Anton-Vargas, J., Joaquim-Luis, G.: Schemes of combination of decision trees as a strategy for anomaly detection. In: Proceedings of the LACCEI International Multi-Conference Engineering Education Technology (2020). https://doi.org/10.18687/LACCEI2020.1.1.306
18. Mosquera, R., Castrillón, O.D., Parra, L.: Support vector machines, Naïve Bayes classifier and genetic algorithms for the prediction of psychosocial risks in teachers of Colombian public schools. Inf. Tecnol. **29**, 153–162 (2018). https://doi.org/10.4067/S0718-076420180 0600153
19. Godoy Viera, A.F.: Machine learning techniques used for text mining. Bibl. Res. **31**, 103–126 (2017). https://doi.org/10.22201/IIBI.0187358XP.2017.71.57812
20. Bagnato, J.I.: Logistic regression. In: Learn Machine Learning in Spanish - Theory + Practice Python. p. 43. España (2020)
21. Zhang, D.: Support vector machine. In: Fundamentals of Image Data Mining. TCS, pp. 179–205. Springer, Cham (2019). https://doi.org/10.1007/978-3-030-17989-2_8
22. Kanani, P., Padole, M.: Deep learning to detect skin cancer using google colab. Int. J. Eng. Adv. Technol. **8**(6), 2176–2183 (2019). https://doi.org/10.35940/ijeat.F8587.088619
23. Bagnato, J.I.: Install the python development environment. In: Learn Machine Learning in Spanish - Theory + Practice Python, p. 7 (2020)
24. Zárate-Valderrama, J., Bedregal-Alpaca, N., Cornejo-Aparicio, V.: Classification models to recognize patterns of desertion in university students. Ingeniare **29**, 168–177 (2021). https://doi.org/10.4067/S0718-33052021000100168
25. Bagnato, J.I.: Metrics and confusion matrix. In: Learn Machine Learning in Spanish - Theory + Practice Python, pp. 79–82 (2020)

Predicting Academic Performance in Mathematics Using Machine Learning Algorithms

Carlos Alberto Espinosa-Pinos[1]([✉]) [iD], Ignacio Ayala-Chauvín[2] [iD],
and Jorge Buele[3,4] [iD]

[1] Carrera de Psicología, Facultad de Ciencias Humanas y de la Salud, Universidad Tecnológica Indoamérica, Ambato 180103, Ecuador
carlosespinosa@indoamerica.edu.ec
[2] Centro de Investigaciones de Ciencias Humanas y de la Educación CICHE, Universidad Indoa-mérica, Ambato 180103, Ecuador
mayala@uti.edu.ec
[3] Carrera de Ingeniería Industrial, Facultad de Ingeniería y Tecnologías de la Información y la Comunicación, Universidad Indoamérica, Ambato 180103, Ecuador
jorgebuele@uti.edu.ec
[4] Department of Electronic Engineering and Communications, University of Zaragoza, 44003 Teruel, Spain

Abstract. Several factors, directly and indirectly, influence students' performance in their various activities. Children and adolescents in the education process generate enormous data that could be analyzed to promote changes in current educational models. Therefore, this study proposes using machine learning algorithms to evaluate the variables influencing mathematics achievement. Three models were developed to identify behavioral patterns such as passing or failing achievement. On the one hand, numerical variables such as grades in exams of other subjects or entrance to higher education and categorical variables such as institution financing, student's ethnicity, and gender, among others, are analyzed. The methodology applied was based on CRISP-DM, starting with the debugging of the database with the support of the Python library, Sklearn. The algorithms used are Decision Tree (DT), Naive Bayes (NB), and Random Forest (RF), the last one being the best, with 92% accuracy, 98% recall, and 97% recovery. As mentioned above, the attributes that best contribute to the model are the entrance exam score for higher education, grade exam, and achievement scores in linguistic, scientific, and social studies domains. This confirms the existence of data that help to develop models that can be used to improve curricula and regional education regulations.

Keywords: Supervised learning · Academic performance · Machine learning · Random forest

1 Introduction

The educational system is incorporating essential changes in its conventional models. Technology is becoming a pillar of support to improve the academic environment and teaching conditions. Several applications and devices are being developed daily to strengthen educational methodologies [1]. Educational technologies focus on facilitating the planning and orientation of the learning process [2]. Among its benefits are acquiring new knowledge and promoting teamwork, creativity, and autonomy [3, 4]. All this interaction generates a considerable amount of data that, if properly analyzed, can create guidelines to improve the quality of education. Using data mining methods, machine learning, and other statistical techniques allows the discovery of patterns of student behavior [5]. The objective of this new trend in research is to contribute to the improvement of student skills. They can also provide information explaining their limitations or obstacles to better performance [6].

Low performance in mathematics is a widespread problem in educational systems in a large part of the world. The Program for International Student Assessment [7] has investigated this condition, confirming this problem. Students from Bhutan, Cambodia, Honduras, Paraguay, Panama, and Ecuador do not reach level 2, which refers to the essential acquisition of mathematical skills. Evaluated students can only obtain information from a single source and apply basic methods to solve problems with integers with the help of formulas or algorithms. Ecuador participated for the first time in the PISA-D 2018 tests, where a sample of 6,108 students from 173 fiscal, fiscomisional, municipal and private schools was taken. 70.9% of the students did not obtain level 2 (377/1000) in mathematics. In reading competence (ability to understand, use, reflect on and interact with written texts), the average was 409, which in this case is equivalent to level 2. While in science, 52.7% of students also did not reach the basic level of skills [8].

Several factors are related to low academic performance in the subject of mathematics. Internal factors positively affect academic performance, such as self-esteem, self-concept, previous knowledge, attitude towards the subject, perceived self-efficacy, and motivation. External factors can also be named, which can be family and other socioeconomic factors. Parents' educational level and expectations directly correlate with academic performance [9]. Numerous studies positively link the educational level of parents with good academic performance. It is assumed that the greater the number of years of study of the parents, the greater the time dedicated to supervising and accompanying their children's schoolwork [10]. Gender may also be a factor to consider, as females obtained higher scores than males. Students who have not failed subjects also perform better than those who have. Finally, there is a high correlation between English test scores and cumulative grade point averages [11].

This has led to the development of several research studies in which attempts are made to identify the conditions that influence academic performance [12]. Most commonly, these conditions are assessed in school-age children, as developed in [13]. Physical activity, diet, and parental education can influence their academic performance and quality of life. STEM (Science, Technology, Engineering, and Mathematics) education as shown in [14]. Here, eight machine learning (ML) algorithms are used to generate different models that aim to predict student performance.

Considering the WHO recommendations, evaluating people's mental health at all stages is essential. In [15], they review various psychological aspects and analyze whether they influence the performance of those who begin their university education. Also, the changes in modern societies, interconnectivity, and Internet use could affect human behavior. In [16], they propose identifying an association between academic performance and using machine learning to use Internet resources. It could even be evaluated whether social networks distract students from meeting their academic objectives using ML, as proposed in [17]. Current algorithms offer so many variants that it is already submitted to combine them to obtain hybrid models that could have better results [18].

While several types of research include the most current machine learning algorithms, the existing approaches still require further analysis [19]. Current aspects such as social networks or internet usage have been evaluated, but most focus on which algorithm has the best results. No emphasis is placed on knowing which variables have the most significant impact on student performance in Ecuador. Even though studies already exist in other parts of the world, the study's objective is to learn about the behavior of this population in particular. Therefore, in this article, three different models were developed, which allow us to identify which one has higher percentages of pre-accuracy, memory, and retrieval. At the same time, socio-economic indicators, demographics, and academic performance in other subjects are evaluated to define whether they can be used as predictors of good performance in mathematics.

This paper consists of four sections, including the introduction in the first section. Section 2 describes the proposed methodology, and Sect. 3 the results. Finally, the conclusions are presented in Sect. 4.

2 Methodology

The model application methodology was based on CRISP-DM (Cross Industry Process for Data Mining), frequently applied in data mining and machine learning projects. This consists of the model's debugging, adequacy and evaluation when processing the data, as stated by Bronson [20]. The structure begins with the database's construction and the variables' definition. Then the descriptive analysis of the data is presented, and correlations between independent variables are identified. When applying the selected Machine Learning model, the model's performance is evaluated. Subsequently, the results of the chosen model are communicated, and a test is executed together with the operations area.

2.1 Construction of the Base and Definition of Variables

The database corresponds to informative data on high school students in Ecuador, which is freely accessible for download from the Ministerio de Educación y Cultura (MEC) official website[1]. A space in the cloud was designated for storage with the help of "Colaboratory"[2]. Finally, the database was loaded with 34 variables and 514852 records

---

[1] https://educacion.gob.ec/datos-abiertos/.

[2] https://colab.research.google.com/notebooks/welcome.ipynb?hl=es.

using open-source Python code. There are eight numerical variables, six ordinal categorical variables, and 20 nominal categorical variables. The variables related to socioeconomic indexes are ethnic self-identification, disabilities, sex, evaluation regime, natural region, province, and year of birth, among the main ones. Quantitative and qualitative achievement variables include the scientific, mathematical, linguistic, and social studies domains. The variables used in this study are shown in Table 1.

Table 1. Description of variables used.

Type	Variable	Label
Numeric	imat	Grade obtained in the mathematical domain
	inev	Grade obtained in the grade exam
	pes	Grade obtained for application to higher education
	ilyl	Grade obtained in the linguistic domain
	icn	Grade obtained in the scientific domain
	ies	Grade obtained in social studies
Categoric	es_regeva	Evaluation system
	id_zona	Educational planning area
	tp_sost	Type of support of the educational institution
	tp_sexo	Gender
	id_prov	Province
	tp_area	Area of settlement of the educational institution
	etnibbe	Ethnicity
	financiamiento	Type of financing of the educational institution

2.2 Descriptive Analysis

When a respondent has not completed the respective information, the record is completed with "999999". These records are identified and replaced with blanks as the first filtering filter. The numbering above indicates no data recorded for the individual surveyed. Then the records mentioned above are replaced by the median in the case of numerical variables because there are outliers in each case. In the case of categorical variables, the mode is used because it is the most representative value and thus reduces the bias in the information. Box plots were also used for each variable, and their mean was analyzed to avoid bias in the processing and to interpret the data. The code developed in Python is presented in Program code 1.

Program code 1. Median and mode replacement code

```
data['isec'] = data['isec'].fillna(data['isec'].median())

data['inev'] = data['inev'].fillna(data['inev'].median())

data['pes'] = data['pes'].fillna(data['pes'].median())

data['imat'] = data['imat'].fillna(data['imat'].median())

data['ilyl'] = data['ilyl'].fillna(data['ilyl'].median())

data['icn'] = data['icn'].fillna(data['icn'].median())

data['ies'] = data['ies'].fillna(data['ies'].median())

data['ies'] = data['financiamiento'].replace({np.nan:1})

data['tp_sost'] = data['tp_sost'].replace({np.nan:4})

data['etnibbe'] = data['etnibbe'].replace({np.nan:4})

data['quintil'] = data['quintil'].replace({np.nan:1})

data['nl_inev'] = data['nl_inev'].replace({np.nan:1})

data['nl_imat'] = data['nl_imat'].replace({np.nan:1})

data['nl_ilyl'] = data['nl_ilyl'].replace({np.nan:1})

data['nl_icn'] = data['nl_icn'].replace({np.nan:1})

data['nl_ies'] = data['nl_ies'].replace({np.nan:1})

data['deshonestidad'] = data['deshonestidad'].replace({np.nan:2})
```

The next step is to evaluate the variables that can be considered predictors of the output variable "imat". In the first instance, the categorical variables are analyzed, and, as an example, the zone category (id_zona) is presented about the grade obtained in mathematics (Fig. 1). The variable "zona_id" is a good predictor because the median for each subcategory tends to be the same, approximately between 7.75 and 8.1. This criterion is repeated with all the categorical variables and allows us to define those that can be qualified as good predictors. These are "es_regeva", "id_zona", "tp_sost", "tp_sexo", "id_prov", "tp_area", "etnibbe" and "financiamiento".

2.3 Correlations

To select the numerical attributes related to "imat" we determined a correlation matrix by applying Spearman's statistic. The data obtained are shown in Table 2. The numerical variables that best predict mathematics achievement are "inev" with a correlation of 0.78 and "pes" with 0.65. Also, with a lower value are "ilyl" with 0.65, "icn" with 0.60, and "ies" with 0.59. The variables "inev" and "pes" are directly related since they result from students' tests at the end of their secondary school studies. It should be considered that a test may not be an indicator of good knowledge but rather reflect the ability to memorize or analyze a particular problem. On the other hand, the variables "ilyl", "icn", and "ies" are the grades obtained in the remaining domains (language, natural sciences, and social sciences), which show the student's tendencies in a multiple-knowledge assessment. The other numerical and sociodemographic variables present low correlation values and are not part of the analysis.

```
[  ]  sns.boxplot(x="id_zona", y="imat", data=data) #buen predictor
```

```
<matplotlib.axes._subplots.AxesSubplot at 0x7fb38915ad10>
```

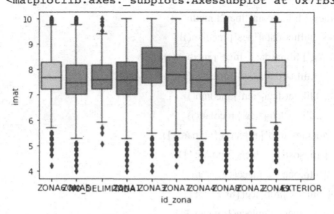

Fig. 1. Box plot for categorical variable.

Table 2. Correlation matrix obtained in Python.

	V1	V2	V3	V4	V5	V6	V7	V8	V9	V10
V1	1.0000	0.9956	−0.010	0.0176	0.0188	0.0409	0.0037	0.0069	0.0189	0.0302
V2	0.9956	1.0000	−0.010	0.0158	0.0180	0.0398	0.0028	0.0060	0.0183	0.0293
V3	−0.010	−0.010	1.0000	0.1666	0.2483	0.3252	0.2299	0.2208	0.1767	0.1726
V4	0.0176	0.0158	0.1666	1.0000	0.2343	0.2672	0.1993	0.2381	0.2067	0.1983
V5	0.0188	0.0180	0.2483	0.2343	1.0000	0.7305	0.7782	0.8380	0.8363	0.8130
V6	0.0409	0.0398	0.3252	0.2671	0.7305	1.0000	0.6513	0.6715	0.6180	0.6050
V7	0.0037	0.0028	0.2299	0.1993	0.7782	0.6513	1.0000	0.6457	0.6043	0.5853
V8	0.0069	0.0060	0.2208	0.2381	0.8380	0.6715	0.6457	1.0000	0.6834	0.6557
V9	0.0189	0.0183	0.1767	0.2067	0.8363	0.6180	0.6043	0.6834	1.0000	0.6684
V10	0.0302	0.0293	0.1726	0.1983	0.8130	0.6050	0.5853	0.6557	0.6684	1.0000

V1 = id_cant, V2 = id_parr, V3 = na_eano, V4 = isec, V5 = inev, V6 = pes, V7 = imat, V8 = ilyl, V9 = icn, V10 = ies.

2.4 Machine Learning Model

Supervised learning consists of taking a series of inputs x and outputs y to train the model with the statistical algorithms offered according to the structure of the data. So that when the system encounters a new input, it can decide on its output [21, 22]. For this application, a cutoff value of 8 is established in the database, making a relationship of a score of 800/1000 in the university entrance exam. With this information, we generate a model with each machine learning tool: Decision Tree, Random Forest, and Naive Bayes. Based on the literature, different authors agree on the need to test other models.

After configuring their hyper-parameters, the results are evaluated under the metrics of interest to solve the problem, choose the one with the best performance, and go deeper [23].

Decision Trees. With this nonparametric supervised learning method, classification and regression can be performed. The objective is to create a model that predicts the value of a target variable by learning simple decision rules inferred from the characteristics of the data [24]. The mathematical formulation, according to [25, 26]. Given the training vectors R $x_i \in R^n, i = 1, ..., l$ and a label vector $y \in R^l$, a decision tree recursively divides the feature space. This way, it obtains clusters of samples with the same labels or similar target values. The data at node "m" are represented by Q_m con N_m samples. Each applicant division $\theta = (j, t_m)$ which consists of a characteristic "j" and threshold t_m, distributes the data in $Q_m^{left}(\theta)$ and $Q_m^{right}(\theta)$ subsets, thus obtaining the Eqs. (1) and (2).

$$Q_m^{left}(\theta) = \{(x, y)|x_j \leq t_m\} \tag{1}$$

$$Q_m^{right}(\theta) = Q_m/Q_m^{left}(\theta) \tag{2}$$

The quality of a candidate node split "m" is calculated using a loss impurity function, where the choice depends on the task to be solved (classification or regression), as presented in (3). Then, parameters are selected that minimize the impurity. $\theta^* = \arg \min_\theta G(Q_m, \theta)$

$$G(Q_m, \theta) = \left(N_m^{left}/N_m\right)H\left(Q_m^{left}(\theta)\right) + \left(N_m^{right}/N_m\right)H\left(Q_m^{right}(\theta)\right) \tag{3}$$

Recursion for subsets $Q_m^{left}(\theta^*)$ and $Q_m^{right}(\theta^*)$ until the maximum allowable depth is reached is $N_m < \min_{samples}$ or $N_m = 1$ [25].

Random Forests. Decision trees tend to present problems when the number of characteristics (columns) is significant; in most cases, it tends to overfit, so the initial problem to be solved increases its level of complexity. The problem is solved by selecting each column randomly and making decision trees for each set of columns, thus developing a learning clustering algorithm that combines a series of weaker models to create a more robust one. Individual decision trees often exhibit considerable variation and tend to over-fit.

The gradient increase for classification is very similar to the regression case. However, the sum of $F_M(x_i) = \sum_m h_m(x_i)$ is not homogeneous for a prediction: it cannot be a class, as trees produce continuous values. The mapping of $F_M(x_i)$ to a class or probability depends on the loss. For the deviation (or logarithmic loss), the probability that x_i belongs to the positive class is modeled as $p(y_i = 1|x_i) = \sigma(F_M(x_i))$, where σ is the sigmoid function. For multiclass classification, k trees (for k classes) are constructed in each M iteration. The probability that x_i belongs to class k is modeled as a softmax of the $F_{M,k}(x_i)$ values [25].

Naïve Bayes. It is related to a set of supervised learning algorithms based on Bayes theorem classification, assuming the naivety of conditional independence between each feature given a class variable value. Bayes' theorem establishes the following relation, given the class variable "y" and the vector of dependent characteristics using and obtaining (4) [25]. These classifiers can be extremely fast compared to more sophisticated methods, but their performance may be inferior depending on the application.

$$P(y|x_1, ..., x_n) = P(y)P(x_1, ..., x_n|y)/P(x_1, ..., x_n) \tag{4}$$

Using the naive assumption of conditional independence described in (5), for all "i", this relation is simplified in (6).

$$P(x_1|y, x_1, ..., x_{i-1}, x_{i+1}, ..., x_n) = P(x_i|y) \tag{5}$$

$$P(y|x_1, ..., x_n) = P(y) \prod_{i=1}^{n} P(x_i|y)/P(x_1, ..., x_n) \tag{6}$$

Since $P(y|x_1, ..., x_n)$ is constant at the input, the classification rule shown in (7) can be used.

$$P(y|x_1, ..., x_n) \propto P(y) \prod_{i=1}^{n} P(x_i|y) \Rightarrow \hat{y} = \arg \max_y P(y) \prod_{i=1}^{n} P(x_i|y) \tag{7}$$

3   Results

After testing the three models, we obtained data that are described below:

3.1   Decision Tree

The training base corresponded to 70% of the total base, and the remaining was used for testing purposes. The results presented below correspond to the test base only. These are encouraging since, for the classification of achievement, 88% accuracy was identified in the model for high scores and 96% for low scores. As for the memory or retrieval process of the model, 86% efficiency for high scores and 97% for low scores. Ultimately according to the f1-score, the model has a classification efficiency of 87% for high scores and 96% for low scores, as presented in the Table 3.

Regarding the confusion matrix of the model, it can be observed that it classifies 86% of true positives and 97% of true negatives. As for the errors, there are 3.1% in false positives and 14% in false negatives (Fig. 2).

3.2   Random Forest

The results for the achievement classification are also good since, according to the precision metric, 94% accuracy was identified in the model for high grades and 97% for

Table 3. Decision tree metrics.

	Precision	Recall	f1-Score	Support
High	0.88	0.86	0.87	33138
Low	0.96	0.97	0.96	121318
Accuracy			0.94	154456
Macro avg	0.92	0.91	0.92	154456
Weighted avg	0.94	0.94	0.94	154456

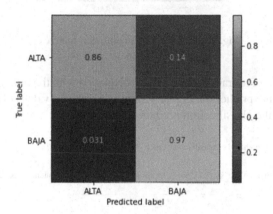

Fig. 2. Decision tree confusion matrix.

Table 4. Random forest metrics.

	Precision	Recall	f1-Score	Support
High	0.94	0.90	0.92	44072
Low	0.97	0.98	0.98	161869
Accuracy			0.97	205941
Macro avg	0.96	0.94	0.95	205941
Weighted avg	0.97	0.97	0.97	205941

low rates. As for the memory or retrieval process, there is 90% for high and 98% for low grades. According to the f1-score, the model has a classification efficiency of 92% for high and 98% for low, as shown in Table 4.

For the model's confusion matrix analysis, it can be observed that it classifies 90% of true positives and 98% of true negatives. The error is 1.6% in false positives and 10% in false negatives, as shown in Fig. 3.

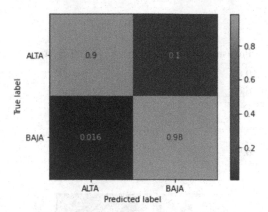

Fig. 3. Random forest confusion matrix.

In addition, using Program code 2, a list is displayed with the individual contribution of each variable in the prediction. Figure 4 shows the relative values of the variables that contribute most to the classification prediction of this model.

Program code 2. Code to visualize the contribution of each predictor variable

---

predictors =
data[['tp_area','etnibbe','tp_sexo','tp_sost','id_prov','id_zona','es_regeva','financiamiento','inev','pes','ilyl','icn','ies']]
targets = data.notas_altas

---

list(model.feature_importances_)	list(predictors)
[0.005484728442717092 , 0.008439363336006242 , 0.012991898676069766 , 0.03308892813657683 , 0.0207099001130441878 , 0.017796969027645413 , 0.00875393697341941 , 0.022389220716036665 , 0.2794456450582253 , 0.1515849074862936 , 0.14298028306744393 , 0.15859983246250228 , 0.13773438650402156]	['tp_area' , 'etnibbe' , 'tp_sexo' , 'tp_sost' , 'id_prov' , 'id_zona' , 'es_regeva' , 'financiamiento' , 'inev' , 'pes' , 'ilyl' , 'icn' , 'ies']

Fig. 4. List each variable's contribution to the Random Forest model.

3.3 Naïve Bayes

The results for the achievement classification are high since 93% accuracy was identified in the model for high scores and 71% for low scores. As for the memory or retrieval process, 92% was found for high grades and 76% for low rates. According to the f1-score, the model has a classification efficiency of 93% for high scores and 74%, as shown in Table 5.

Table 5. Metrics for Bayes' model.

	Precision	Recall	f1-Score	Support
0	0.93	0.92	0.93	80934
1	0.71	0.76	0.74	22037
Accuracy			0.88	102971
Macro avg	0.82	0.84	0.83	102971
Weighted avg	0.89	0.88	0.88	102971

The confusion matrix of the Bayes model classifies 92% of true positives and 76% of true negatives with an error of 24% in false positives and 8.3% in false negatives, as shown in Fig. 5.

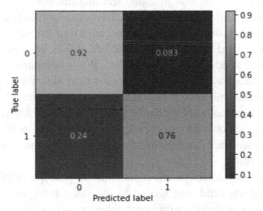

Fig. 5. Confusion matrix for Bayes' model.

According to the model obtained with the random forest, there are characteristics (attributes) that Ecuadorian students possess, according to the information presented in the database downloaded from the MEC. The variables that best contribute to the classification of achievement in mathematics are "inev" with 27.94%, "pes" with 15.16%, "ilyl" with 14.30%, and "icn" with 15.86%, and "ies" with approximately 13.77%. As for the categorical attributes, the variable "tp_sost" contributes 3.3%, "financiamiento" 2.2%, "id_prov" 2.1%, "id_zona" 1.8% and "tp_sex" 1.3%.

The metrics for the Decision Tree model are 87%, 96%, and 94%, respectively, while for Naïve Bayes, there are 93%, 74%, and 88%, respectively. The best model according to precision, recall, and accuracy metrics is the Random Forest with 92%, 98%, and 97%, respectively. This indicates that the model has a classification power of 92000 per 100000 data, classification recall of 98000 per 100000 data, and 97000 hits per 100000 classification observations.

3.4 Discussion

This study has considered that machine learning offers essential tools to identify human behavior and predict future actions. This will depend on the age group involved in the study and the objectives of the research. Ecuador was chosen as a case study, where the evaluation method for admission to a higher education institution is through a general knowledge test. This evaluation includes verbal, mathematical, abstract, and natural science reasoning. A good performance in mathematics is a determining factor during the student's school life and allows them to increase their chances of entering the career of their choice. The weighting scale of the "transformar test" (name of the national test) is 1000 points, and knowing the conditions that influence a better academic performance is relevant. Concerning neighboring countries, Colombia follows a similar methodology with the so-called "state exam", while in Peru, each education center decides the requirements for student admission. Despite this, it is clear that performance in mathematics is vital in the process of admission and studies in universities.

Regarding the computational side, although linear and nonlinear regressions could be used, Froud et al. [13] show that machine learning has better results in this type of research. If we talk about children's education, it has been identified that the best predictor of academic performance is that the child's mother has a fourth-level education. Our study was based on data provided by the MEC; therefore, it was not possible to review this variable, but it will be considered in future studies. While comparing our study with that of Uskov et al. [14], they have focused on evaluating the algorithms but do not provide information on variables that could influence performance. Something similar occurs in [18], where they use various sociodemographic data in their study; in the end, these are not analyzed, and they only focus on evaluating the models' performance. As in our research, it has been identified that NB has the poorest performance, while RF is the one that offers the best results.

Halde et al. [15] showed that student motivation, perception of information, and study aids influenced the predicted score. At the same time, our study has focused on assessing the grades obtained in different subjects and the main sociodemographic variables. The approaches are different, but ML algorithms receive relevant information on student behavior. There are also other variables that the EQF has not considered, such as the frequency of Internet connection, discussed in [16]. This frequency is shown to be positively correlated with academic performance, while the volume of Internet traffic is negatively associated. It has also been identified that the support vector machine (SVM) has the highest accuracy percentages. This study recommends using demographic data to improve predictions, which has been considered in our study. The use of social networks is another variable that the SCM has not considered; therefore, we have not evaluated it. Although the study by Nti et al. [17] shows that the rate of use of social networks and their use in class partially affects academic performance, it is a topic that should be expanded.

4 Conclusions

The available machine learning techniques allow a high volume of data to be analyzed. In this application, three algorithms have been used to identify the variables that could be predictors of academic performance in the subject of mathematics. Numerical variables (attributes) are the ones that best contribute to the classification model, where grades in other sciences, graduation exams, and entrance exams to higher education stand out. Likewise, categorical variables have been analyzed to show that sociodemographic factors directly affect grades. The analysis of the performance of the various algorithms shows that the Random Forest has higher percentages of the most critical variables in the performance of the different algorithms. The bibliography shows several related studies but has different methodologies and scopes. The objective has been fulfilled, emphasizing that a new learning algorithm was not developed, but several existing techniques were evaluated to understand the situation of a specific country. Also, we chose simple methods to reduce the computational expense (improving its replicability), obtaining good performance.

To enhance the results obtained in this study, the application of other models is proposed as future work. These could be regressions or other models such as logit, linear multiple, etc. Forecasting models could also be performed as a prior regression, a segmentation of the base in more than two groups to minimize biases or avoid unbalance. In addition, it is possible to work with another cut-off value for classification according to the minimum score requirement for access to higher education. In Ecuador, different minimum scores depend on the career to apply for; for example, 950 points are required on average for medicine and 750 for other careers.

It has also been identified that variables could be disaggregated to obtain more information and details in the predictions. The variable "isec" has information on parental education, goods, and services, which could be disaggregated according to the needs of the study. This will allow us to apply the classification models studied in this research and determine how the results are affected or verify if they are maintained.

A limitation is that the information used in the analysis comes only from academic tests to facilitate the mathematical analysis. However, it has been statistically determined that the sociodemographic variables do not influence the study. Other economic variables have not been evaluated, so their inclusion is proposed for future work. Other authors are also encouraged to review different methodologies and compare this study, improving the field of knowledge that has been addressed.

Acknowledgment. Universidad Tecnológica Indoamérica for its support and financing under the "Big data analysis and its impact on society, education and industry" project.

References

1. Jalil, N.A., Hwang, H.J., Dawi, N.M.: Machines learning trends, perspectives and prospects in education sector. ACM Int. Conf. Proc. Ser. 201–205 (2019). https://doi.org/10.1145/334 5120.3345147
2. Buele, J., et al.: Interactive system to improve the skills of children with dyslexia: a preliminary study. In: Rocha, Á., Pereira, R.P. (eds.) Developments and Advances in Defense and Security. SIST, vol. 152, pp. 439–449. Springer, Singapore (2020). https://doi.org/10.1007/978-981-13-9155-2_35
3. García-Magariño, I., Gonzalez Bedia, M., Palacios-Navarro, G.: FAMAP: a framework for developing m-health apps. In: Advances in Intelligent Systems and Computing. pp. 850–859. Springer Verlag (2018). https://doi.org/10.1007/978-3-319-77703-0_83/COVER/
4. Varela-Aldás, J., Buele, J., Lorente, P.R., García-Magariño, I., Palacios-Navarro, G.: A virtual reality-based cognitive telerehabilitation system for use in the covid-19 pandemic. Sustain. **13**, 1–24 (2021). https://doi.org/10.3390/su13042183
5. Shah, D., Patel, D., Adesara, J., Hingu, P., Shah, M.: Exploiting the capabilities of blockchain and machine learning in education. Augment. Hum. Res. **6**(1), 1–14 (2021). https://doi.org/10.1007/s41133-020-00039-7
6. Buele, P.A., Avilés-Castillo, F., Buele, J.: Repercusiones en la Salud Mental de los Estudiantes de Tercero de Bachillerato: Un Caso de Estudio. Publicare **1**, 26–30 (2021)
7. Schneider, B.R., Estarellas, P.C., Bruns, B.: The politics of transforming education in Ecuador: confrontation and continuity, 2006–2017. Comp. Educ. Rev. **63**, 259–280 (2019). https://doi.org/10.1086/702609
8. Ward, M.: PISA for Development Out-of-school-assessment Results in Focus. PISA Focus **110**, 26 (2020)
9. Broc, M.Á.: Rendimiento Académico Y Otras Variables Psicosocio-Familiares En Alumnos De Educación Secundaria Obligatoria. Eur. Sci. J. **13**, 50 (2017). https://doi.org/10.19044/esj.2017.v13n5p50
10. Paseka, A., Schwab, S.: Parents' attitudes towards inclusive education and their perceptions of inclusive teaching practices and resources. Eur. J. Spec. Needs Educ. **35**, 254–272 (2020). https://doi.org/10.1080/08856257.2019.1665232
11. Villamizar Acevedo, G., Araujo Arenas, T.Y., Trujillo Calderón, W.J.: Relación entre ansiedad matemática y rendimiento académico en matemáticas en estudiantes de secundaria. Ciencias Psicológicas. **14**, 1–13 (2020). https://doi.org/10.22235/cp.v14i1.2174
12. Fahd, K., Venkatraman, S., Miah, S.J., Ahmed, K.: Application of machine learning in higher education to assess student academic performance, at-risk, and attrition: a meta-analysis of literature. Educ. Inf. Technol. **27**(3), 3743–3775 (2021). https://doi.org/10.1007/s10639-021-10741-7
13. Froud, R., Hansen, S.H., Ruud, H.K., Foss, J., Ferguson, L., Fredriksen, P.M.: Relative performance of machine learning and linear regression in predicting quality of life and academic performance of school children in Norway: data analysis of a quasi-experimental study. J. Med. Internet Res. **23**, e22021 (2021). https://doi.org/10.2196/22021
14. Uskov, V.L., Bakken, J.P., Byerly, A., Shah, A.: Machine learning-based predictive analytics of student academic performance in STEM education. In: 2019 IEEE Global Engineering Education Conference (EDUCON), pp. 1370–1376 (2019). 0.1109/EDUCON.2019.8725237
15. Halde, R.R., Deshpande, A., Mahajan, A.: Psychology assisted prediction of academic performance using machine learning. In: 2016 IEEE International Conference on Recent Trends in Electronics, Information and Communication Technology, RTEICT 2016 - Proceedings. pp. 431–435. Institute of Electrical and Electronics Engineers Inc. (2017). https://doi.org/10.1109/RTEICT.2016.7807857

16. Xu, X., Wang, J., Peng, H., Wu, R.: Prediction of academic performance associated with internet usage behaviors using machine learning algorithms. Comput. Human Behav. **98**, 166–173 (2019). https://doi.org/10.1016/j.chb.2019.04.015

17. Nti, I.K., Akyeramfo-Sam, S., Bediako-Kyeremeh, B., Agyemang, S.: Prediction of social media effects on students' academic performance using Machine Learning Algorithms (MLAs). J. Comput. Educ. **9**, 195–223 (2021). https://doi.org/10.1007/s40692-021-00201-z

18. Sokkhey, P., Okazaki, T.: Hybrid machine learning algorithms for predicting academic performance. Int. J. Adv. Comput. Sci. Appl. **11**, 32–41 (2020). https://doi.org/10.14569/ijacsa.2020.0110104

19. Talahua, J.S., Buele, J., Calvopina, P., Varela-Aldas, J.: Facial recognition system for people with and without face mask in times of the covid-19 pandemic. Sustainability **13**, 6900 (2021). https://doi.org/10.3390/su13126900

20. Bronson, S.: The Data Mining Guide For Novices And Dummies (2020)

21. Sarkar, D., Bali, R., Sharma, T.: Practical Machine Learning with Python. Apress (2018). https://doi.org/10.1007/978-1-4842-3207-1

22. Varela-Aldás, J., Fuentes, E.M., Buele, J., Meló, R.G., Barat, J.M., Alcañiz, M.: Support vector machine as tool for classifying coffee beverages. In: Rocha, Á., Ferrás, C., Montenegro Marin, C.E., Medina García, V.H. (eds.) ICITS 2020. AISC, vol. 1137, pp. 275–284. Springer, Cham (2020). https://doi.org/10.1007/978-3-030-40690-5_27

23. Musso, M., Kyndt, E., Cascallar, E., Dochy, F.: Predicting mathematical performance: the effect of cognitive processes and self-regulation factors. Educ. Res. Int. **2012**, 1–13 (2012). https://doi.org/10.1155/2012/250719

24. Bzdok, D., Krzywinski, M., Altman, N.: Points of significance: machine learning: supervised methods. Nat. Methods. **15**, 5–6 (2018). https://doi.org/10.1038/nmeth.4551

25. Pedregosa, F., et al.: Scikit-learn: machine learning in Python. J. Mach. Learn. Res. **12**, 2825–2830 (2011)

26. Guevara, C., et al.: Detection of student behavior profiles applying neural networks and decision trees. In: Ahram, T., Karwowski, W., Pickl, S., Taiar, R. (eds.) IHSED 2019. AISC, vol. 1026, pp. 591–597. Springer, Cham (2020). https://doi.org/10.1007/978-3-030-27928-8_90

Analysis of Classification Algorithms for the Prediction of Purchase Intention in Electronic Commerce

Maritza Aguirre-Munizaga[1,2]($\boxtimes$) (iD), Javier Del Cioppo Morstadt[3] (iD),
and Teresa Samaniego-Cobo[1] (iD)

[1] Facultad de Ciencias Agrarias "Dr. Jacobo Bucaram Ortiz", Universidad Agraria del Ecuador, Av. 25 de Julio, Guayaquil, Ecuador
{maguirre,tsamaniego}@uagraria.edu.ec
[2] Universidad Internacional de La Rioja, Av. Logroño, La Rioja, Spain
[3] Facultad de Economía Agrícola, Universidad Agraria del Ecuador, Av. 25 de Julio, Guayaquil, Ecuador
jdelcioppo@uagraria.edu.ec

Abstract. The analysis focuses on data from an e-commerce retailer to identify the classification techniques for obtaining the best performances of validated classification algorithms. It is essential to highlight that this type of prediction is used in the commerce sector since it is a sector in constant development and allows to identify the consumer's behaviour to variables such as average time on the website, transactions completed, pages rated, among others. The research focuses on Business to Consumer commerce, collecting data from the purchase sessions for 12 months. This allowed the comparison of the Naive Bayes model of Gaussian type, Random Forest and Extra Trees Classifier, which are finally validated against the results of Dummy classifier, highlighting the efficiency of Extra Trees Classifier. This type of study and the selection of the variables provide a higher correlation with the Revenue attribute, which is the one used as a prediction class. The efficiency of Extra Trees Classifier stands out in this type of study, together with the selection of the variables that provide the highest correlation with the Revenue attribute, which is the one used as the prediction class.

Keywords: Classification algorithms · Electronic commerce · Machine learning · Prediction of purchase

1 Introduction

E-commerce is now an indispensable part of global retail trade, and like other areas, the industry has undergone a digital transformation helping consumers benefit from online transactions. At the same time, the number of digital buyers is increasing every year, establishing a comparison of the increase of online purchases by category in this study. According to a projection made by the data provider Statista, the growth of online shopping establishes a higher percentage in consumer electronics [1]. This increase

R. Valencia-García et al. (Eds.): CITI 2022, CCIS 1658, pp. 30–42, 2022.
https://doi.org/10.1007/978-3-031-19961-5_3

in sales is projected primarily for electronics. However, the growth in online grocery shopping is expected to increase with the various confinement periods that have occurred worldwide due to the pandemic.

Globally in 2020, during the COVID-19 crisis, consumers' behaviour and shopping habits changed fundamentally. Approximately 2 billion people purchased goods or services online, and, during the same year, retailers reported over US$4.2 billion in global retail sales [2]. Therefore, it concludes that the COVID-19 crisis generated a change in consumer behaviour, represented by an increase in the use of digital media to acquire goods and services.

Some relevant figures reported to ECLAC [3] indicate that during the pandemic, they had more than 1.7 million new buyers on their platform, of which 80% of regular buyers made a food purchase for the first time, and 20% made their first purchase at this time.

At the onset of the pandemic, daily deliveries grew by more than 1.1 million, evidencing that consumers tend to shop online from their computers or smartphone, highlighting that the convenience of online shopping makes it an emerging trend among consumers, especially Generation Y [4].

This study aims to demonstrate that, by collecting information from consumer shopping sessions, the pattern of customer behaviour can detect to target advertising, marketing and offers to potential customers. According to a 2021 survey, about 70% of shoppers use a cell phone, while 30% indicate that they use a computer [5]. The dataset used in this analysis comes from a Bussiness to Consumer site in Ecuador and shared by Sakar C. and Kastro [6]. The same has been complemented with information collected locally. The data belong to one year of monitoring, so a data mining analysis of the purchase intention of visitors to the site is presented, which allows recognizing a pattern of consumer behaviour according to the trend of the sessions.

One of the techniques of data mining analysis is classifying such a voluminous amount of data into two or more distant classes. Labelled data is used to generate a model to predict the buying influence on a retail site by applying supervised learning.

The proposed work compares the accuracy of various classification techniques. Among these are classification algorithms that examine the characteristics of an item present in the data set and assign it to one of the predefined classes. The elements to be classified are generally represented by records of elements in a database table or file. The classification task characterises by having a correct definition of the classes and a training set consisting of pre-classified examples. The task is to build a model to be used on unclassified data in order to classify it.

From this problem, the research question generates: How would a predictive algorithm of online purchase intention help the exponential growth of a retail store?

We are identifying as a dependent variable the efficiency of the executed algorithms and the amount of evaluated and classified sessions in the dataset as an independent variable.

2 Related Works

Artificial intelligence has helped to discover data mining, a new and influential field of computer science. This process of extracting or discovering patterns from data sets is used in health, agriculture [7], environment, marketing [8], and fraud detection, among others [9].

Data classification is a mining technique used to predict the class of objects whose class label is unknown. Many classification techniques are available in data mining to classify data into two or more classes. Some classification techniques are k-nearest neighbour (KNN), Bayesian network, decision trees, and support vector machines. This paper compares various classification techniques that seek to "learn" from previous shopping patterns and run functions that generate good predictions.

This tool is vital for the sustained development of companies to become more competitive in this globalized market where marketing trends are increasingly biased or selective for the decision-making of a target consumer [10]. In turn, these algorithms help to provide real-time feedback on changing market situations.

The main benefits of implementing this algorithm in e-commerce include: a framework for implementing digital marketing strategies on retail sites, reduced market research costs, accurate and up-to-date information on customer purchase intent by region and reduced operational and logistical costs within administrations.

This proposal attempts to determine the purchase intent of visitors to a website from their current session information and how to use it to predict whether the session will end with a purchase. In this context, reference is made to work done by Mokryn, Bogina and Kuflik [11]. They compare data from two retail e-commerce sites to model purchase dynamics and generate the purchase intent of anonymous visitors from their clickstream information.

In the research conducted by Shi [12], three online purchase intention prediction models were built based on the corresponding classical machine learning models (logistic regression, decision tree and random forest). More than 85% accuracy was obtained in the predictions generated.

A project experimenting with individualized e-commerce recommendation technology was generated by using machine learning technology. It examines in-depth the related technologies and algorithms of the recommender system and proposes an architecture [13].

3   Methodology

In the analysis methodology, an exploratory analysis with a quantitative approach was carried out in the sampled units, which belong to 12,546 purchasing sessions captured in one year[1], thus generating a numerical correlation analysis.

The sessions belong to different users of an online shopping store and the data has been collected through Google analytics.

For this purpose, several types of research have been used, having in the first instance the documentary research through which it has been possible to describe and explain the knowledge previously established in the reliable sources of information for the consolidation of the project.

The research design is observational and longitudinal based on the following variables:

---

[1] https://github.com/maguirre2017/Online_ecommerce.

- Effect of the number of different types of pages visited in that session and the total time spent on each of the page categories.
- Effect of the percentage of visitors who enter the site from that page and then leave ("bounce") without triggering another request to the analytics server during that session.
- Effect of the average value of a web page a user visited before completing an e-commerce transaction "Page Value".

As an information analysis technique, a Pearson correlation analysis is applied, recognizing the dependence between the identified attributes. The recommendation of the most efficient algorithm will be generated for practical application purposes using a predictive scope. Table 1 describes the attributes of the dataset used in this analysis which come from a Bussiness to Consumer site shared by Sakar C. and Kastro [6]. The same has been complemented with information collected locally on an e-commerce website with data belonging to one year of monitoring.

Table 1. Atributes and description

Attributes	Description
Administrative	Number of visited pages
Administrative_Duration	Time of each visit
Informational	Pages of the same type visited by the user
Informational_Duration	Time spent visiting pages of this type
ProductRelated	Product-related pages
ProductRelated_Duration	Time on product-related pages
BounceRates	Percentage of site visitors
ExitRates	Percentage of page views that trigger a visit to our site
PageValues	Average between page value and transaction completed
SpecialDay	Approach to special days (Mother's Day, Valentine's Day, etc.)
Month	Month of visit
OperatingSystems	Operating system from which it was accessed
Browser	Browser
Region	Numerical value of the access canton
TrafficType	Numeric value of the type of web traffic
VisitorType	New visitors, returning visitors or other
Weekend	Boolean represents whether it is a weekend or not
Revenue	Boolean represents whether the purchase was completed or not

3.1 Descriptive Analysis of Collected Data

In this phase, the information corresponding to the purchase sessions was analysed. First, it verified that there were no invalid data in the dataset. Additionally, it found that of the operating systems used to access the e-commerce site, the most used is Android Mobile, and the least used is Linux. As for the browsers, it can highlight that the most significant number of sessions are from Google Chrome.

Since quantitative data is available, graphs were generated to present the representative characteristics of the study variables [14].

According to the descriptive analysis of the data collected from the shopping sessions, no purchases were made through the website in January and April.

Figure 1 describes the percentage of buyers who completed the transaction with the True value and those who didn't make a purchase with False. For effect, it seems that in November, 6.06% of visitors did make purchases, unlike May, which despite having had a more significant number of visits, only 2.98% completed the purchase. The trend line shows that the Pages Values attribute tends to increase in November and December, representing that the most significant number of users have completed an e-commerce transaction in these months.

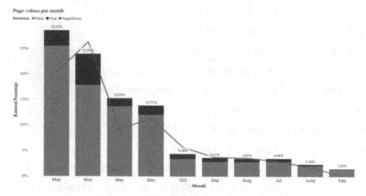

Fig. 1. Percentage of sessions in which a transaction concluded per month

Figure 2 shows on the left graph the trend of visitors who did or didn't make a purchase on weekends and the right those who have generated purchase transactions on weekends, which shows that the highest number of transactions took place on weekdays in May, followed by November, March and December.

The Revenue class was evaluated using Pearson's correlation method to identify the correlation factor between the dataset's attributes and the class. Based on this analysis, the attributes month, informational_duration, weekend, browser, operatingsystems, traffictype were eliminated (Fig. 3).

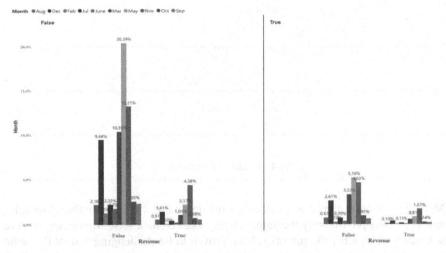

Fig. 2. Percentage of customers who purchased by month, divided into weekends, and working days

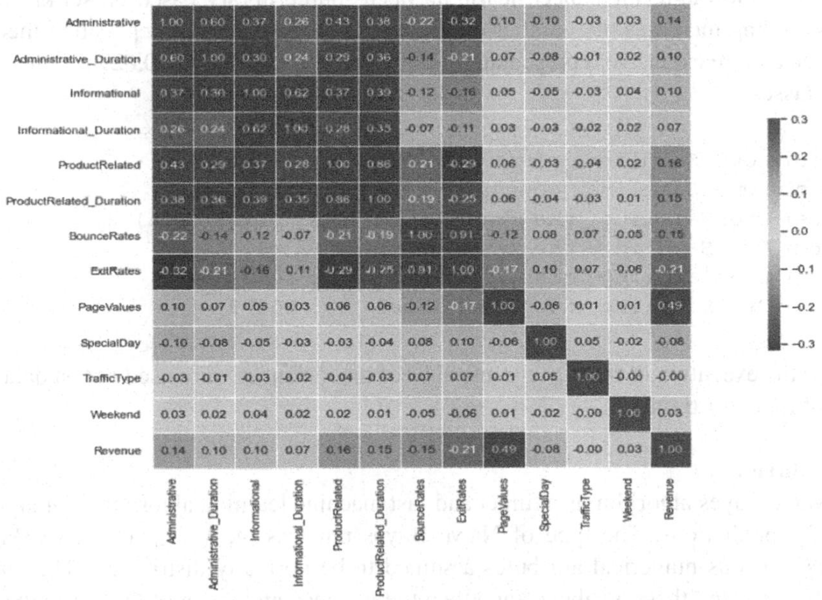

Fig. 3. Ranked of atributes

3.2 Classification Algorithms

When analyzing the data, it was found that it was impossible to guarantee a balance in the Revenue attribute, as shown in Fig. 4, so it was decided to apply a technique that would allow the generation of a balance in the sampled data.

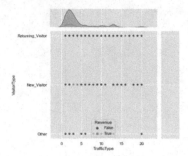

Fig. 4. Ranked of atributes

Most classification algorithms will only work optimally when the number of samples in each class is approximately the same. Highly skewed data sets, where one or more classes vastly outnumber the minority, have proven to be challenging and, at the same time, become increasingly common [15]. So, one way to address this problem is to resample the dataset to compensate for this imbalance to arrive at a more robust and fair decision boundary. The synthetic minority oversampling technique (SMOTE) [16], was applied through Imbalanced-learn, an open-source library based on sci-kit-learn. Oversampling increases the number of minority class instances by replicating them to generate a more extensive representation of the dataset resulting in 10,629 instances for both classes:

```
Before OverSampling, counts of label '1': 1917
Before OverSampling, counts of label '0': 10629
After OverSampling, the shape of train_X: (21258, 16)
After OverSampling, the shape of train_y: (21258,)
After OverSampling, counts of label '1': 10629
After OverSampling, counts of label '0': 10629
```

For the execution of the algorithms, 30% of the instances were used as test data and 70% of them for training.

Naive Bayes.
The Naive Bayes algorithm is a direct and fast machine learning algorithm that is often used for predictions. The type of Naive Bayes ran was the Gaussian Naïve Bayes, with continuous numerical attributes assumed to be normally distributed. The output class fractionated these attributes, and then the variance and mean of the attribute were calculated for each class.

We proceed to run different models; in the first instance, we run Gaussian Naive Bayes obtaining an accuracy of 85.54%.

Random Forest.
Afterwards, Random Forest was run due to the generalization capability of this model, which works as a set of decision trees combined with bagging. The execution of this

algorithm, randomized cross validation is used, in this method it is divided in each inter-action and thus there is the possibility of overlapping subsets in the different interactions. When using bagging, what is happening is that different trees see different portions of the data. No single tree sees all the training data, which results in training each tree with different data samples for the same problem. Different hyperparameters are applied to validate the accuracy of this algorithm, which is shown in the Table 2:

Table 2. Execution with different hyperparameters

Execution	max_depth	n_estimators	Random_state	Accuracy (in %)
1	10	10	3	90.28
2	6	550	2	87.99
3	5	950	2	86.72
4	5	750	2	86.74
5	4	550	2	86.11

Extra Trees Classifier.
Extra-Trees or Extremely Randomised Trees take the randomness of Random Forest to another level. This model considers a subset of the trees' predictive characteristics to be created. When choosing a character and a threshold value to divide each node, instead of choosing the threshold that best divides each characteristic, a random cut-off value is made for each characteristic proposed, choosing the best of them as the division rule. Another difference with Random Forest is that the samples with which each trainee are not observations.

An additional tree classifier used in Phyton performs a meta estimator that fits a series of random decision trees on several subsamples of the dataset and uses averaging to improve predictive accuracy and control overfitting [17]. We parameterised n_estimators according to the run that obtained the best accuracy in Random Forest, resulting in 90.75% efficiency. Figure 5 shows the variation of the accuracy depending on the model.

Support Vector Machine SVM.
SVM is known to use the kernel trick to solve nonlinear problems, while decision trees derive hyperrectangles in the input space to solve the problem. In this case, an accuracy of 85.60% was obtained.

Decision trees are observed in this case to be better for categorical data and handle collinearity better than SVM, with an accuracy of 86.95%.

With the training data, we highlight the execution in Jupyter Notebook [18] of the classification algorithms shown in Fig. 5 with the resulting accuracy. In turn, libraries such as seaborn [19], matplotlib, sklearn, numpy, pandas, among others, have been used to generate the descriptive statistics of the data used, as well as the execution of the models with the training data.

	Algorithms	Accuracy Score
0	Random Forest	90.276302
1	K-NN Algorithm	86.503719
2	SVM	85.680128
3	Decision Tree	86.955367
4	Extra Trees Classifier	90.756972
5	Gaussian NB	85.547290

Fig. 5. Accuracy score

3.3 Results

In the test set using accuracy, precision, recall, F1 score, specificity and area under the receiver operating characteristic curve (AUC-ROC). The extra three classifier model was evaluated, giving the results shown in Fig. 6.

	precision	recall	f1-score	support
0	0.96	0.92	0.94	3101
1	0.93	0.96	0.94	3277
accuracy			0.94	6378
macro avg	0.94	0.94	0.94	6378
weighted avg	0.94	0.94	0.94	6378

Fig. 6. Accuracy scores

Figure 7 shows the variation of the accuracy depending on the model.

The test data results are presented in the Table 3, for the three models with the highest accuracy.

The AUC (Area Under Curve) was the metric selected to quantify classifier performance [20], derived from the calculation of the area under the ROC (Receiver Operating Characteristics) curve, which is the result of plotting the rate of true positives against the rate of false negatives. Different studies have used the AUC as a metric for classifier performance and demonstrated its advantages, although others have pointed out its shortcomings. This measure can be misleading mainly for unbalanced data sets where the minority class represents less than 10% of the data set. For that reason, we first applied the oversampling technique in this dataset. For model training, 70% of the data were used, and for testing, the local data used corresponded to 30% of the total number of sessions in the dataset. Figure 8 generates a ROC curve for the best performing classifier, verifying the area under the ROC curve using the sklearn.metrics.roc_curve function.

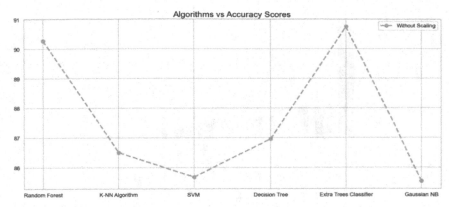

Fig. 7. Accuracy scores

Table 3. Modelling and accuracy with test data

Model	Accuracy(in %)
Extra Trees Classifier model accuracy	93.99%
Gaussian Naive Bayes model accuracy	78.35%
Random Forest Classifier model accuracy	87.24%

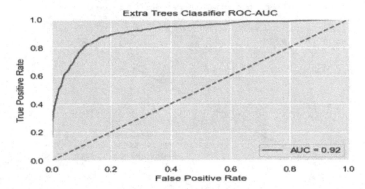

Fig. 8. Represents the ratio of the true positive rate (sensitivity) to the false positive rate ("1 - specificity").

The random forest and the other trees also allow estimating the importance of each characteristic in the model; thus, Fig. 9 shows the importance according to the attributes identified as most significant.

The results of the model run are presented through a receiver operating characteristic (ROC) analysis, a graphical approach to analysing the performance of a classifier [18]. This shows the relative performance of the Extra Trees Clasifier model, generating an AUC of 0.92.

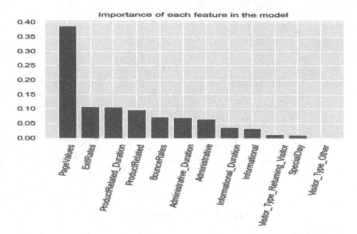

Fig. 9. Importance of attributes concerning the executed model

Finally, DummyClassifier is used to compare the behaviour of the Extra Trees Classifier with a fictitious classifier that handles the conjectures based on a stratified data set. It shows that our model generates a high performance and allows us to deduce that it can be used as a prediction model in conjunction with the identified attributes of greater importance (Fig. 10).

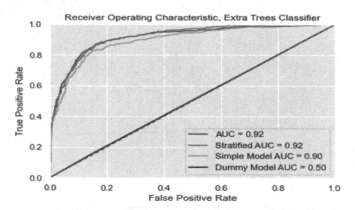

Fig. 10. Model comparison, including DummyClassifier

4   Conclusions and Future Work

E-commerce is the action of conducting transactions of buying and selling goods and services online, and it is one of the many fields revolutionised by data science [21]. E-commerce companies need to increase the percentage of website visitors who complete the purchase in online stores. To achieve this goal, e-commerce companies and academic researchers have devoted efforts to analysing and modelling the behaviours of website users, especially in recent years, where there has been a trend in research to use machine learning methods to predict user behaviour.

In this research, we propose analysing classification algorithms and a purchase prediction model to predict the intention to finalise a purchase in a session. The proposed model is tested with data from a website in Ecuador that maintains locations in the central cantons of the province of Guayas. This paper aims to help and illustrate how to work with labelled data and classification models.

The experiments show that machine learning models generate excellent performance in identifying purchase intent, so it concludes that the Extra Trees Classifier model can help stores generate a personalised shopping experience through product recommendations and offer generation concerning each session's data.

References

1. Statista: eCommerce report 2021. https://www.statista.com/study/42335/ecommerce-report/. Last accessed 3 June 2022
2. Jílková, P., Králová, P.: Digital consumer behaviour and eCommerce trends during the COVID-19 crisis. Int. Adv. Econ. Res. **27**(1), 83–85 (2021). https://doi.org/10.1007/s11294-021-09817-4
3. CEPAL: Recuperación económica tras la pandemia COVID-19: empoderar a América Latina y el Caribe para un mejor aprovechamiento del comercio electrónico y digital (2020)
4. Lim, Y.J., et al.: Online purchase behavior of generation Y in Malaysia. Procedia Econ. Financ. **37**, 292–298 (2016). https://doi.org/10.1016/s2212-5671(16)00050-2
5. Statista: Ecuador: online shopping devices 2021 | Statista. https://www.statista.com/statistics/921189/ecuador-online-purchases-device/. Last accessed 6 June 2022
6. Sakar C., Kastro, Y.: Online Shoppers Purchasing Intention Dataset (2018)
7. Colombo-Mendoza, L.O., Paredes-Valverde, M.A., del Salas-Zárate, M.P., Valencia-García, R.: Internet of things-driven data mining for smart crop production prediction in the peasant farming domain. Appl. Sci. **12**, 1940 (2022). https://doi.org/10.3390/app12041940
8. Hervert-Escobar, L., López-Pérez, J.F., Esquivel-Flores, O.A.: Optimal pricing model: case of study for convenience stores. In: Pichardo-Lagunas, O., Miranda-Jiménez, S. (eds.) Advances in Soft Computing: 15th Mexican International Conference on Artificial Intelligence, MICAI 2016, Cancún, Mexico, October 23–28, 2016, Proceedings, Part II, pp. 353–364. Springer International Publishing, Cham (2017). https://doi.org/10.1007/978-3-319-62428-0_28
9. Alejandro, R.H., Trejo, L.A., Hervert-Escobar, L., Hernández-Gress, N., Enrique, G.N.: Mexican stock return prediction with differential evolution for hyperparameter tuning. In: Batyrshin, I., Gelbukh, A., Sidorov, G. (eds.) Advances in Computational Intelligence: 20th Mexican International Conference on Artificial Intelligence, MICAI 2021, Mexico City, Mexico, October 25–30, 2021, Proceedings, Part I, pp. 355–368. Springer International Publishing, Cham (2021). https://doi.org/10.1007/978-3-030-89817-5_27
10. Lim, Y.J., Osman, A., Salahuddin, S.N., Romle, A.R., Abdullah, S.: Factors influencing online shopping behavior: the mediating role of purchase intention. Procedia Econ. Financ. **35**, 401–410 (2016). https://doi.org/10.1016/s2212-5671(16)00050-2
11. Mokryn, O., Bogina, V., Kuflik, T.: Will this session end with a purchase? inferring current purchase intent of anonymous visitors. Electron. Commer. Res. Appl. **34**, 100836 (2019). https://doi.org/10.1016/J.ELERAP.2019.100836

12. Shi, X.: The application of machine learning in online purchasing intention prediction. In: ACM International Conference Proceeding Service, pp. 21–29 (2021). https://doi.org/10.1145/3469968.3469972

13. Esmeli, R., Bader-El-Den, M., Abdullahi, H.: Towards early purchase intention prediction in online session based retailing systems. Electron. Mark. **31**(3), 697–715 (2020). https://doi.org/10.1007/s12525-020-00448-x

14. Charry, K., Coussement, K., Demoulin, N., Heuvinck, N.: Descriptive analysis. In: Charry, K., Coussement, K., Demoulin, N., Heuvinck, N. (eds.) Marketing Research with IBM® SPSS Statistics: A Practical Guide, pp. 31–47. Routledge (2016). https://doi.org/10.4324/9781315525532-2

15. Lemaître, G., Nogueira, F., Aridas, C.K.: Imbalanced-learn: a python toolbox to tackle the curse of imbalanced datasets in machine learning. J. Mach. Learn. Res. **18**, 1–5 (2017)

16. Chawla, N.V., Bowyer, K.W., Hall, L.O., Kegelmeyer, W.P.: SMOTE: synthetic minority over-sampling technique. J. Artif. Intell. Res. **16**, 321–357 (2011). https://doi.org/10.1613/jair.953

17. Ampomah, E.K., Qin, Z., Nyame, G.: Evaluation of tree-based ensemble machine learning models in predicting stock price direction of movement. Information **11**(6), 332 (2020). https://doi.org/10.3390/info11060332

18. Silaparasetty, N.: Machine Learning Concepts with Python and the Jupyter Notebook Environment: Using Tensorflow 2.0. Apress, Berkeley, CA (2020). https://doi.org/10.1007/978-1-4842-5967-2

19. Bisong, E.: Matplotlib and seaborn. In: Building Machine Learning and Deep Learning Models on Google Cloud Platform, pp. 151–165. Apress, Berkeley, CA (2019). https://doi.org/10.1007/978-1-4842-4470-8_12

20. Muschelli, J.: ROC and AUC with a binary predictor: a potentially misleading metric. J. Classif. **37**(3), 696–708 (2019). https://doi.org/10.1007/s00357-019-09345-1

21. Chaubey, G., Gavhane, P.R., Bisen, D., Arjaria, S.K.: Customer purchasing behavior prediction using machine learning classification techniques. J. Ambient Intell. Humaniz. Comput. (2022). https://doi.org/10.1007/s12652-022-03837-6

Knowledge Based Systems

Alignment Techniques in Domain-Specific Models

Paola Grijalva-Arriaga[1,3]($\boxtimes$) , Galo Cornejo-Gómez[2] , Raquel Gómez-Chabla[1] ,
Leandro Antonelli[3] , and Pablo Thomas[4]

[1] Carrera de Ingeniería en Ciencias de la Computación, Universidad Agraria
del Ecuador, Av. 25 de Julio y Pio Jaramillo, P.O. BOX 09-04-100, Guayaquil, Ecuador
{pgrijalva,rgomez}@uagraria.edu.ec
[2] Carrera de Computación, Universidad Católica de Santiago de Guayaquil, Av. Carlos Julio
Arosemena Km 1, Guayaquil, Ecuador
galo.cornejo@cu.ucsg.edu.ec
[3] LIFIA - Facultad de Informática, Universidad Nacional de La Plata, 50 esquina 120,
Buenos Aires, Argentina
leandro.antonelli@lifia.info.unlp.edu.ar
[4] LIDI - Facultad de Informática, Universidad Nacional de La Plata, 50 esquina 120,
Buenos Aires, Argentina
pthomas@lidi.info.unlp.edu.ar

Abstract. During the requirements specification stage, conceptual descriptions
of the Domain Universe (DU) are used through several representations such as
glossaries, ontologies and other models. However, a complete representation of
a domain is difficult to achieve. Different ways a domain can be conceptualized
result in a heterogeneous representation, which often makes consistent description challenging. This work aims to identify techniques used in different projects
for domain alignment and their behaviour with a lexical model. In the applied
methodology, a search for the domain alignment was carried out in various scientific databases such as IEEE Explore, ACM and Springer. The obtained result
showed that tools used to align domain specifications are concentrated in ontologies and glossaries, using techniques with similarities in the semantic, lexical,
structural and syntactic fields. When applying semantic and lexical level measures in glossaries called Extended Language Lexicon (LEL) it was obtained the
degree of similarity between the different glossaries, at the semantic level the one
with the best precision was the Cosine Similarity method, while at the lexical
level, the one with the best precision was Jaro Winkler. It is concluded that the
application of the techniques independently does not allow the identification of
similarities, omissions or correspondences between the domains, so it is necessary
to develop a method that contemplates heuristics and integrates the different lexical
and semantic measures as a support to improve the completeness and consistency
of the domain.

Keywords: Aligning domain specifications · Domain alignment · Domain
glossary · Extended language lexicon

R. Valencia-García et al. (Eds.): CITI 2022, CCIS 1658, pp. 45–61, 2022.
https://doi.org/10.1007/978-3-031-19961-5_4

1 Introduction

Domain knowledge is one of the most important factors when choosing high-quality requirements, and it is the knowledge that only domain experts have. The little knowledge [1, 2] that requirements analysts have about a specific domain can cause low-quality requirements [3].

During the requirements specification stage, conceptual descriptions of the UD are used through various representations such as Glossaries, Ontologies and other models. Domain specification glossaries contain definitions of terms that are important in the domain and are written in natural language. A glossary is a collection of definitions of terms that are relevant in some domain that contains cross-references, synonyms, homonyms, acronyms, and abbreviations [4]. Another definition states that a glossary is an important part of any software requirements document [5] that makes technical terms in a domain explicit and provides definitions for them, helping to mitigate imprecision and ambiguity.

A glossary describes the vocabulary of the application without the need to understand the functionality of the business process, also called the domain [6]. The glossaries allow the clarification of the meaning of concepts by joining the terms used in the different models, improving communication between those involved.

On the other hand, domain ontologies are another way to represent concepts that belong to a specific part of the world [7]; it can be considered that it manages highly specialised knowledge and is integrated by concepts, relationships, functions, instances and axioms. A complete domain specification is a challenging goal to achieve [8]. The different ways in which a domain can be conceptualized, result in a heterogeneous representation, often on the same domain, which might cause the interoperability of the systems. The more complete the conceptualization of the domain, the more complete requirements of a system will be obtained.

A way to check requirements is to reuse them in similar systems, but unfortunately, this is not a straightforward process. While requirements (specifications) from the same domain can be reused, it is not certain that the different organizations in the same domain will use precisely the same vocabulary. In this case, an alignment of the domain vocabularies is needed to compare them. For example, in private banks we talk about "clients", while in state banks we talk about "citizens". We can even talk about "users" as a synonym for "clients" because in this context, the client is who uses the computer system platform. From this simple example, reusing specifications to increase completeness cannot be done directly, because it's necessary to join also the languages.

The purpose of this document is to submit a literature review related to the techniques used in different projects to align domain specifications with glossaries and ontologies. The methods that contributed to the alignment were identified and, subsequently, in the context of natural language, these methods were applied in the glossaries of the extended language lexicon (LELs), comparing the results of the alignment.

The document is structured as follows: Sect. 2 presents the literature review process; Sect. 3 shows the results of the literature review; Sect. 4 presents the application of the techniques using a tool based on NLP (glossaries); and in Sect. 5, conclusions and ideas for future work are presented.

2   Alignment Techniques in Specific Domains

This section describes the literature review process carried out in this work, which consists of three steps: formulation of questions, search strategy and selection of studies. This review analyzes the research efforts and projects related to domain-specific alignment techniques, used with the aim of improving the completeness and knowledge of these domains.

2.1   Definition of Research Questions

It was considered that the research question should address the techniques used to align domain specifications in ontologies and glossaries, thus promoting the collection of related works. The research questions defined were:

Table 1. Research questions formulation

Question	Goal
What are the tools used to align domain specifications?	Identify the tools used for domain specification
Will the application of alignment techniques and methods, in LELs domain glossaries, allow their alignment?	What techniques are used to align domain specifications using glossaries, ontologies and other models?
Establish whether the application of similarity techniques in tools based on natural language will allow domain alignment	Identify the techniques used for the alignment of glossaries and other models

Thus, the questions defined were about the tools and techniques used.

2.2   Selection of Articles: Exclusion Criteria

Based on the question presented in Table 1, jobs were searched in the following databases: IEEE Xplore, Springer, ACM, Google Scholar, and Scielo. The search terms consulted were "domain alignment" or "aligning domain specifications"; "aligning domain specifications" or "alignment of specific domains", and "ontology matching" or "ontology alignment". Only publications after 2015 were considered. Finally, the search for scientific articles was carried out using the academic search engine Lens, allowing filters to be applied by years, sources, topics, authors, and other criteria. In Table 2, we can see each search string and each database's selected results.

The articles found were consolidated by eliminating duplicates. Later, a selection of articles was made considering the title and abstract, obtaining a total of 139 scientific documents for a complete reading.

While reading the 139 articles, 67 were excluded since they focused on other aspects not considered in this study. The topics addressed in the excluded documents are the

Table 2. Initial search results

Sources	Search strings	Results obtained
ACM	Techniques aligning domain specifications	36
Springer	Techniques used for aligning domain	52
IEEE Xplore	Aligning domain specifications	35
Google Scholar	Techniques aligning domain specifications	11
Scielo	Techniques aligning domain specifications	5

following: 1) Security Standards with Semantic Technologies Used in Industrial Environments. 2) Studies based on interoperability technologies. 3) Other types of studies related to image-based domain alignment. Finally, 72 articles were selected to analyze in the next stage. Also, three articles found in the bibliographic references of these 72 selected scientific documents were added, which were considered articles of interest for systematic mapping, as seen in Fig. 1.

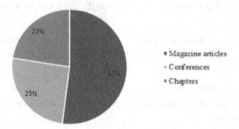

Fig. 1. Classification of the articles

Figure 1 shows the classification of the articles, for this analysis articles were classified according to the technique used, by type of publication (conferences, magazine, chapter) and according to the classification source. According to the type of publication, 52% of the articles are concentrated in magazine articles, 25% in congress and conference articles and 23% in book chapters.

2.3 Classification Results

A total of 75 articles were considered for the next phase of analysis, whose distribution is detailed in Table 3.

The articles considered for the analysis phase are based on projects that have used ontologies or glossaries as tools for domain specification. Most of the literature is cited at the ontology level. Although there is literature related to glossaries, these have not been explored as much, due to the difficulties related to the ambiguities of being written in natural language.

Table 3. Articles classification distribution

Domain specification tool	Quantity	Relevant references by alignment technique
Ontology	11	Lexical Similarity [9–12]
	7	Linguistic Similarity [13–17]
	21	Semantic Similarity [18–22]
	9	Structural Similarity [23–25]
Glossaries	10	Semantics [26–29]
	13	Structural [30–32]
	4	Syntactical [33, 34]

3 Literature Review Results

Results of the literature review answer the established research questions by obtaining the techniques used to align domain specifications.

3.1 Tools for the Alignment of Specific Domain

An alignment process can be defined as the comparison between two or more elements, from which the similarities or differences can be identified. Among the tools used for domain specification are ontologies and glossaries.

In the O1 and O2 ontologies [35], alignment is defined as the process of creating correspondences in the form $(c1, c2, s)$, where $c1 \in O1$ and $c2 \in O2$ are the concepts of the two ontologies and $s \in [0.1]$ is the estimated similarity between the two concepts. An alignment between two ontologies O1 and O2 is a set of correspondences, where each correspondence is defined as: $A(O1, O2) = \{(c1, c2, s) \mid c1 \in O1, c2 \in O2, s \in [0,1]\}$. Correspondences can also have the extended form $(c1, c2, s, r)$, where r is the type of relationship (for example, equivalence or generalization), or a reduced form $(c1, c2)$, where the coefficient of correspondence is not it specifies.

Yuan X et al. [36] use a variety of ontologies to define and represent knowledge in many domains in requirements engineering. To successfully exploit different ontologies, the researchers focused on diverse ontology fusion techniques, showing that no serious attempts have been made in the area of requirements election where ontology fusion has the potential to be successful by generating requirements specifications rapidly through combined ontology-based reasoning means, and attempting to define an approach needed to combine ontologies effectively to improve the requirements elicitation process. They proposed a methodology whereby domain knowledge involved in existing ontologies is combined with an ontology being developed to capture requirements, so that requirements engineers can deliver outcomes based on refined requirements.

On the other hand, with domain glossaries, an alignment process consists of looking for conflicts, completeness, missing parts, omissions, similarities, and differences. Wang, C. [4] proposes an approach for building glossaries from software source code and documentation, using a set of high-quality initial terms identified from code identifiers and definitions of natural language concepts to train a domain-specific prediction model able to recognize glossary terms based on the lexical and semantic context of sentences that mention domain-specific concepts.

3.2 Techniques for the Alignment of Specific Domains

Domain alignment projects considering Glossaries and Ontologies have used lexical, semantic and structural similarity techniques, as shown in Fig. 2.

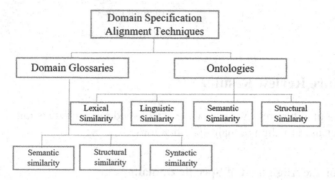

Fig. 2. Classification of techniques according to domain specification tool

From the application of each of these techniques, a measure of similarity is obtained, which is a mathematical expression that allows expressing through a numerical data the degree of relationship between two elements, their similarity or their inequality based on their qualities or attributes of these two elements [37]. Table 4 shows the types and methods for calculating similarity referring to the most commonly used alignment techniques.

Table 4 briefly explains the 3 types of similarity referring to the alignment techniques.

3.3 Alignment Techniques in Domain Glossaries

For the review of alignment techniques in domain specification glossaries, the glossary called Extended Language Lexicon (LEL) has been considered, with studies that include the improvement of their quality, looking for lack of completeness, ambiguities, conflicts or omissions.

Litvak C et al. [41] present an approach that consists of analyzing the entire LEL glossary looking for conflicts according to the following classification developed by the authors: semantic, structural and syntactic. The authors also developed guidelines and a specific process for conflict resolution. The preliminary evaluation showed the importance of identifying the conflicts and their solutions to reach better quality models. Sebastián V et al. [42] presented a variant of the inspection technique to detect defects in the source code, or in design and requirements models; the technique is based on the construction of concept diagrams which are able to verify a lexical model (LEL) that usually presents completeness and ambiguity problems due to the use of natural language.

Table 4. Similarity type

Alignment techniques	Description	Similarity calculation methods
Lexical	It measures the degree of similarity between a series of words. A lexical similarity of 1 (or 100%) corresponds to a total recurrence between the vocabularies, while 0 means that there are no words common between them [38]	Levenshtein distance Damerau-Levenshtein distance Jaro distance Jaro-Winkler distance Match rating approach comparison Hamming distance
Semantic	It aims to measure when two texts are similar in meaning [39]	Euclidean Overlap Manhathan Dice Number of synonyms they share Number of hypernyms they share Jaccad coefficient with synonym expansion Cosine similarity with n-grams and character skip-grams Leacock & Chodorow word similarity Lesk word similarity Word similarity of Wu & Palmer Word similarity of Resnik´s Lin word similarity Conrath's Jiang word similarity Inheritance similarity method (MSI) Sibling similarity method (MSS)
Structural	It uses syntactic information and dependencies between the words of a sentence. This method comprises a set of modules that are executed sequentially, addressing tasks of tree construction, filtering, detection of embedded trees and calculation of similarity between them [40]	

The proposed inspection mainly detects omissions and ambiguities. This inspection proposal discards the analysis of LEL glossary with syntactic conflicts and is part of the construction of conceptual diagrams, through which defects are identified. The process consisted of three phases: 1) constructing a conceptual diagram for each LEL symbol; 2) concept analysis of diagrams; and 3) relationship analysis of each conceptual diagram and between diagrams. Through conceptual diagrams, it was possible to detect through

4 different LEL models: omission of symbols, total or partial omission of notions and impacts, grammatical ambiguity due to different factors like redundant terms, compound sentences not complying with the principles of circularity and minimal vocabulary, and non-relevant symbols.

Hadad GDS et al. [43] address the incompleteness problem by proposing heuristics to facilitate LEL creation. These heuristics were developed based on the identification of the causes that originated the omissions detected, both real and apparent, the latter causing other shortcomings, such as a decrease in the compression of the model, lack of homogeneity in the descriptions contained in it, concealment of relevant information and difficulties in its validation. In [44] they use a checklist as an inspection variant, in order to detect omissions, ambiguity, inconsistencies or errors, performing an experiment applied to the LELs.

3.4 Alignment Techniques in Ontologies Using Lexical Similarity, String Analysis, and Linguistic Similarity

Among the works related to the alignment of ontologies are those that use measures of linguistic similarity or string analysis, which determine the relationship between two or more domains. Ontology alignment or ontology matching are used to identify entities contained in two or more ontologies that are similar or equivalent.

Chandranegara DR et al. [45] propose an approach to find similar entities in the bibliography created by Bibtex and IFLA (International Federation of Library Associations and Institutions). In this research, they combine several similarity methods, such as: Jaro Winkler Distance which finds the similarity between two-character strings where the highest similarity value indicates that the character strings are similar, and Jac-card distance which is used to find the similarity between two sentences. The method Edit Distance is used to convert one character string into another, obtaining the editing distance to be normalized later and finally calculating the maximum distance between both strings. In this study, the authors used an alignment process, where two ontologies are the process's input, then the similarities were compared by applying different methods, and lastly, finding the similarity between the ontologies. This study also aimed to determine whether using the proposed combined similarity method can increase the similarity value. The limitation of the research was the alignment, ontology matching is performed in the class, data properties and object properties in both ontologies, ignoring the relationships between the entities.

Kuntarto GP et al. [17] present Dwipa + Ontology III, a new version of Dwipa Ontology III, one of many sources of knowledge about the domain of tourism in Indonesia, which stores information and its relationships about lodging, attraction, activity and amenities. However, this ontology was missing information related to climate. The project aimed to align two sources of meteorological ontologies: the general meteorological ontology and the meteorological ontology for smart cities, to create a new concept of meteorological ontology with a more precise time-based approach. This new concept of meteorological ontology was generated by measuring its linguistic similarity using tools such as Falcon-AO that provide automatic linguistics. The ontology alignment method successfully mapped the two weather ontologies into a new weather concept showing that there are 14 similar data between the two ontologies named: Weather

Condition, Weather Report, DewPointemperature, Unit, Gust Wind, Celsius, Humidity, AtmospherePressure, Velocity, Temperature, Interval, hasDate, hasSpeedValues, and hasUnit enriched with a new class concept called weatherReport which consists of four subclasses: Unit, Interval, Weather and Temperature for a total of 255 instances.

Karam N et al. [13] describe the alignment of ontologies related to biodiversity and ecology. About biodiversity, they study the variability and diversity of organisms, including the variability within and between species, with special attention to the functional diversity of traits and their relationship with the environment. In the preparatory phase, a set of reference mappings is produced and used to evaluate the performance of ontology matching systems in ontologies related to biodiversity and ecology. They used ontology matching systems: AML, Lily, LogMap (with its different variants), POMap and Extended Mapping (XMap) which are primarily based on lexical matching techniques with an emphasis on the use of prior knowledge and include structural components for matching and filtering. In addition to having a logical repair algorithm that guarantees that the final alignment is consistent and has the desired cardinality. In the case of Lily [14], this is a comprehensive ontology matching system, a scalable matcher that implements reduction anchors to support large-scale ontology matching and uses semantics and both linguistic and structural information for the calculation of similarities.

3.5 Domain Alignment Techniques, Using Ontologies with the Use of Semantics

Another important group is related to studies that, through ontology verification, use semantics to determine if two concepts are similar in terms of their meaning in a domain ontology.

Alhassan BB [22] proposes a technique to find semantic correspondences between a pair of input ontologies to convert them semantically. In this study, an extension of Falcon-AO is used to find synonyms in two different ontologies and combine alignments for the result. Extension is achieved through the use of WordNet, a source of lexical knowledge. The extension of Falcon-AO preserves input ontologies and matching techniques like Falcon-AO. All alignments by WordNet are considered to be correct with a similarity value of 1.0. Falcon-AO has five components that were added to find semantically related terms between two given sources. The first step is pre-processing, the second step is WordNet search, the third is model creation, the fourth is the rule specification, and the final step is the data structure and fusion. Comparative analysis revealed that the extended Falcon-AO is better in terms of accuracy.

Ngo D, Bellahsene Z [46] presents a semantic verification work to efficiently detect conflicts between a set of mappings, especially large-scale ontology matching; performed structural indexing to match both ontologies. If no disjoint relationships are found in those ontologies, a semantic similarity measure is proposed to determine whether two classes in a large ontology are potentially disjoint. Then, patterns are defined to detect conflict maps. Once the conflicting assignments are located, an algorithm is applied to eliminate this inconsistency. A prototype called YAM++ implemented these contributions and participated in OEAI2013 [47] obtaining the first positions verifying the efficacy and efficiency of the results.

Zhu B et al. [19] present an asymmetric semantic similarity measure for the semantic matching of works related. By applying semantic similarity techniques, matching applications can help match information lexically and semantically. To calculate the asymmetric similarity of conceptual abilities, a case of matching programming work is proposed and validated. Semantic matching approaches focus on the semantic similarity between different entities to find suitable matches between requirements and existing descriptions. First, it determines the match between descriptions with all or a significant number of the requirements. Then, it sorts the matching descriptions. Since most descriptions do not meet all the desired requirements, semantic similarity techniques are used in the classification process so that descriptions are taken into account instead of exact matches. In this case, the classification problem was dealt by elaborating the taxonomy of specific skills formalized in a Simple Knowledge Organization System (SKOS).

Hu X et al. [20] propose a four-stage ontology matching framework (FOMF) to improve matching performance. It is based on the only accepted claim that an external exhaustive knowledge base can be used as a semantic bridge between domain ontologies for ontology matching. FOMF semantically maps domain ontologies to a knowledge base and then produces different types of alignments, including equivalence, subclass, and instance alignments. Similarities between two domain ontologies are used to improve equivalence and alignment discovery. Finally, based on the acquired alignments, the inferred alignments are deduced to ensure the integrity of the matching results.

3.6 Domain Alignment Using Ontologies Based on Structural Similarity

Based on the ontology structure, the matching is based on graphical ontologies or ontologies based on taxonomies. Scharffe F et al. [48] consider the alignment of ontologies as a design problem, where for each correlation it is necessary to build the correspondence between pairs or sets of ontological entities; for this purpose they present ontology alignment patterns as reusable templates of recursive correspondences, based on a detailed analysis of frequent ontology mismatches. They developed a library of standard patterns to refine the matches, either by the alignment designer or by pattern detection algorithms. The authors distinguish three levels of abstraction for the representation of ontological alignment, going from executable transformation rules to concrete correspondences between two ontologies, to ontology alignment patterns at the third level. They express patterns using an ontology alignment representation language, extract mismatches from vocabularies associated with datasets published as linked open data and assess the ability of matching patterns to provide suitable alignments for these mismatches. Finally, it creates instances and uses patterns to solve ontology alignment problems. The work carried out provided more support to the user in the application of patterns, making the task easier.

Research [49] proposes a similarity extension based on the structure method for ontology matching. First, they select concepts from both ontologies using similarities between entities based on their linguistic information. Then, it partitions each ontology based on the set of recognized concepts using the clustering method. Finally, it uses the similarity diffusion method to update the similarities between entities of two ontologies and apply a comparison method to establish the results of the mapping. The experimental results show that the approach is very efficient and can obtain better results than others based on similarities and similarity-based algorithms.

Ouali I et al. [23] propose two matching methods based on the graph's structure. Labels, relationships between concepts and their positions in the ontology tree are considered. The first method, called the Inheritance Similarity Method (ISM), emphasizes parent/child relationships by calculating the similarity between two concepts. The second method, called the Sibling Similarity Method (MSS), considers the concept of sibling relationships. In addition, an improvement of the mapping selection strategy is offered by including efficient optimization techniques through the stable marriage algorithm used to improve the alignment quality of the ontology, this improved matching approach allowed to obtain a high-quality level of alignment of two ontologies.

3.7 Alignment of Domains, Using NLP

Y. Liu et al. [50] propose an approach to build and develop a semantic network of concepts and phrases of software engineering, starting with a set of existing glossaries, using explicitly defined terms and associations as a starting point, using techniques based on machine learning to dynamically identify and document additional associations between terms, leverages the network to interpret natural language queries in the glossary, and finally augments the resulting semantic network with feedback provided by users, allowing queries to be improved through natural language interfaces.

Aydemir FB et al. [51] propose a flexible, language-independent technique based on natural language processing (NLP) that analyzes several models included in a project and provides suggestions to modellers based on what is represented in the models they analyze. The method uses a domain ontology with the essential terms of concepts that are expected to appear in the model. The technique analyzes part of the model's NLP. It then compares the identified concepts to the other model, then suggests concepts to be modelled based on the missing concepts, and the domain ontology learns from model feedback to refine future suggestions.

4 Application of Alignment Techniques and Methods, in Domain Glossaries (LELs)

In this section, a comparison is made between semantic and lexical techniques used in document review alignment projects. For this, a lexical model is used, such as the glossaries called Extended Language Lexicon (LEL), which contain information from a specific domain, expressed through its different symbols, notion states and impact. With a case study, it is intended to determine if through the application of these techniques, it is possible to identify omissions, similarities and correspondences between the domains represented with the LELs.

The LELs glossaries correspond to the domain on "Tomato Crop" and were created for the exemplification of the case study. Table 5 represents the content of the symbols of the LELs.

The number of products of each LEL is represented, LEL1: 144 products, LEL2: 119 products, LEL3: 119 products and contains synonyms.

For the comparison of the LEL Glossaries, consider the following levels: a) the LELs are on the same domain and speak the subject in the same language. b) they contain the

Table 5. Topics contained in the LEL symbols

Product	LEL1		LEL2		LEL3	
	Qty	Topics	Qty	Topics	Qty	Topics
Subject	4	Farmer Producer Illness Plague	3	Farmer Producer Plague	3	Farmer Producer Plague
Object	5	Tomato Tomatoes mecatetoma Seedbed irrigation plan	3	Tomato Tomatoes Hotbed	3	Tomato plant Tomato Hotbed
verbs	8	Prepare the soil sow, water, transplant, fumigate, fertilize, ferti-irrigation, harvest	7	Prepare the soil, sow to water transplant, fertilize fertigation, harvest	7	Condition the ground plant, water transplant fertilize fertigation gather,
Condition	5	Vegetative, flowering, development, maturation, harvested	4	Vegetative flowering Ripening harvested	4	Vegetative Bloom Maturation harvested
Notions	50		44		44	
Impact	72		58		58	
Total	144		119		119	

same symbols with very similar meanings and the most important ideas in notions and impacts of the larger text (LEL1) are represented in the smaller texts (LEL2 and LEL3), c) LEL 2 has 20% fewer symbols than LEL1 d) LEL 3 has 40% of symbols that are synonymous with LEL1. For each case, they were separated by type of symbol and compared by elements, symbols, types, notions and impact.

For the comparison, Python is used as a tool and the TF-IDF standard is applied to the texts with application of lexical and semantic techniques. To apply the semantic techniques, the TF-IDF technique is applied to convert each of the words in the document into vectors, necessary for the application of the corresponding measures such as: Euclidean, Cosine Similarity and Jaccard Coefficient, in three different comparison cases: equal LELs (LEL1-LEL1), LELs with a slight difference in number of symbols (LEL1-LEL2) and LELs with the presence of synonyms (LEL1-LEL3). Table 6 shows the results of the semantic comparison made with the LEL documents.

The results shown in Table 6 show that the comparisons are in accordance with the expected values: value 1, equal LEL; 0.9947 LEL with LEL with difference in number of symbols; and, 0.7253 for the presence of synonyms.

Table 6. Semantic comparison

Cases	Euclidean	Cosine Similarity	Jaccard
LEL1, LEL1	1.00	1.00	1.00
LEL1, LEL2	0.8975	0.9947	0.4690
LEL1, LEL3	0.2589	0.7253	0.4497

For the comparison of lexical similarity, the Jaro Distance, Jaro-Winkler and Hamming Distance techniques were used. The symbol sets of the LELs indicated in Table 5 were compared. In the cases LEL1-LEL2 and LEL1-LEL3 in the Hamming technique, the last 5 symbols of LEL1 were omitted, because the sets must match in size.

Table 7 shows the results of the lexical comparison made with the LEL symbols.

Table 7. Lexical comparison

Cases	Elements	Mesures		
		Hamming	Jaro	Jarowinkler
LEL1-LEL1	Symbols	1	1	1
	Notions	1	1	1
	Impact	1	1	1
LEL1-LEL2	Symbols	0.76	0.84	0.87
	Notions	0.69	0.73	0.73
	Impact	0.58	0.74	0.74
LEL1-LEL3	Symbols	0.23	0.55	0.56
	Notions	0.2	0.28	0.28
	Impact	0.16	0.16	0.16

In the lexical comparison, LEL1 compared to itself is 1 among all measures, thus indicating complete similarity. In the comparison between LEL1-LEL2, the similarity values were 0.87 in symbols, 0.73 in notions and 0.74 in impact. Among the LEL1-LEL3, the best similarity values were 0.56 in symbols, 0.28 in notions and 0.16 in impact, corresponding to the Jaro Winkler mean, since it compares characters and their transpositions in each word of the set.

5 Conclusions and Future Work

Among the most used tools for domain specification are ontologies and glossaries. Studies have concentrated greater effort on the use of ontologies, which exceed by a large percentage the works related to tools based on natural language such as domain glossaries.

At the lexical level, among the most used methods we find Jaro Distance, Jaro Winkler, Jaccard Distance, Edit Distance, and Hamming, applied in projects to convert character strings or find the similarity between two-character strings, comparing the similarities and testing whether a combined method can increase the similarity value.

Among the most used methods at the semantic level in the different projects were Euclidean, Manhathan, Jaccad Coefficient with expansion in synonyms, cosine similarity, applied in the search for synonyms, translation machines, automatic construction of summaries, attribution of authorship, tests of comprehensive reading, information retrieval, which need to measure the degree of similarity between two given texts. A project of great importance in this field is Falcon-AO where they added five components to semantically find corresponding terms between two given sources, creating a method that included: 1) pre-processing, 2) WordNet search, 3) model creation, 4) rule specification, and 5) data structure and merging.

At the structural level, projects such as pattern library development apply two matching methods, the Inheritance Similarity Method (MSI) and the Sibling Similarity Method (MSS), based on the structure of the graph, where labels, and relationships between concepts and their positions in the ontology tree are considered.

Using NLP, projects such as the construction of semantic networks of software engineering concepts and phrases were found, from existing glossaries that use the explicitly defined terms and associations as a starting point and that use techniques based on machine learning, identifying and documenting dynamically additional associations between terms, which have been used to interpret queries in natural language in the glossary, and increase the resulting semantic network with the feedback provided by users, allowing queries to be improved through natural language interfaces.

At the LEL glossary level, work developed looks for conflicts related to semantic, structural and syntactic levels. The projects seek to find ambiguities, gaps, omissions between the LEL symbols, which reduce the quality of the glossaries due to the use of natural language, where the alignment process is carried out with requirements engineers who perform the search through different heuristics.

With the application of semantic and lexical techniques in the LEL domain glossaries, it was possible to determine the degree of similarity between the different glossaries, at the semantic level the one with the best precision was the Cosine Similarity method, while at the lexical level, the one with best precision was Jaro Winkler, where the values obtained are low, because the sets differ in size and in the position of the elements. The application of these methods by themselves does not allow to detect where the missing or omissions were, as well as the variations between the LELs, which is a limitation if we want to align domains in order to improve the completeness and understanding of this.

The NLP is a wide field that has currently allowed text processing even with limitations. Natural language understanding presents an area open to many challenges.

As future work, these techniques and methods should be executed, through a process that contemplates heuristics and considers natural language variants such as synonyms, hyponyms, hyperonyms, with the use of a thesaurus that has the domain terms, which allows to obtain similarities, correspondences and omissions between LELs, in order to improve the completeness of the domain and as a support to achieve interoperability between systems.

References

1. Litvak, C., Antonelli, L., Rossi, G., Gigante, N.: Improving the identification of conflicts in collaborative requirements engineering. In: 2018 International Conference on Computational Science and Computational Intelligence (CSCI). IEEE, pp. 872–877 (2018)
2. Aldekhail, M., Chikh, A., Ziani, D.: Software requirements conflict identification: review and recommendations. Int. J. Adv. Comput. Sci. Appl. **7**, 326–335 (2016). https://doi.org/10.14569/IJACSA.2016.071044
3. Landhauser, M., Komer, S.J., Tichy, W.F.: Synchronizing domain models with natural language specifications. In: 2012 First International Workshop on Realizing AI Synergies in Software Engineering (RAISE). IEEE, pp. 22–26 (2012)
4. Wang, C., et al.: 2019. A learning-based approach for automatic construction of domain glossary from source code and documentation. In: Proceedings of the 2019 27th ACM Joint Meeting on European Software Engineering Conference and Symposium on the Foundations of Software Engineering (ESEC/FSE 2019). Association for Computing Machinery, pp. 97–108, New York, NY, USA (2019)
5. Arora, C., Sabetzadeh, M., Briand, L., Zimmer, F.: Automated extraction and clustering of requirements glossary terms. IEEE Trans. Softw. Eng. **43**, 918–945 (2017). https://doi.org/10.1109/TSE.2016.2635134
6. do Leite, J.C.S.P., Franco, A.P.M.: A strategy for conceptual model acquisition. In: [1993] Proceedings of the IEEE International Symposium on Requirements Engineering. IEEE Comput. Soc. Press, pp. 243–246 (1993)
7. Sadoun, D., Dubois, C., Ghamri-Doudane, Y., Grau, B.: From natural language requirements to formal specification using an ontology. In: Proceedings of the International Conference Tools with Artificial Intelligence ICTAI, pp. 755–760 (2013). https://doi.org/10.1109/ICTAI.2013.116
8. Ivanova, T.: Ontology alignment. Int. J. Knowl. Syst. Sci. **1**, 22–40 (2010). https://doi.org/10.4018/jkss.2010100102
9. Bulygin, L.: Combining lexical and semantic similarity measures with machine learning approach for ontology and schema matching problem. CEUR Workshop Proc. **2277**, 245–249 (2018)
10. Thi, N., Anh, T.T.T.: Ontology Matching Based on Combination of Lexical and Structural (2015)
11. Li, Q., Li, T., Chang, B.: Learning word sense embeddings from word sense definitions. In: Lin, C.-Y., Xue, N., Zhao, D., Huang, X., Feng, Y. (eds.) ICCPOL/NLPCC -2016. LNCS (LNAI), vol. 10102, pp. 224–235. Springer, Cham (2016). https://doi.org/10.1007/978-3-319-50496-4_19
12. Bayomi, M., Levacher, K., Ghorab, M.R., Lawless, S.: OntoSeg: a novel approach to text segmentation using ontological similarity. In: 2015 IEEE International Conference on Data Mining Workshop (ICDMW). IEEE, pp. 1274–1283 (2015)
13. Karam, N., Khiat, A., Algergawy, A., Sattler, M., Weiland, C., Schmidt, M.: Matching biodiversity and ecology ontologies: challenges and evaluation results. Knowl. Eng. Rev. **35**, e9 (2020). https://doi.org/10.1017/S0269888920000132
14. Wu, J., Pan, Z., Zhang, C., Wang, P.: Lily results for OAEI 2019. In: CEUR Workshop Proceedings, vol. 2536, pp. 153–159 (2019)

15. Schalley, A.C.: Ontologies and ontological methods in linguistics. Lang Linguist Compass **13**, 1–19 (2019). https://doi.org/10.1111/lnc3.12356
16. Medina, D., Maturana, G., Villa, F.: A prototype for a serious digital game to teach linguistic ontologies. arXiv:1909.07371 (2019)
17. Kuntarto, G.P., Alrin, Y., Gunawan, I.P.: The key role of ontology alignment and enrichment methodologies for aligning and enriching Dwipa ontology with the weather concept on the tourism domain. In: 2019 3rd International Conference on Informatics and Computational Sciences (ICICoS). IEEE, pp. 1–6 (2019)
18. García, A.C.H., Vidal, M.T., de Jesús, J., Martínez, L.: Medidas de similitud semántica aplicadas a una ontología de dominio. Res. Compu. Sci. **147**(6), 119–131 (2018). https://doi.org/10.13053/rcs-147-6-9
19. Zhu, B., Li, X., Sancho, J.B.: A novel asymmetric semantic similarity measurement for semantic job matching. In: 2017 International Conference on Security, Pattern Analysis, and Cybernetics (SPAC), pp. 152–157. IEEE (2017)
20. Hu, X., Feng, Z., Chen, S., Huang, K., Li, J., Zhou, M.: Accurate identification of ontology alignments at different granularity levels. IEEE Access **5**, 105–120 (2017). https://doi.org/10.1109/ACCESS.2016.2614759
21. Maheshwari, G., Trivedi, P., Sahijwani, H., Jha, K., Dasgupta, S., Lehmann, J.: SimDoc: Topic sequence alignment based document similarity framework. In: Proceedings of the Knowledge Capture Conference, pp. 1–8 (2016). https://doi.org/10.1145/3148011.3148016
22. Alhassan, B.B.: Extending an ontology alignment system with a lexical database. Sci Res J **III**, 12–17 (2015)
23. Ouali, I., Ghozzi, F., Taktak, R., Hadj Sassi, M.S.: Ontology alignment using stable matching. Procedia Comput. Sci. **159**, 746–755 (2019). https://doi.org/10.1016/j.procs.2019.09.230
24. Nguyen, T., Conrad, S.: Emparejamiento de ontología utilizando múltiples medidas de similitud. In: International Joint Conference Knowledge Discovery Knowledge Engineering Knowledge Management. https://ieeexplore.ieee.org/document/7526985 (2015). Accessed 14 Aug 2022
25. Tamizhmaran, S.V., Vivekanandan, V., Vijayaragavan, P.: Theoretical strategies to devise structural semantics of ontology inferencing graph techniques. Int. J. Sci., Res. Sci. Eng. Technol. **2**, 217–220 (2015)
26. Martinc, M., Montariol, S., Zosa, E., Pivovarova, L.: Capturing evolution in word usage: just add more clusters? In: Companion Proceedings of the Web Conference 2020. ACM, New York, NY, USA, pp. 343–349 (2020)
27. Hadad Graciela, D.S., Alberto Sebastián, R.: Estudio Comparativo de Variantes de Inspección sobre el Modelo Léxico Extendido del Lenguaje. 2512 (2019)
28. Yao, Z., Sun, Y., Ding, W., Rao, N., Xiong, H.: Dynamic word embeddings for evolving semantic discovery. In: WSDM 2018 – Proceedings of the 11th ACM International Conference Web Search Data Min 2018, pp. 673–681 (2018). https://doi.org/10.1145/3159652.3159703
29. Delpech, J.-F.: Unsupervised word sense disambiguation in dynamic semantic spaces. 1–7 (2018)
30. Ridao, M.N., Doorn, J.H., Kaplan, G.N.: Construcción de grafos de glosarios guiada por el estilo del discurso. In: Workshop de Investigadores en Ciencias de la Computación (WICC 2020, El Calafate, Santa Cruz), pp. 405–409 (2020)
31. Zeng, W., Zhao, X., Wang, W., Tang, J., Tan, Z.: Degree-aware alignment for entities in tail. In: Proceedings of the 43rd International ACM SIGIR Conference on Research and Development in Information Retrieval, pp. 811–820. ACM, New York, NY, USA (2020)
32. Wu, Y., Liu, X., Feng, Y., Wang, Z., Zhao, D.: Jointly learning entity and relation representations for entity alignment. In: Proceedings of the 2019 Conference on Empirical Methods in Natural Language Processing and the 9th International Joint Conference on Natural Language Processing, pp. 240–249. Hong Kong, China, 3–7 Nov 2019

33. Jean Luc, R., Mahatody, T., Razafimandimby, J.P.: Elaborate lexicon extended language with a lot of conceptual information. Int. J. Comput. Sci. Eng. Appl. **5**, 1–18 (2015). https://doi.org/10.5121/ijcsea.2015.5601

34. Sebastián, A., Hadad, G.D.S.: Mejoras a un modelo léxico mediante mapas conceptuales In:. XXI Congr Argentino Ciencias la Comput (Junín, 2015) (2015)

35. David, J., Euzenat, J., Scharffe, F., Trojahn dos Santos, C., Dos Santos, C.T.: The Alignment API 4.0. Semant Web **2**, 3 (2011). https://doi.org/10.3233/SW-2011-0028

36. Yuan, X., Tripathi, S.: Combining ontologies for requirements elicitation. In: 2015 IEEE International Model-Driven Requirements Engineering Workshop (MoDRE), pp. 1–5. IEEE (2015)

37. Amón, I., Jiménez, C.: Funciones de Similitud sobre Cadenas de Texto: Una Comparación Basada en la Naturaleza de los Datos. In: Int. Conf. Inf. Resour. Manag. 13 (2010)

38. Micol, D., Mu, R., Palomar, M.: Técnicas léxico-sintácticas para el reconocimiento de Implicación Textual (2007)

39. Vilariño, D., Tovar, M., Beltrán, B., León, S.: Un modelo para detectar la similitud semántica entre textos de diferentes longitudes. Res. Comput. Sci. **85**, 57–64 (2014). https://doi.org/10.13053/rcs-85-1-5

40. Fernandez, S., Marsa-Maestre, I., Velasco, J.R., Alarcos, B.: Ontology alignment architecture for semantic sensor web integration. Sensors **13**, 12581–12604 (2013). https://doi.org/10.3390/s130912581

41. Litvak, C., Rossi, G., Antonelli, L.: Conflict management in the collaborative description of a domain language (S), pp. 524–577 (2018)

42. Sebastián, A., Hadad, G.D.S., Robledo, E.: Inspección centrada en Omisiones y Ambigüedades de un Modelo Léxico. In: CIbSE 2017 - XX Ibero-American Conf. Softw. Eng., pp. 71–84 (2017)

43. Hadad, G.D.S., Litvak, C.S., Doorn, J.H.: Heurísticas para el modelado de requisitos escritos en lenguaje natural. In: CACIC 2014 - XX Congr. Argentino Ciencias la Comput. (2014)

44. Hadad, G.D.S., Sebastián, A.: Inspecciones para Mejorar la Calidad de Modelos en Lenguaje Natural. In: XXV Congreso Argentino de Ciencias de la Computación, pp. 737–746 (2019)

45. Chandranegara, D.R., Sarno, R.: Ontology alignment using combined similarity method and matching method. In: 2016 International Conference on Informatics and Computing (ICIC), pp. 239–244. IEEE (2016)

46. Ngo, D., Bellahsene, Z.: Efficient semantic verification of ontology alignment. In: 2015 IEEE/WIC/ACM International Conference on Web Intelligence and Intelligent Agent Technology (WI-IAT), pp. 141–148. IEEE (2015)

47. Ngo, D.H., Bellahsene, Z., Results, Y.A.M., Semantic, I.: YAM ++ - Results for OAEI 2012. In: International Semantic Web Conference, United States. fflirmm-00758720f (2012)

48. Scharffe, F., Zamazal, O., Fensel, D.: Ontology alignment design patterns. Knowl. Inf. Syst. **40**(1), 1–28 (2013). https://doi.org/10.1007/s10115-013-0633-y

49. Wang, Y., Liu, W., Bell, D.A.: A structure-based similarity spreading approach for ontology matching. In: Deshpande, A., Hunter, A. (eds.) SUM 2010. LNCS (LNAI), vol. 6379, pp. 361–374. Springer, Heidelberg (2010). https://doi.org/10.1007/978-3-642-15951-0_33

50. Liu, Y., Lin, J., Cleland-Huang, J., Vierhauser, M., Guo, J., Lohar, S.: SENET: a semantic web for supporting automation of software engineering tasks. In: 2020 IEEE Seventh International Workshop on Artificial Intelligence for Requirements Engineering (AIRE). IEEE, pp. 23–32 (2020)

51. Aydemir, F.B., Dalpiaz, F.: Towards aligning multi-concern models via NLP. In: Proceedings of the 2017 IEEE 25th International Requirement Engineering Conference Work REW 2017, pp. 46–50 (2017). https://doi.org/10.1109/REW.2017.82

IVRMaker, An Interactive and Customizable Telephone Chatbot Services Platform

Miguel Ángel Rodríguez-García[1]([✉]), Camilo Caparrós-Laiz[2], Pedro José Vivancos-Vicente[3], José Antonio García-Díaz[2], and Rafael Valencia-García[2]

[1] Departamento de Ciencias de la Computación, Universidad Rey Juan Carlos, 28933 Madrid, Spain
miguel.rodriguez@urjc.es
[2] Facultad de Informática, Universidad de Murcia, Campus de Espinardo, Murcia 30100, Spain
{camilo.caparrosl,joseantonio.garcia8,valencia}@um.es
[3] Vócali Sistemas Inteligentes S.L, Campus de Espinardo, Murcia, Spain
pedro.vivancos@vocali.net

Abstract. Chatbots are systems that imitate human conversation by using Artificial Intelligence. They have been designed to interact with users by using natural language in a way that they think they are having a dialogue with a human. The relevance of these is gaining impact in our society, being widely applied to numerous fields, from Health Care to Education. Although their usage is associated with different purposes such as virtual assistant, entertainment, domotic, and routing, they are becoming increasingly popular in business domains, managing the customer services since they can automate, optimize and manage business processes and marketing campaigns. However, it is an arduous task to integrate them into the business data flows to take advantage of their potential and stand out from the competence. Therefore, in this work, we have described IVRMaker, an interactive and customizable telephone chatbot services platform. The target behind the IVRMaker is to help companies to integrate a conversational assistant into their business process. The platform is mainly based on cutting-edge research areas in Natural Language Processing to facilitate easy integration into the business data model. The evaluation of the platform was carried out in two use cases relating to disparate domains. The results obtained were interesting in demonstrating the applicability and adaptability of these assistants and their direct impact on the automatization of customer services and marketing campaigns.

Keywords: Chatbot · Natural Language Processing · Marketing campaigns

R. Valencia-García et al. (Eds.): CITI 2022, CCIS 1658, pp. 62–74, 2022.
https://doi.org/10.1007/978-3-031-19961-5_5

1   Introduction

Chatbots have rapidly invaded and occupied the Internet, becoming the next relevant technological leap in conversational services [10]. Recent advances in Natural Language Processing have made possible the intelligent Human-Computer interaction, allowing the development of computer programs capable of having a natural dialogue through text or voice as a human user responding to the user automatically [1]. While it is a relatively new research area for the community, its application has risen substantially over the last few years in several domains [19]. Although they are widely used virtual assistants in various fields, chatbots have a tremendous impact on diverse applications concerning marketing management, providing direct interaction with users via to promote products or even customer service managing situations to seek dissatisfactions in users' sales or recommend products.

Artificial Intelligence has been one of the primary factors for triggering the wide usage of chatbots in our society. Recent developments in related research fields have enabled the proliferation of techniques that reduce the understanding drawback between humans and machines [13]. Deep Neural network models or multi-task learning mechanisms are some of the methods that are being explored by the community to improve computer reading comprehension [5,14]. In particular, much work has been developed in those research lines focusing on improving the conversational assistant answer accuracy. For instance, in the neural network field, several models have been developed for labelling words and phrases in sentences to indicate their semantic role [16]; analysing the textual entailment to measure the directional relation between text fragments in a sentence [11]; and breaking the sentence into elemental components [18]. On the contrary, in the area of multi-task learning, specific problems related to the Natural Language Understanding system are attracting attention, such as sentence-to-vector encoders [9], labelled data [21] or natural language inference [17].

As we can observe, a chatbot is a complex system composed of several models, making the setting an arduous task for non-expert users. We proposed IRV Maker, an interactive and customizable telephone chatbot services platform, to address this drawback. The primary idea behind the platform is to assist companies with cutting-edge technologies for integrating these conversational agents into their data ecosystem. The platform provides an infrastructure that helps the company with the chatbots' configuration and deployment to have benefited from their advantages swiftly.

The remainder of the work is organized as follows: Sect. 2 provides a survey regarding chatbot usage. Section 3 details the method developed, carrying out a modular decomposition that explains how it works in depth. Section 4 describe the variety of use cases designed for conducting the validation of the platform proposed. Finally, Sect. 5 itemizes the most relevant obtained findings and future research lines to explore.

2   Related Works

Chatbots are systems that have been designed to improve the conversation between machines and humans, offering models that increase the understanding and efficiency of machines [13]. In literature, various approaches can be distinguished concerning determined application domains. In education, Charizia et al., in [2] propose a chatbot prototype for the educational domain that aims to identify the students' needs and answer accordingly. The described system utilises a knowledge base that formally describes the application domain. It was developed to infer students' intentions, even when they do not know what they want exactly. The system is composed of several modules from which we pointed out the inference engine that utilises the Dirichlet Allocation Algorithm for providing answers accordingly and Human-Computer Interaction Supervisor, which aims to monitor the dialogue between students and the chatbot for identifying aspects such as undetermined questions or non-convergent interaction conversations. In a completely different domain, Comendador et al. [3] describe Pharmabot, a chatbot developed for prescribing, suggesting and giving information about generic medicines for children. The proposed system is based on a purely natural language matching technique, the Left-Right Parsing Algorithm, also known as LL parser, which consists of parsing the inputs given by the users from left to the right in a controlled technical and medical dictionary. The system is making questions to patients to figure out their health problems. Each answer is analysed by using the LL parser to identify medical keywords that provide pieces of evidence about such a problem. As a result of the consultation, generic medicines are prescribed, detailing specific aspects such as intake, dosage or drug reactions. Lastly, in a closer domain to the business side, Li et al., [8] proposed AliMe Assist, an intelligent assistant designed to improve customers' shopping experiences in E-commerce. AliMe is based on question answering (QA). It provides customers with different interaction services for managing any problems with their purchases and two different ways for interaction, voice and text. The system is configured in four layers where the first corresponds to the processing of the inputs, where customers' questions are classified by analysing their content. The analysis is conducted by a trie-based pattern matcher called business rule parser, by which the customer query is analysed to figure out the intention. The second layer determines the routing of each costumers' question. The third layer is composed of relevant tools like a semantic parser, slot filling engine, and chat engine, among others, that are responsible for processing the elements of the customers' questions. Finally, the fourth layer is the persistence layer, where the knowledge is stored.

So far, a study of various alternative chatbots has been analyzed to demonstrate their impact in diverse application domains. The study showed the increasing usage of these intelligent agents to automatize specific tasks in which some dialogues need to be carried out to accomplish them. However, despite this multitude of applications, finding a strategy focused on helping non-experts users configure and deploy such a system in their industry ecosystem has not been easy in the literature. Some approaches propose tools for solving some drawbacks related to their initial functioning states, such as compiling enough conversational data to train the system [7] or improving their access to data repositories [6]. However, tools that assist companies, besides developing strategies to enhance precision and facilitate usability, integrability and deployment in different domains are required. Therefore, in response to this need, it has been developed IVRMaker. Its architecture is specified in the following section.

3   Architecture

The platform proposed is composed of two main modules: chatbot and campaign manager and chatbot. The former is, in turn, constituted by three submodules: i) dashboard, an information management tool responsible for monitoring, analysing and visually displaying a set of specific key performance indicators that track system condition, chatbots functioning and campaign status; ii) chatbot builder and configurator, a user assistant that helps users to create chatbots. It enables users to set different configurations regarding the application domain, connections to other platforms, and Natural Language Understanding (NLU) model, among others; and, iii) configuration manager with outside responsible for facilitating a via to access external data repositories. Other three submodules also form the latter: i) Input/Output interfaces that represent the interaction via by which clients and chatbot talk; ii) Natural Language Processing module (NLP module) that employs several tools to analyse the conversation between both entities, clients and chatbots. It aims to capture specific features from text exchange between chatbots and clients for understanding the context;

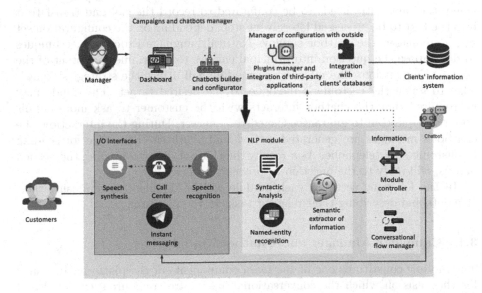

Fig. 1. Architecture of IVRMaker platform

and, finally, iii) the information module that aims at guiding the flow of dialogue between chatbots and clients to a pre-specified target. Figure 1 depicts the architecture designed, representing the modules analysed and their interactions.

Although the two main modules that constituted the platform have been significantly delimitated, conducting separately different services in parallel, they complement each other to address the target of understanding precisely and answering correctly to users. To carry out this target, the platform works as follows: first, the company manager who wants to utilise a chatbot must sign up. Then, it is required to use the builder and configuration module to create a new instance of a chatbot. The module provides a friendly user interface for creating and configuring a chatbot from scratch. Here, the manager can select a multitude of parameters, such as the NLU model, static messages to interact with customers, call centre type, metrics or indicators to monitor, credentials settings to enable chatbots to interact with social networks or even actions to handle events, define hooks for external web services or implement connections to external data sources. As a result, the manager obtained the configured chatbot ready for deployment. Depending on the configuration selected, different modules will be activated. For instance, if metrics or indicators are set to analyse the performance of the chatbot's service, then the dashboard will provide an interface with several ways of visualising such information in real-time. Similarly, if an external repository is required to be utilised by the chatbot to, for instance, set a marketing campaign for a determined product, the configuration manager outside provides tools to examine the status of such connection.

In a use case scenario, a chatbot correctly configured and deployed works as follows: initially, a customer calls the call centre to ask a question concerning, for instance, a specific marketing campaign published by the company. At this stage, the call centre needs to be configured to record the call and translate it into the text to be processed later. Next step, depending on the configuration set by the manager, the chatbot employs Natural Language Processing techniques to decompose the question into principal entities to determine the intent of the customer's question. The information module will utilise the strategies' knowledge to guide the customer's dialogue to the desired target. This guide may be required that the chatbot interacts with the customer to ask more details about the question to guarantee the correct answer. During the interaction, the chatbot's messages are generated in text and synthesised to voice for sending to customers by telephone. As a result, the chatbot, after compiling the needed details, will reply to the question as precisely as possible.

In the following sections, each module will be detailed, decomposing their elements and describing their relevant tasks in the platform.

3.1   Campaign Manager and Chatbot Module

The module constitutes one of the main components of the platform. It stands for the basis on which the conversational agents are configured, executed and monitored. The module is formed by three principal components: Dashboard, chatbots builder and configurator and the manager of configuration with outside. Each one will be described in detail in the following subsections.

Dashboard Component. The Dashboard is a data visualization component that implements various alternatives to graph in real-time metrics and indicators related to platform and chatbots performance. Concretely, in the platform, managers can monitor functioning variables such as memory usage, disk capacity, and the amount of the process executing. Alternatively, chatbot managers can analyze the users' behaviours through relevant indicators such as activity volume rate, bounce rate, response volume, conversation length, and interaction rate. The visualizer is based on two main libraries Matplotlib[1] as a mathematical and graphics support and Flask[2] as a web framework container, which implements several graphs to represent data.

Chatbot Builder and Configurator Component. It is a multi-step setup wizard to assist managers in configuring the conversational agent. The tool is defined as a multi-step setup wizard because the chatbot configuration process has been organized in different steps, one per configurable parameter. Here, it will analyze the four main parameters required to fulfil a proper configuration of a chatbot:

- Domain: this parameter is used by managers can define the arena where the conversational agent will work. It represents the primary instructions that an agent needs to understand the components of the customers' messages that need to be identified to infer their intentions. Therefore, defining the domain requires parameters such as entities to specify elements in the messages that the chatbot must pay particular attention to because they may make out the direction of the conversation. It also defines intentions that aim at identifying directions of dialogue flow. The intentions represent a very useful tool since it allows you to predefine the conversation diagram, where it can be specified the paths in which the customers' dialogue can be guided to reach the target. In addition, in some dialogues, a chatbot could require minimal memory space to store details provided by consumers that can be required later on for answering, taking intended decisions or carrying out determined actions. We have designed an easy key-value structure to store this type of information. This structure makes managing the chatbots' memory easy, fitting out an optimized method to insert and retrieve data. Finally, a chatbot can also perform actions in certain situations, such as accessing an external database or calling an external API. We have included the parameter action to specify the set of determined actions that a chatbot can do.
  We have defined a configuration file for each described parameter based on YAML, a data serialization language that provides a basic structure to store

---

[1] https://matplotlib.org/.
[2] https://flask.palletsprojects.com/en/2.1.x/.

information based on key-value. Thus, we have represented intentions, entities, slots and actions using the keywords intent, entity, slot and action, respectively.

- Credential: It has been defined to enable chatbots to interact with external web services such as social networks. Its configuration is mainly based on two attributes: token_access and url_webhook. The former contains the token given by the external service to access. The latter includes the URL, where the accessible web services have been configured to receive requests. This parameter gains importance when companies want to advertise their services on social networks or offer them by using an instant messaging platform. In both scenarios, chatbots require mechanisms to access these external platforms and interact with them since one of the services that may be offered could be customer service. Consequently, to resolve this drawback efficiently, we decided to include the credential parameters with these two parameters to make its configuration and operation easier.
- Rules: In this platform's context, a rule has been defined to model specific parts of conversations that should always follow the same direction. For instance, when a customer greets, the conversational agent must reply with a greeting back. The conversion pattern is specified by actions and intents defined in the domain. Thus, in a rule definition, intent indicates the start point of a conversation when a rule will be executed. In contrast, an action stands for the operation that will be accomplished when the rule is executed. Hence, the coupling parameters specify the two required attributes to complete a rule; first, the intent indicates the place in a dialogue where a rule will be executed, and the action, the operation assigned to the conversational agent to carry out. As a result, by using this tool, it can be possible to link determined actions to users' intentions in patterns that repeatedly occur in conversations. This mechanism is advantageous for redirecting the users' conversational flow to the specific target.
- Natural Language Understanding Model is responsible for analysing users' messages carefully to figure out their intentions. Note that the model specified here will be trained by the details specified above.

Manager of Configuration with Outside Component. This component has been developed to facilitate the chatbots' interaction with organizational datasets. This interaction has to do with the marketing campaign configuration since it can require details stored in a corporate database about a particular product for advertising it. The exchanges can also help improve corporate customer service, since it can require information stored on its databases. Alternatively, this component is also responsible for managing the third-party plugins installed in the conversational agent. Its primary target is to enable a way to easily extend the functionalities of a chatbot, integrating plugins developed by third parties.

3.2   Chatbot Module

It stands for other big block inside the IVR Maker platform, the chatbot. It defines the structure that a chatbot should have to be deployed. In particular, three primary elements need to be set: IO interfaces as a costumer communication vias, NLP module as a tools for processing costumers' messages and inferring their intends, and information module to control the dialogue between costumers and conversational agents. In the following sections, each mentioned module will be scrutinized.

I/O Interfaces Component. The component is formed by a set of tools that are in charge of recognizing customers' voice and transcribing it to text; managing the customers' calls operating as a call centre; synthesizing voice from the text replies given by chatbot, and enabling communication via to interact with external instant message platforms. During the chatbot configuration, the manager can easily configure this component with any supported Natural Language Processing tool in the builder and configuration chatbots. Thus, a possible structure could be: Asterisk[3] as a call centre, Kaldi[4] as a synthesizer and voice recognizer, and Telegram API[5] as an external communication to allow customers to interact by using this messaging platform.

Natural Language Processing Component. It aims to process the customers' messages to understand their intentions. It can be seen as a set of analysis natural language tools that have a primary target of identifying and extracting relevant entities that produce tangible evidence about the customers' purposes. The analysis process comprises three main analyzer tools: Syntactic Parser, Name Entity Recogniser and Semantic Information Extractor. The objective of the first tool is to employ techniques that segment, tokenize and part-of-speech tag natural text to assign a graph structure that reveals the relationships between the identified tokens, considering syntax rules from grammar. Alternatively, the entity recognizer is responsible for seeking, locating and classifying named entities mentioned in unstructured text into a set of pre-defined categories such as locations, organizations, and person names, among others. In particular, one of the key functions of the recognizer is to harvest details from the customers' conversations to use for future interactions. Finally, the Semantic extractor is devoted to capturing relations between the meanings of words, phrases or sentences. These relations are defined by synonymy, antonymy, homonymy, polysemy and metonymy [12]. Their identification is crucial to understanding the customers' intentions.

---

[3] https://www.asterisk.org/.
[4] https://kaldi-asr.org/.
[5] https://core.telegram.org/.

Information Component. This component has been developed to cover an essential task inside the chatbot module, to orchestrate the modules to operate together, making the chatbot work correctly. Therefore, its main target is to control which module interacts with which other module, maintaining the coherence in their execution and controlling the knowledge flow through the chatbot's pipeline. In other words, it manages the inputs and outputs of each component, overseeing the execution order and passing the knowledge generated from each pipeline member to their following. This control enables it to accomplish a very relevant task for the chatbot, managing the conversational user flows, from the dialogue between customers and the chatbot, and redirecting the conversation to achieve the customer's objectives.

4   Validation

The validation of the presented platform was carried out by two case studies conducted in two different scenarios. The first case study was on the Technical Inspection of Vehicles, where it is emulated a proactive chatbot behaviour scenario. The second case study was oriented in the practitioner's domain. Concretely, the chatbot was prepared for customer care, receiving calls from patients and making appointments.

4.1   The Ministry of Transport (MOT) Test Use Case

This use case is devoted to simulating proactive behaviour, where a chatbot initiates the conversation to advertise to a client about the due date of Ministry of Transport (MOT) test of a vehicle that is the owner, recommending new appointments to conduct it. The chatbot utilized for this use case had the following configuration: i) Spacy[6] for the NLP component, we utilized the pipeline provided by Spacy to analyze the content of the users' messages. Taggers, morphologizers and parsers form the pipeline to extract the tokens, rule-based strategies to capture determined expressions relevant for inferring users' intentions, and Name Entity Recognizer for identifying entities related to time expressions. ii) Botpress[7] for the conversational user interface where actions, hooks and events are utilised to trigger the proactive behaviour, allowing the conversational agent access to databases where the car customers' profiles are stored; iii) Asterisk software as a call centre to directly interact with customers. It implements all functionalities to establish, control and manage telephone calls. Furthermore, it provides services to sample the customers' voices and transcribe them into text. In this scenario, the key functionality is to analyze the content of customers' messages and understand their timetable preferences.

As an example of this scenario, the chatbot would start the conversation, access an internal database, and check technical inspection certifications going

---

[6] https://spacy.io.
[7] https://www.bootpress.org/.

to the due date in the weeks ahead. Then, it will retrieve the information related to owners and send a memo to remind them of the due date of the certified technical inspection. Then, it will start the dialogue between the user and chatbot to establish the appointment, which is adapted to the user's preference timetable. For instance, let's suppose that the certification of a car whose plate number is 'PZ65 BYV' will expire two weeks ahead. Then, once the chatbot realised this situation, it will make a call to its owner with the following message: "Dear customer, the certified of Ministry of Transport of the vehicle 'PZ65 BYV' is going to be expired 15/08/2022. We are contacting you to suggest an appointment to renew the certification. The date will be following Monday on 1/08/2022 from 9.00 to 10.00 am". Then, the chatbot will wait for the customer's reply, where different answers could be given, since an easy answer accepting the appointment, to suggest the customer the slot or even change the choice to another day. Although the set-out scenario looks like an accessible dialogue to model, it offers a comprehensive alternative to which the chatbot must be trained to give a precise and appropriate answer.

4.2 Medical Appointments Use Case

The target of this use case is to simulate health customer service, where the patient sends a message by using an instant messaging platform to ask for an appointment. Then, the chatbot needs to harvest specific details about the patient to assign the corresponding practitioner. Name, surname, and health insurance number, among others, are the details that the chatbot will require to be able to set a time slot with a practitioner. Note that the scrutinized information can be given in different formats or through various questions, and the chatbot has to have techniques to analyze the message, identify the determined entities and store it for later purposes such as registering the appointment in the system.

In this scenario, we have considered the following components to configure the chatbot: i) NLTK[8] library for the NLP module to carry out tasks such as tokenization, stemming, tagging, parsing and entity classification; ii) Botpress as a chatbot interface to interact with users. Its sources have been published in a repository under an open source license, allowing developers to maintain the code and include new functionalities. In particular, for this use case, it is required that the chatbot interacts with users by using an instant messaging platform. Therefore, it is necessary to manipulate the chatbot's code to include new functionality that facilitates this interaction, and we believe that it was the best option, given the accessibility to the code and the documentation online; and finally iii) Telegram API was used to connect chatbots to patients by using Telegram as an instant messaging platform.

---

[8] https://www.nltk.org/.

5   Conclusions and Future Work

In this work, we proposed IVRMaker, an interactive and customizable telephone chatbot services platform. IVRMaker has been developed to assist companies in taking advantage of the benefits of chatbots. The platform proposed a complex architecture divided by modules that are based on cutting-edge Natural Language Processing techniques, focused on extracting, analyzing and understanding the customers' messages from two distinguishable vias, voice and text. The platform integrated natural language processing tools such as voice synthesizer and recognizer, semantic knowledge extractor, and syntactic analyzers, among others, for a primary objective to be capable of understanding the customers' intents and answering accordingly. The evaluation of the platform was carried out in two different application domains, health and vehicle safety. Concretely, it is configured as a chatbot for customer service and managing patient appointments in the health domain. Alternately, in the vehicle domain, the chatbot was configured with proactive behaviour, addressing the assignments time slots to carry out the test for renewing the certification of the Ministry of Transport.

For future work, there are a variety of work lines that we would like to explore. Firstly, the Machine Learning libraries available for building chatbots are limited. We would like to include more Machine Learning libraries and tools for natural language processing. Secondly, the evaluation has only tested the proper functioning of the platform. However, the wide variety of techniques implied in the chatbot operation opens the possibility of conducting diverse, interesting evaluations. For instance, the accuracy of the intention prediction by the NLU model. Consequently, we believe it would be interesting to conduct several experiments to assess their accuracy. Thirdly, the metrics and indicators available for the Dashboard are currently essential. Therefore, it would be interesting to develop tools that enable companies to design their metrics and indicators, including parameters for conducting data analytics consumed/produced by their chatbots. Although the platform provides different interfaces in the chatbot module to extend its functionality, for instance, the plugin manager, we would like to include more interfaces to facilitate its interoperability to other platforms and plugin extensibility. Finally, it is planned to include knowledge extraction technologies such as the ones presented in [4, 15, 20] to improve the name entity recognition technologies in specialised domains such as medicine.

Acknowledgements. This work has been funded by INFO and the European Regional Development Fund (FEDER/ERDF) under the RIS3MUR COVID-19 program through project IVRMAKER (2020.08.ID+I.0020). This work has been also partially supported by the projects "Programa para la Recualificación del Sistema Universitario Español 2021–2023", and the Community of Madrid, through the Young Researchers R+D Project. Ref. M2173 - SGTRS (co-funded by Rey Juan Carlos University) and PEJD-2019-PRE/TIC-16151.

References

1. Adamopoulou, E., Moussiades, L.: An overview of chatbot technology. In: Maglogiannis, I., Iliadis, L., Pimenidis, E. (eds.) AIAI 2020. IAICT, vol. 584, pp. 373–383. Springer, Cham (2020). https://doi.org/10.1007/978-3-030-49186-4_31
2. Clarizia, F., Colace, F., Lombardi, M., Pascale, F., Santaniello, D.: Chatbot: an education support system for student. In: Castiglione, A., Pop, F., Ficco, M., Palmieri, F. (eds.) CSS 2018. LNCS, vol. 11161, pp. 291–302. Springer, Cham (2018). https://doi.org/10.1007/978-3-030-01689-0_23
3. Comendador, B.E.V., Francisco, B.M.B., Medenilla, J.S., Mae, S.: Pharmabot: a pediatric generic medicine consultant chatbot. J. Autom. Control Eng. 3(2) (2015)
4. García-Sánchez, F., Valencia-García, R., Martínez-Béjar, R.: An integrated approach for developing e-commerce applications. Expert Syst. Appl. 28(2), 223–235 (2005). https://doi.org/10.1016/j.eswa.2004.10.004
5. Hashimoto, K., Xiong, C., Tsuruoka, Y., Socher, R.: A joint many-task model: Growing a neural network for multiple NLP tasks. arXiv preprint arXiv:1611.01587 (2016)
6. Kaimakis, N.J., Davis, D., Breck, S., Nye, B.: Domain-specific reduction of language model databases: Overcoming chatbot implementation obstacles. In: the Proceedings of the MODSIM World Conference, Norfolk, Virginia (2018)
7. Kushwaha, A.K., Kar, A.K.: Language model-driven chatbot for business to address marketing and selection of products. In: Sharma, S.K., Dwivedi, Y.K., Metri, B., Rana, N.P. (eds.) TDIT 2020. IAICT, vol. 617, pp. 16–28. Springer, Cham (2020). https://doi.org/10.1007/978-3-030-64849-7_3
8. Li, F.L., et al.: AliMe assist: an intelligent assistant for creating an innovative e-commerce experience. In: Proceedings of the 2017 ACM on Conference on Information and Knowledge Management, pp. 2495–2498 (2017)
9. May, C., Wang, A., Bordia, S., Bowman, S.R., Rudinger, R.: On measuring social biases in sentence encoders. arXiv preprint arXiv:1903.10561 (2019)
10. Molnár, G., Szüts, Z.: The role of chatbots in formal education. In: 2018 IEEE 16th International Symposium on Intelligent Systems and Informatics (SISY), pp. 000197–000202. IEEE (2018)
11. Parikh, A.P., Täckström, O., Das, D., Uszkoreit, J.: A decomposable attention model for natural language inference. arXiv preprint arXiv:1606.01933 (2016)
12. qizi Qodirova, D.B.: Analysis of changes in the semantic structure and lexical and semantic relations of English words in Uzbek. In: International Conferences, vol. 1, pp. 3–7 (2022)
13. Ranoliya, B.R., Raghuwanshi, N., Singh, S.: Chatbot for university related FAQs. In: 2017 International Conference on Advances in Computing, Communications and Informatics (ICACCI), pp. 1525–1530. IEEE (2017)
14. Ruder12, S., Bingel, J., Augenstein, I., Søgaard, A.: Learning what to share between loosely related tasks. arXiv preprint arXiv:1705.08142 (2017)
15. Ruiz-Sánchez, J.M., Valencia-García, R., Fernández-Breis, J.T., Martínez-Béjar, R., Compton, P.: An approach for incremental knowledge acquisition from text. Expert Syst. Appl. 25(1), 77–86 (2003). https://doi.org/10.1016/S0957-4174(03)00008-3
16. Seo, M., Kembhavi, A., Farhadi, A., Hajishirzi, H.: Bidirectional attention flow for machine comprehension. arXiv preprint arXiv:1611.01603 (2016)

17. Sha, L., Chang, B., Sui, Z., Li, S.: Reading and thinking: Re-read LSTM unit for textual entailment recognition. In: Proceedings of COLING 2016, the 26th International Conference on Computational Linguistics: Technical Papers, pp. 2870–2879 (2016)
18. Stern, M., Andreas, J., Klein, D.: A minimal span-based neural constituency parser. arXiv preprint arXiv:1705.03919 (2017)
19. Suhaili, S.M., Salim, N., Jambli, M.N.: Service chatbots: a systematic review. Expert Syst. Appl. **184**, 115461 (2021)
20. Valencia-García, R., Ruiz-Sánchez, J.M., Vicente, P.J.V., Fernández-Breis, J.T., Martínez-Béjar, R.: An incremental approach for discovering medical knowledge from texts. Expert Syst. Appl. **26**(3), 291–299 (2004). https://doi.org/10.1016/j.eswa.2003.09.001
21. Wieting, J., Kiela, D.: No training required: Exploring random encoders for sentence classification. arXiv preprint arXiv:1901.10444 (2019)

Digital Transformation of Health Care Services: Médikal Case Study

José Medina-Moreira[1]([⊠]) [iD], Katty Lagos-Ortiz[2] [iD], and Andrea Sinche-Guzmán[2] [iD]

[1] Médikal, Av. Guillermo Pareja Rolando, Guayaquil, Ecuador
jmedina@medikal.com.ec
[2] Facultad de Ciencias Agrarias, Universidad Agraria del Ecuador, Av. 25 de Julio, Guayaquil, Ecuador
{klagos,asinche}@uagraria.edu.ec

Abstract. The digital transformation of healthcare companies in times of Covid-19 was a relevant factor in sustaining the great demand for healthcare services, allowing the establishment of new communication channels, forms of payment, information processing, and online medical consultation services, among other services. This transformation implies substantial changes in people's culture and businesses, through a systematic, strategic and cultural change process, supported by the application of cutting-edge technologies that allow the systematization of processes and adequate data analysis. This research shows the digital transformation of the Médikal Center, which integrated technological changes within its processes such as migration to a cloud computing scheme allowing optimization of investment costs in IT infrastructure; migration to a more stable ERP; replacement of manual clinical laboratory processes by automated processes; generation of dynamic reports using data analytics thus improving decision-making at the managerial level; and establishment of new contact channels with the user such as the chatbot and mobile applications that allowed greater attention to customer demand. In short, this digital transformation process has allowed improving the quality of service, customer satisfaction, and supporting the decision-making of the company's executives, but in order to achieve this purpose, it was necessary to use methodologies supported by the best practices in the management of planning and implementation of IT projects.

Keywords: Digital transformation · Medical services · Innovation · BPM · Cloud computing · Telemedicine · ERP

1 Introduction

The new technological era has impacted all sectors and social spheres, digital transformation is a continuous, multidimensional and complex process, following these new paradigms implies having a mentality open to change. Digital solutions have incorporated mechanisms and tools that facilitate user experiences [1]. One of the most benefited sectors has been health.

R. Valencia-García et al. (Eds.): CITI 2022, CCIS 1658, pp. 75–89, 2022.
https://doi.org/10.1007/978-3-031-19961-5_6

The healthcare sector is one of the fastest-growing technology areas. For this reason, it has drawn the attention of the World Health Organization (WHO), and the Digital Health or eHealth "Cyber Health" guidelines that include a wide range of concepts on the application of information and communication technologies (TIC) in monitoring, prevention and promotion. The health system, as well as education, knowledge and research, have fostered long-term strategic plans for the development of technical infrastructure and its implementation in health services [2].

The COVID-19 pandemic has strengthened the need to rapidly adopt digital solutions in healthcare. It emphasizes the need to introduce systematic changes to find an effective digital solution. These changes may lead to innovative ways to improve compliance with medical services for citizens.

One of the most significant challenges facing the health sector is having the ability to involve the user or patient in the transformation of their processes. The COVID-19 pandemic, which affected the entire world in a very high percentage, accelerated the process of digital transformation in medical centers, clinics and hospitals, which have chosen to implement virtual communication channels, virtual reports, chatbots, telemedicine, and other processes that help patients to have better care without leaving home and improve their quality of life [3].

To manage change, we must first understand organizational changes and how they affect people. Organizational change begins when a need for change arises in one or more units of the organization. To talk about organizational change, it is necessary to consider social change, which, from a systems approach, can be defined as "any change in the status quo or quasi-static equilibrium of an organism, situation or process that affects the structure, technology and human resources of a global organization" [4]. The digital transformation process in the health field includes the predisposition of medical staff, doctors and patients who are open to change and the constant use of technology.

People who need the health system the most often have the least access to it. Digital technologies can help increase access, but the most health-vulnerable population groups typically have the lowest levels of connection and awareness of digital health. In the Region of the Americas, hundreds of millions of people face structural discrimination, exclusion, and inequality due to a lack of access to digital technologies and the potential health benefits associated with their use. There is an urgent need to make a digital transformation of the health sector, but it must be a transformation that specifically aims to guarantee equitable access for all population groups, especially those who are in a situation of vulnerability [3]. A biased approach to digital transformation could backfire and disadvantage vulnerable groups even more.

Some of the new processes in the health area consist of the inclusion of safer systems, health control and monitoring devices, and also keeping digital medical records, electronic patient records, among others [5]. These technological processes, apart from identifying problems in patients early, also improve medical management, helping to streamline care, reduce costs, reduce face-to-face consultations, and improve operational efficiency by facilitating clinical and administrative tasks linked to the assessment, transmission, evaluation and accuracy of medical treatment.

Organizations in charge of medical care are considered perfect environments for digital transformation, in their desire to promptly provide patients with the best results.

Transformation takes place through three steps: digital business environment; digital user experience and digital business models [6].

The idea of implementing intelligent solutions in the medical area is not only focused on medical services but also on the business processes that surround them in order to obtain the maximum benefits from the implementation, this in turn ensures offering a quality service and a pleasant experience to patients [7]. It is necessary to adopt data management mechanisms efficiently to provide real-time processing and facilitate the delivery of timely information, that's where data mining and big data come into play to perform the analysis of stored data. However, it should be considered that when working with large amounts of data, the challenge of guaranteeing network and data security arises [8].

The digital transformation process has made it possible to improve the quality of service, internal and external customer satisfaction, and support the decision-making of the company's executives. To achieve this purpose, methodologies supported by the best practices in the industry have been used. IT project planning and implementation management. The use of TIC can improve patient care, either as support and monitoring of the administrative part, keeping a clinical record, drug registration, monitoring patients, giving consultations in remote areas, or training your staff in remote areas. For technology to be accepted by people who provide a health-related service and by patients, there are several important factors related to quality.

This work is structured as follows: Sect. 2 describes the digital transformation of health services that has led them to include new ways of working in their processes. Then, Sect. 3 describes the methodology used in Médikal for the digital transformation of its processes. Section 4 presents the evaluation and results of the processes carried out. Finally, Sect. 5 presents conclusions and future lines of research.

2 Digital Transformation in Healthcare Services

Digital transformation is not just digitizing documents, developing applications or incorporating equipment in health institutions. It requires integrating new technologies and methodologies into each process of the institution, the work and the culture of its workers, and in an ecosystem that includes the population it attends and the relationships with its environment. It means transforming how services are provided and the population assisted. The fulfilment of the essential functions of promotion, prevention, care and cure of people's health involves decision-makers and people who use technologies creatively and actively [9]. Modern technology serves to help health professionals work more efficiently and improve the quality of health services. Health care facilities must respond to a technology-enabled care environment; developments must prepare for the future, facilities and buildings must meet the needs of patients, and staff anticipating future requirements [10].

A digital transformation implies changes in the structure and culture of people and institutions, to facilitate the work of medical personnel, through a continuous, disruptive, strategic and cultural change process based on the intensive use of technologies, TIC, systematization and data analysis. This seeks a higher quality and efficiency of medical care and its processes at all health system levels [11].

An organization comprises people with interests, motives, abilities, and limitations that come together and influence their job performance. Thus, the characteristics of the organizational culture in institutions that provide health services can impact positively or negatively the development and implementation of organizational transformation processes. To manage change, we must first understand organizational changes and how they affect people. The organizational change process begins when the forces that create the need to generate change appear in one or more organizational units. Any change in an environment or process affects a global organization's structure, technology and human resources [12].

Healthcare institutions, pharmaceutical companies, and hospital systems deliver better patient experiences and health outcomes through digital technology. Telemedicine and access to personal health services are two points of contact. But improving patient care is just one of the benefits of digital disruption. Those responsible for digital transformation must be able to facilitate the transformation of the organization's human resources towards the digital scenario. This means they must "move" from traditional to new ways of working; in other words, as the regulatory ecosystem evolves, unique digital capabilities should be developed. To achieve a successful digital transformation, organizational change management must be integral to this new workflow. Eligible employees to occupy and dominate digital issues are the key to the success of any digital transformation initiative, in which "digital transformation" is the means. Organizational change is a two-way process in which there must be a strategic plan that defines the expected objectives, specific actions and management indicators and the employees of the organization must have a clear understanding of this new business opportunity, the tools that they have been offered and what to expect from this new scenario [13].

3   Methodology Used

The methodology used in the digital transformation process carried out in Médikal is detailed, which consisted of several schemes that allowed moving from the client/server scheme to a Cloud Computing as Service (CCaS) infrastructure that defined the parameters that allowed to automate the processes. Figure 1 shows the technologies applied to achieve the objective.

3.1   Cloud Computing

For the transformation process of the IT platform in Médikal, the initial "client/server" architecture was abandoned, which was very unstable due to the ongoing problems of overloading resources in low-performing server equipment. It was designed and implemented a Cloud Computing as Service (CCaS) [14, 15] with "self-service" services on demand, achieving greater scalability and efficient control of the quantification of resources as seen in Fig. 2.

Microservice architecture is a software application development method that works as a set of small services that run independently and autonomously, requiring full business functionality. The use of microservices in the system architecture has allowed a more efficient development, while using fewer resources. This architecture has made it

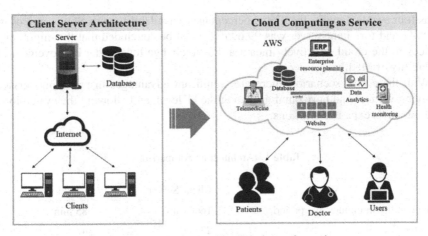

Fig. 1. Technologies used in digital transformation

possible to abstract the processing, storage, network, security, and application services in containers and instances, using the services of the Amazon Web Service (AWS) provider [16], improving the productivity and availability time of services.

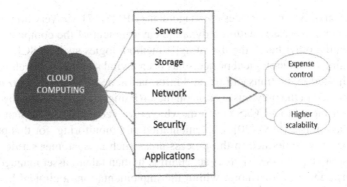

Fig. 2. Cloud computing as service

Cloud Computing has allowed the incorporation of new care services, such as telemedicine, which can be performed on-demand by users, during extended hours and on weekends. On the other hand, it will allow the evaluation of a horizontal growth of the company, with the implementation of new attention centers in different points of the city and the country, at a lower cost and time.

To measure the efficiency of the availability of both architectures, the events and historical logs of the years 2020 (client-server) and 2021 (Cloud services) have been reviewed. As can be seen in Table 1, the availability service of the cloud platform significantly outperforms the client-server architecture. As a result of the analysis, it was obtained that in the client-server platform the estimated total time of unavailability of the service was 1600 min, while in the cloud it was 85 min. In the case of the client-server architecture, the number of reported events was 237, while in the cloud services, it was four events. Finally, the global percentage of availability with cloud services was 99.983% and for client-server was 99.695%. It can be concluded that the migration of services to the cloud effectively meant a drastic change toward the improvement and availability of Médikal services.

With these new scenarios, there are significant advantages in providing services, achieving vertical and horizontal growth at the IT level, and allowing the evaluation of the company's expansion options.

Table 1. Architecture comparison

	Client-Server	Cloud
Unavailability in minutes per period	1600 min	85 min
Reported Events	237	4
Availability of services	99.983%	99.695%

3.2 ERP (Enterprise Resource Planning)

The application of Business Process Management (BPM) [17] was very important to add value to business processes within a dynamic environment of the company's Strategic Planning. On the other hand, the use of agile methodologies such as SCRUM [18, 19] for the planning of technological projects has been a vital step in the development of an ERP tool adjusted to the transactional and information needs of the organization.

As mentioned in the previous section on the ERP migration, the company went from a client-server model to a CCaS platform, which involved a process of planning, training, quality assurance (QA) [20], implementation and monitoring, for this purpose the relevant aspects were defined in the process areas such as customer service, financial and administrative processes such as accounting, human talent, asset management, and corporate insurance. Furthermore, within the implementation, a clinical history module was developed, which would be integrated with the ERP, allowing better care and the collection of relevant clinical information for the personalization of treatments for patients.

The processes were unified and followed a flow from appointment scheduling to patient care. In Fig. 3, the process diagram is outlined in a general way.

Within this context, the patient can schedule 3 main services: medical consultation, clinical laboratory tests and imaging corresponding to X-rays, ultrasounds and tomography.

Each one of them will have a different flow; for example in the case of scheduling a medical consultation, the patient must previously go to have his vital signs taken, where data such as weight and blood pressure are recorded. Then, the patient is activated in the system so that the doctor can enter the clinical history, at this point, the doctor evaluates the patient and enters the diagnosis, generates observations, prescriptions or certificates if applicable, and all these reports are sent to the patient's mail, they are also validated with the electronic signature of the treating physician to guarantee its authenticity. Later, the doctor can schedule the next appointment or make an interconsultation with another specialty. Additionally, the patient will be able to consult and monitor the data generated [21].

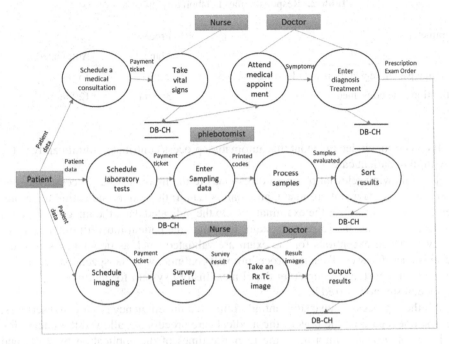

Fig. 3. Process diagram

The process of clinical laboratory tests begins when the user makes the payment transaction and approaches the sample collection area; in this area, there is a mobile device in which all the users of the day appear with their respective order of payment here the phlebotomist receives or takes the sample and performs a checklist of all the exams in the order, once the available exams have been validated, the identification codes for the exams are automatically printed. Then these exams go to the laboratory area where the teams process them according to the category (blood count, immunological, among others), these teams read the bar codes and assign the results to the respective user; at that point the laboratory manager validates the results, and the results are recorded in the clinical history database. Finally, they are sent to the patient by email, considering the restrictions of tests that have another treatment for their delivery to the patient.

Regarding the time of results recording, two scenarios are observed, the processes carried out manually and the processes done with the automation. For the first case, the time it takes to record the exams in the log plus generate a manual label is on average 4 min. In the second case, the checklist registration of exams and automatic label printing takes an average of 1 min. From a sample of 120 patients, we observed that the manual process takes 360 min and the automated process takes 120 min. Finally, the time difference between both processes with the referred sample is 240 min, with a general ratio of 3:1, as seen in Table 2. Note: Times of taking the sample by nursing are not considered.

Table 2. Response times in laboratory processes

Parameter	Processes	
	Manual	Automated
Average patient registration and identification time	4 min	1 min
Attention time consumed	360 min	120 min

It can be concluded then that this automation process contributes significantly to the flow time of patient care.

The following relevant process corresponds to the image-taking process. Once the reservation and payment are made, an email is sent to the patient indicating the afore-mentioned conditions for the examination. On the indicated date, the imaging therapist will be able to view the respective exam, for which the patient must fill out a previous survey in which exceptions for the exam are validated, such as pregnancy status and pre-existence diseases. Then the procedure will continue, with the specialist generating the medical report and completing the clinical history system for the final analysis by the specialist who referred it.

All these processes have substantially improved the efficiency of care and services; the first one regarding the flow of the medical care process has allowed the integration of the whole process, improving the response times of the application by 20%, and facilitating the availability of information in friendly interfaces that will enable the doctor to have data to support their diagnoses.

In the flow of the laboratory process, it was possible to eliminate the manual labelling of the samples, which eventually caused human errors, accompanied by the time it took for the specialist to write down the manual codes in a notebook and then pass it on to laboratory for comparison. The redesign and automation of this process reduced the error by 7%, while the processing time was reduced by 23%, serving more patients in the same period.

In the imaging flow, the optimization falls on the use and loading of the patient's clinical history of images in DCOM format (three-dimensional images) which allows the doctor to compare the report of the imaging specialist with the system image to support his diagnosis.

3.3 Data Analytics

The use of data analytics has allowed business stakeholders to obtain timely and reliable information for strategic decision-making [22]; for the purpose of this research, infor-mation cubes were designed, which allowed obtaining required metrics by directors of the main business units [23].

For the design of the information boards, the techniques of extraction, transformation and loading (ETL) were used [24, 25]; for the extraction process, it was necessary to integrate different databases (information sources), among them the transactional information database, clinical history database and historical database, to form what is known as the company's Data Warehouse [26], In the transformation process, techniques were applied to analyze atypical data (empty fields, out of range, type of field unit, among others) and give it a particular treatment according to established criteria; in the loading process through the online analytical processing (OLAP) [27] the data was loaded into information cubes for data consumption and in this way to elaborate the Key Performance Indicators (KPIs) [28] for data analytics.

Among the main dashboards that were designed, we have: the sales dashboard, which contains all the information regarding daily sales, global sales, and the most demanded services, among others. The production board shows the installed capacity, number of daily queries, and number of services attended. In the laboratory case, it is possible to obtain patients' health information by age, sex or condition according to laboratory results.

For those interested in the information that can satisfy their requirements, training has been carried out for administrative personnel in data analytics tools in such a way that the user can consume the data and personalize the visualization of the data according to their specific needs.

Dashboards will be generated based on the requirements of each area of the medical center. Figure 4 shows the number of appointments scheduling made by WhatsApp according to medical specialties.

Fig. 4. Appointments scheduled by WhatsApp according to specialty

Figure 5 shows the graphs based on the number of appointments planned, reserved and attended in the cardiology area, which helps to confirm the absenteeism of patients and to know if the service offered to patients was effective.

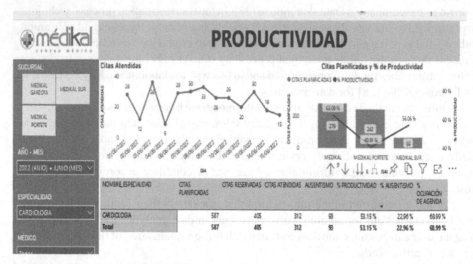

Fig. 5. Productivity per specialist

3.4 Website

Offering online information to patients is a tool of significant impact that gives added value to the services provided by the company. For this, a website was designed, as shown in Fig. 6, in which the patient, after an authentication process, could access different services such as appointment scheduling, consultation of laboratory test results, consultation of current and historical orders, medical history checking, consulting medications and prescribed prescriptions, consulting health packages and promotions, viewing the history of vital signs and finally consulting his transactional information.

To evaluate the use of this service, an online survey was conducted with 650 patients in terms of design and usability. As shown in Fig. 7, 98% of the patients are delighted with the interface design in terms of structure and organization of the website (P1); in terms of usability, 93% of the patients considered that the information presented had been helpful to them based on their requirements (P2).

3.5 Telemedicine

The use of telemedicine is a service that acquired great relevance due to the COVID-19 pandemic, so its implementation and use today constitutes a service that has a considerable level of demand due to the benefits of virtuality and reduction of time that it represents [29]. However, providing this service requires unique logistics to achieve efficiency in the service and customer satisfaction.

Fig. 6. Médikal website

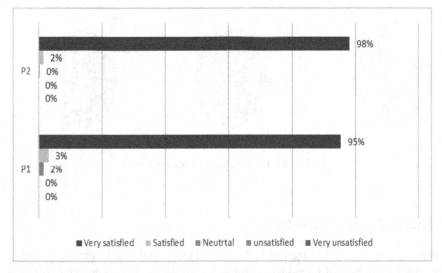

Fig. 7. Questions about design and usability to patients

The virtual care unit was created for this purpose, which is responsible for monitoring the patient-client process from start to finish, evaluating and recommending best practices in providing this service.

In general, the telemedicine process, begins in phase 1, with the scheduling of the medical appointment for telemedicine through any of the available channels (Web, Chat-bot, Call Center, On-site), an automatic email with the appointment date and the session link is sent to the patient. The virtual appointment is inserted in the doctor's agenda on the indicated date and time; the doctor activates the option for the video conference simultaneously by opening the patient's medical history patient. In phase 2: On the scheduled date, the patient enters the teleconsultation service link and communication is established in both ways. After a credential certification protocol, the doctor begins the virtual consultation, consulting and feeding the patient's medical history; in phase 3: According to the patient's diagnosis, the doctor generates the medical prescription or orders for clinical examinations, and orders are sent via mail to the patient for their processing. In phase 4: After verifying the conformity of the service, the query is terminated, and the virtual session is released.

To have a criterion of the viability of the telemedicine service, surveys related to the level of user satisfaction are generated periodically, which is based on three questions; P1: From the last survey carried out, the following results were obtained; for the first question, 84% of the patients considered that the telemedicine process was easy for them, 99% of the patients were satisfied with the doctor's care, and finally, 98% of them would recommend this type of online consultation to family and friends. These results are shown in Fig. 8.

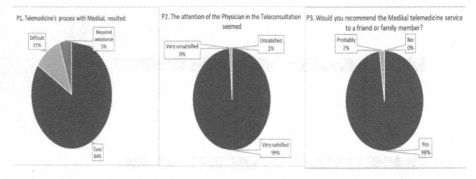

Fig. 8. Telemedicine survey results

4 Evaluation and Results

To demonstrate the results obtained in the case of the digital transformation process, we have that for the case of Cloud Computing, the results were satisfactory in relation to the availability time of the system in the cloud with a result of 99.983%, in contrast to 99.695%, having a difference margin of 0.288%, which in terms of hours corresponds to 25.5 h of difference.

In the case of the process planning and automation system, a 3:1 ratio was obtained in the reduction of care time for patients who use the laboratory service, obtaining substantial efficiency in this specific service.

In the data analytics section, its evaluation may seem imperceptible, however, the significance it has for a company, to have timely information for decision making, generates substantial value in achieving the strategic objectives of the organization.

In the development of the web portal, which allows a better service-patient interaction, considerable results have been obtained in the user experience, by using this new platform in which the user will be able to arrange and manage the attention and demand of services required by the patients.

About the Telemedicine service, according to the results of the surveys in Sect. 3.5, a considerable acceptance of this new service is proved, specifically in reference to the attention and service, however, we observe that there may be a technical-operational limitation according to the geographical location or the population to which the service could be addressed, given that the evaluation of the question about how easy was the telemedicine process for them, obtained the lowest percentage in the evaluation of the service, this analysis may constitute an additional study, which does not cover the scope of this work.

5 Conclusions and Future Work

The COVID-19 pandemic has accelerated the development of new technologies in the different productive and health sectors, including the medical care. Médikal has faced these new transformation challenges at the right time with an innovative vision of services, successfully facing the risks that every transformation process entails and obtaining favorable results for its operations and business units.

The evolution of technology in the cloud ensures high availability of its services, the use of an ERP that integrates the main business areas, will allow to manage business resources effectively, and with the implementation of the Analytics of Data is possible to make strategic decisions based on metrics and performance indicators. On the other hand, the development of the Website and new services for patients, such as telemedicine, payment gateways, and chatbots, allows it to offer agile, timely, and transparent services, focusing on satisfying patients' health and information needs.

In the context of future work and with the commitment to take on new challenges, the projects to be carried out are: to determine the traceability of laboratory samples to determine the time it takes for the samples to be processed throughout the process flow, the analysis of Rx images using artificial intelligence (AI), the use of supervised and unsupervised algorithms to define patterns of future illnesses of patients based on clinical results, use of augmented reality for the area of treatment of psychological problems, and for physical rehabilitation in the area of physiotherapy.

Acknowledgements. The Médikal Center supported this work, we thank its directors for supporting the development of scientific research and providing the opportunity to contribute with their extensive knowledge, experience and initiative for the benefit of one of the most critical sectors of the population, health.

References

1. Shickel, B., Tighe, P., Bihorac, A.: Deep EHR: a survey of recent advances in deep learning techniques for electronic health record (EHR) analysis. IEEE J. Biomed. Heal. informatics. **22**, 1589–1604 (2017)

88   J. Medina-Moreira et al.

2. OMS, O.M. de la S.: CD59/6 - Hoja de ruta para la transformación digital del sector de la salud en la Región de las Américas - OPS/OMS I Organización Panamericana de la Salud. https://www.paho.org/es/documentos/cd596-hoja-ruta-para-transformacion-digital-sector-salud-region-americas. Last accessed 21 June 2022
3. Marques, I.C.P., Ferreira, J.J.M.: Digital transformation in the area of health: systematic review of 45 years of evolution. Heal. Technol. 10(3), 575–586 (2019). https://doi.org/10.1007/s12553-019-00402-8
4. Hu, S., Wang, H., She, C., Wang, J.: AgOnt: ontology for agriculture internet of things. In: Li, D., Liu, Y., Chen, Y. (eds.) CCTA 2010. IAICT, vol. 344, pp. 131–137. Springer, Heidelberg (2011). https://doi.org/10.1007/978-3-642-18333-1_18
5. Kraus, S., Schiavone, F., Pluzhnikova, A., Invernizzi, A.C.: Digital transformation in healthcare: analyzing the current state-of-research. J. Bus. Res. 123, 557–567 (2021). https://doi.org/10.1016/J.JBUSRES.2020.10.030
6. Cavoski, S., Vujovic, V., Devrnja, V., Ferenc, B., Lukic, F.: Digital transformation in healthcare healthcare on demand. In: 2022 21st International Sympoisum INFOTEH-JAHORINA, INFOTEH 2022 – Proceedings, pp. 1–6 (2022). https://doi.org/10.1109/INFOTEH53737.2022.9751335
7. Gopal, G., Suter-Crazzolara, C., Toldo, L., Eberhardt, W.: Digital transformation in healthcare - architectures of present and future information technologies. Clin. Chem. Lab. Med. 57, 328–335 (2019). https://doi.org/10.1515/CCLM-2018-0658/PDF
8. Haggerty, E.: Healthcare and digital transformation. Netw. Secur. 2017, 7–11 (2017). https://doi.org/10.1016/S1353-4858(17)30081-8
9. Fernández, T.: Taxonomía de transformación digital. Rev. Cuba. Transform. 1, 4–23 (2020)
10. Sarris, A., Sawyer, M.G.: Automated information systems in mental health services. Int. J. Ment. Health. 18, 18–30 (2015). https://doi.org/10.1080/00207411.1989.11449141
11. Benech Valdovinos, R.: Study on the impact on the implementation of digital tools in people management in a social security institution. Rev. Gestión las Pers. y Tecnol. 39, (2020)
12. Alagoz, E., Chih, M.Y., Hitchcock, M., Brown, R., Quanbeck, A.: The use of external change agents to promote quality improvement and organizational change in healthcare organizations: a systematic review. BMC Health Serv. Res. 18, 1–13 (2018). https://doi.org/10.1186/S12913-018-2856-9
13. Hanelt, A., Bohnsack, R., Marz, D., Antunes Marante, C.: A systematic review of the literature on digital transformation: insights and implications for strategy and organizational change. J. Manag. Stud. 58, 1159–1197 (2021). https://doi.org/10.1111/JOMS.12639
14. Rahimi, M., Jafari Navimipour, N., Hosseinzadeh, M., Moattar, M.H., Darwesh, A.: Toward the efficient service selection approaches in cloud computing. Kybernetes 51, 1388–1412 (2022). https://doi.org/10.1108/K-02-2021-0129/FULL/XML
15. Wei, Y., Blake, M.B.: Service-oriented computing and cloud computing: challenges and opportunities. IEEE Internet Comput. 14, 72–75 (2010). https://doi.org/10.1109/MIC.2010.147
16. Hota, N., Pattanayak, B.K.: Cloud computing load balancing using amazon web service technology. In: Advance Intellingent Systems and Computing, vol. 1299, pp. 661–669. AISC (2021). https://doi.org/10.1007/978-981-33-4299-6_54/COVER/
17. Nicholas, J.M., Steyn, H.: Project Management for Engineering, Business and Technology. Routledge (2020). https://doi.org/10.4324/9780429297588
18. Ramírez, M., Soto, M., Moreno, H., Rojas, E.M., Millán, N., Cisneros, R.: Metodología SCRUM y desarrollo de Repositorio Digital. Rev. Ibérica Sist. e Tecnol. Informação E17, 1062–1072 (2019)
19. Hayat, F., Rehman, A.U., Arif, K.S., Wahab, K., Abbas, M.: The influence of agile methodology (scrum) on software project management. In: Proceedings of the - 20th IEEE/ACIS

International Conference Softwage Engingeering Artifical Intelligence Netwwork Parallel/Distributed Comput. SNPD 2019, pp. 145–149 (2019). https://doi.org/10.1109/SNPD.2019.8935813

20. Schulmeyer, G.: Handbook of software quality assurance (2007)
21. Medina-Moreira, J., Apolinario, O., Luna-Aveiga, H., Lagos-Ortiz, K., Paredes-Valverde, M.A., Valencia-García, R.: A collaborative filtering based recommender system for disease self-management. Commun. Comput. Inf. Sci. **749**, 60–71 (2017). https://doi.org/10.1007/978-3-319-67283-0_5/COVER/
22. Runkler, T.A.: Data Analytics. Springer Fachmedien Wiesbaden, Wiesbaden (2020). https://doi.org/10.1007/978-3-658-29779-4
23. Raghupathi, W., Raghupathi, V.: Big data analytics in healthcare: promise and potential. Heal. Inf. Sci. Syst. **2**, 3 (2014). https://doi.org/10.1186/2047-2501-2-3
24. Diouf, P.S., Boly, A., Ndiaye, S.: Variety of data in the ETL processes in the cloud: State of the art. In: 2018 IEEE International Conference Innovation Research Development, pp. 1–5. ICIRD (2018). https://doi.org/10.1109/ICIRD.2018.8376308
25. Vassiliadis, P., Simitsis, A., Skiadopoulos, S.: Conceptual modeling for ETL processes. In: ACM International Workshop on Data Warehousing and OlAP, pp. 14–21 (2002). https://doi.org/10.1145/583890.583893
26. Abai, N.H.Z., Yahaya, J.H., Deraman, A.: User requirement analysis in data warehouse design: a review. Procedia Technol. **11**, 801–806 (2013). https://doi.org/10.1016/J.PROTCY.2013.12.261
27. Cuzzocrea, A., Bellatreche, L., Song, I.Y.: Data warehousing and OLAP over big data: current challenges and future research directions. In: International Conference Information Knowlcdge Management Proceedings, pp. 67–70 (2013). https://doi.org/10.1145/2513190.2517828
28. Chan, A.P.C., Chan, A.P.L.: Key performance indicators for measuring construction success. Benchmarking Int. J. **11**, 203–221 (2004). https://doi.org/10.1108/14635770410532624/FULL/XML
29. Waller, M., Stotler, C.: Telemedicine: a primer. Curr. Allergy Asthma Rep. **18**(10), 1–9 (2018). https://doi.org/10.1007/s11882-018-0808-4

Computer Vision and Image Analysis

Texture and Color-Based Analysis to Determine the Quality of the Manila Mango Using Digital Image Processing Techniques

Jacquelin Aguirre-Radilla[1] (ID), Eduardo De La Cruz-Gámez[1]([✉]) (ID),
José Luis Hernández-Hernández[2] (ID), Jorge Carranza-Gómez[1] (ID),
José Antonio Montero-Valverde[1] (ID), and Miriam Martínez-Arroyo[1]([✉]) (ID)

[1] Division of Research and Graduate Studies, National Technology of Mexico, Acapulco
Institute of Technology, Acapulco, Mexico
{mm20320002,eduardo.dg,jorge.cg,jose.mv,
miriam.ma}@acapulco.tecnm.mx
[2] Division of Research and Graduate Studies, National Technology of Mexico, Chilpancingo
Institute of Technology, Chilpancingo, Mexico
joseluis.hh@chilpancingo.tecnm.mx

Abstract. This work shows the development of an algorithm based on image
processing techniques and aims to determine the quality of Manila mango for
export purposes. Currently in Mexico, in most of the mango producing states, the
analysis of this fruit is done manually and the quality of the mango is determined
by considering the state of maturity, cleanliness of the mango´s skin and size.
During this process, the fruit is granding and then classified; in these tasks, human
errors can occur due to fatigue. The consequences of these errors translate into
losses for farmers, since for one fruit detected to be of poor quality, the entire lot is
rejected. Therefore, any attempt made to support the determination of the quality
of this fruit in an automated way will be of great support, especially for small and
medium-sized agricultural enterprises (SMEs). The methodology employed uses
digital image processing techniques by analyzing color and texture, calculating
the mean of the components and using statistical methods (histograms and co-
occurrence matrices) in the regions of interest, in addition to applying the support
vector machine (SVM) algorithm to classify Manila mango based on maturity
and peel damage. The algorithm presented here details a process of obtaining
the image to filter it and identify the edges of the mango, the representation and
manipulation through the histogram is used to improve the image without affecting
aspects that may be relevant in the image such as contours, textures and intensity.
These characteristics will be used later to determine the quality of the fruit. The
results shown so far are satisfactory, reaching 86% Accuracy.

Keywords: Color feature · Texture feature · Digital image processing · SVM

1 Introduction

Mexico is a country, which due to its variety of climates shows a great variety of crops,
among them the mango. This fruit is harvested in 26 of the 32 states of the country,

R. Valencia-García et al. (Eds.): CITI 2022, CCIS 1658, pp. 93–106, 2022.
https://doi.org/10.1007/978-3-031-19961-5_7

the state of Guerrero is one of them. Among the variants of this fruit, one of the most requested is the Manila mango, a fleshy fruit with spherical shape and sweet flavor, which is surrounded by a woody cover that encloses a big seed [31].

According to the agricultural census conducted by the Mexican agency of the National Institute of Statistics and Geography (INEGI), the annual losses caused by a harvest with quality deficiencies can be from 5% to 40% [15]. The selection process for this fruit was documented in the town of San Luis las Lomas in Tecpan de Galeana, a municipality in the state of Guerrero. Currently, in these municipality, the selection is done manually and based on the experience of the people in charge of sorting the fruit.

2   Related Works

In the past, many research Works have been carried for detecting, classify the quality of fruits. In this paper [1], the author proposes a multi-class classifier for fruits and vegetables using a unified approach that allows it to combine various features and classification types. The proposed method requires non-heavy training. Four types of classification tests are developed, their proposal demonstrates to reduce the error factor by up to 15% in a methodology called classifier fusion. The work of [27] addresses the use of computational algorithms for shape detection in fruits, the authors make a comparison of the most popular algorithms as a support solution in fruit inspection processes by automating the classification. [24] The author present the use of a hybrid splitting and fusion algorithm in the analysis of fruit images as a support for the detection of defects in the peels is proposed. The paper by [34] proposes the use of a Gray Level Co-occurrence Matrix (GLCM) to extract mango fruit features using an SVM classifier and the K-means method. Here [30], the author focuses on automatic detection of pomegranate fruits in an orchard. The image is segmented based on color feature using K-means clustering method. The K-means method produces accurate segmentation results only when applied to images defined by regions similar in texture and color. The paper by [37], shows a evaluation method more effective than using only one of the external features or weight combining an expensive nondestructive (NDT) measurement. Grading of fruits is implemented by four models of machine learning as Random Forest (RF), Linear Discriminant Analysis (LDA), Support Vector Machine (SVM), and K-Nearest Neighbors (KNN).

3   The Manual Process of Classify

The characteristics that the classifiers consider to determine the quality of the mango are as follows:

1. **Size**: It is the most important element to categorize the mango, the box containing the largest fruit is the one that offers the highest price.

   a. *Extra*: The mango is called Extra when it is visually larger than the others.
   b. *First*: It is the common size required of a good granding, it is a classification following Extra.

c. *Second*: If the size is smaller than Primera, it is considered Segunda.
d. *Third*: The following classification of Segunda. Some classifiers do not separate the mango by third, if the mango is closer in size to Segunda they place it in that grade, if it is smaller they place it in quarter.
e. *Quarter:* The smallest size.

2. **Texture:** The fruit is classified in boxes with the name "Semi" when the mango´s skin is damaged (cracks, stains, etc.). The size and color of the mango is not relevant in this category.

3. **Color**: Classify is done before the stage of maturity, therefore, the desired color of the skin is green, otherwise the fruit is separated into two classifier:

a. *Ripe*: The mango´s skin begins to take on a yellow-orange color. Because the price of the product is reduced in comparison to green-colored mangoes, the exporter buys it and classifies it in boxes as ripe.
b. *Waste*: If the skin is completely yellow-orange in color, it is no longer suitable for transportation and is discarded and placed in waste boxes. Waste boxes also have semi-sorted mangoes where the texture quality is not enought to be exported and is discarded.

The next step is to fill boxes with the fruits depending on the above aspects. Obviously, the fruit with the highest price is the one that achieves the quality factors mentioned above, with priority being given to size. In this stage, due to human fatigue, a defective mango may be added to a box of good quality fruit. If a purchaser selected a random box and a defective fruit is observed, the whole box is discarded, meaning a loss for the producer. Large companies are supported on technology to solve these problems, while small and medium-sized producers do not. Therefore, any attempt to support the work of this group of farmers in their tasks of harvesting and/or selection of their products is of great interest to them.

In Fig. 1 shows that this work develops a proposed computational methodology based on digital image processing techniques. Unlike other techniques, this procedure is not invasive to the product.

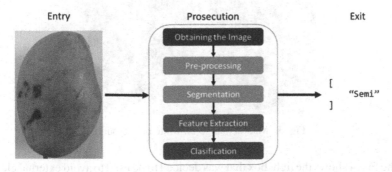

Fig. 1. General schema of the mango Manila classifier algorithm.

4   Methods

The proposed methodology consists of 5 stages shown in Fig. 2.

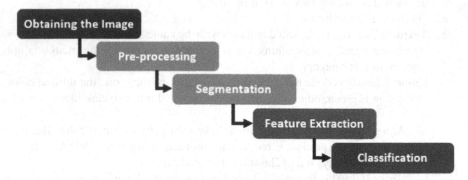

Fig. 2. Methodology for the classification of the Manila mango.

4.1   Obtaining the Image

In the first tests, the user in charge of categorizing places the mango to be classified in a light box for photography with a white background measuring 24 × 23 × 22 cm, then captures a digital photograph of the mango using a mobile device.

In the Fig. 3 shows that the acquired image is exported to a laptop where, together with the different images that the categorizer captures of the Manila mango, it will form part of a DataSet that will be normalized to a format and size suitable to be used in the pre-processing stage, to know the output value of the classified mango.

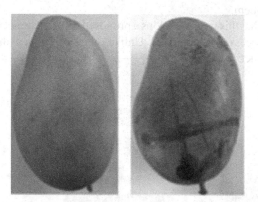

Fig. 3. Manila mango on white background.

In the Fig. 4 shows the light box that was decided to be used to avoid external elements (weather conditions, lighting, among others) that could affect the image acquisition, achieving a DataSet of images making them ideal for a favorable detection (that have the necessary resolution and no distortion).

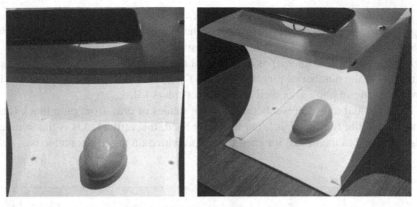

Fig. 4. Light box for photography.

4.2 Pre-processing

After having obtained the image to be processed, we proceed to the stage of reduction
or elimination of unwanted information and improve the quality of the image obtained
to acquire the appropriate characteristics that favor pre-processing, suppress intensity
variations and noise, avoiding compromising edges, contours and textures.

In Fig. 5 shows a comparison of the manila mango before and after processing, in
Fig. 5(a) the acquired digital image of the fruit is shown, in Fig. 5(b) the manila mango is
shown after having gone through a filtering process in which the cross-correlation filter
was used because of its efficiency in returning in the output an array with the data type
equivalent to the array of the input image, The resulting image was then equalized to find
and apply a point operation such that the histogram of the modified image approximates
a uniform distribution [8].Calculate H, S and I:

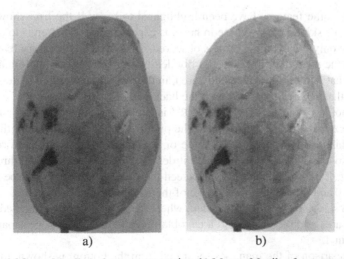

a)   b)

Fig. 5. a) Mango Manila before pre-processing, b) Mango Manila after pre-processing.

The Fig. 6 shows the histograms to appreciate the brightness of the images shown in Fig. 5. In Fig. 6 (a) shows the histogram of the figure before processing and Fig. 6 (b) shows the histogram of the image after processing.

The histogram of an image f is a graph that represents the color intensity levels of f with respect to the number of pixels present in f with each color intensity. It can help to control exposure in photos, as well as to correct colors [8].

The horizontal axis represents the different shades of gray from pure black (on the left) to pure white (on the right). On the other hand, the vertical axis is the number of pixels contained in the image for each tone represented on the horizontal axis.

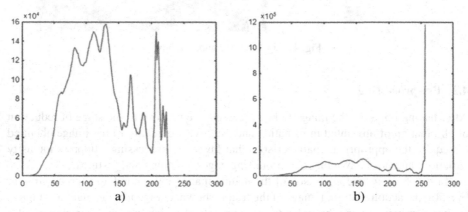

a)   b)

Fig. 6. a) Histogram of the mango in the original image, b) Histogram of the fruit once filtered.

4.3   Segmentation

At this stage some features have been highlighted to know if the fruit shows damage on the mango´s skin and a decrease in noise is expected, the next step is to acquire the image where only the mango region is observed. To obtain the necessary features to be extracted in the next step, the image is divided by transforming it into binary without damaging what is relevant to the study area, in this way it is expected to detect defects of intensity that can be associated with the background.

A threshold of type THRESH_BINARY is applied in order to change the value of a pixel if it exceeds the set threshold (if the pixel is in a hole in the area), the function returns the binarized image and the value of the threshold, tests are performed using histograms to establish a range in which it detects the ideal value of the threshold. As shown in Fig. 7, the pixels that do not exceed the value of the range will be filled with the value of 0 and thus a complete image of the mango will be extracted.

In Fig. 8 shows the result of this step, where the objects to be segmented belong to the affected area and the unaffected area, obtaining the mango´s image separated from the background.

The comparison of the mangoes separated from the bottom is shown, in Fig. 8 (a) the mango is classified by size, in Fig. 8(b) it is classified by texture.

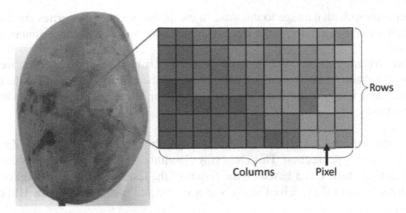

Fig. 7. Digital image of Manila mango.

The "Semi" mango (which has been classified by texture) has had the damage shown in Fig. 5 resalted.

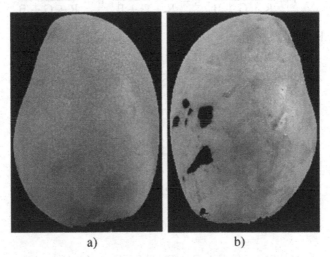

a)   b)

Fig. 8. Manila mango separated from the background. a) Classified by size, b) Classified by texture.

4.4   Feature Extraction

To obtain the characteristics, it was decided to analyze the skin of the fruit to determine the properties of color and texture, since the objective of the algorithm is to classify Manila mangoes based on the following attributes:

- **Semi**: Mango with damage to the skin. In this phase, textural properties are used to extract the relevant data on the skin, if the fruit is not damaged, it continues to be classified.
- **Color**: When the mango is considered "Maduro". Using the color properties, we will know the shade of the skin (if it is yellow-orange, the mango will belong to the color class, taking into account that the green shade is considered an attribute for mangoes with class).

To extract the color feature, the K-means algorithm [21] was used to calculate the number of shades per section. This clustering algorithm requires the number of clusters to be defined, which was 5 based on the results of the tests performed. In addition, the RGB component of the received image was acquired and transformed to the HSI color variant [7, 17]:

The conversion of the HSI model from RGB was performed using the process developed in the paper optimized True-Color Image Processing [25]:

1. Obtain the RGB components of the image:

$$r = \frac{R}{R+G+B}, \quad g = \frac{G}{R+G+B}, \quad b = \frac{B}{R+G+B} \tag{1}$$

2. Calculate H, S and I:

$$h = \cos^{-1}\left\{\frac{0.5.[(r-g)+(r-b)]}{[(r-g)^2+(r-b)(g-b)]^{1/2}}\right\} \tag{2}$$

$$h \in [0, \pi] \, for \, b \leq g \tag{3}$$

$$h = 2\pi - \cos^{-1}\left\{\frac{0.5.[(r-g)+(r-b)]}{[(r-g)^2+(r-b)(g-b)]^{1/2}}\right\} \tag{4}$$

$$h \in [\pi, 2\pi] \, for \, b > g \tag{5}$$

$$s = 1 - 3.\min(r, g, b); \, s \in [0, 1] \tag{6}$$

$$i = (R+G+B)/(3.255); \, i \in [0, 1] \tag{7}$$

3. RGB model conversion from HSI:

$$h = H.\pi/180; \, s = S/100; \, i = I/255 \tag{8}$$

$$x = i.(1-s) \tag{9}$$

$$y = i.\left[I + \frac{s.\cos(h)}{\cos(\pi/3 - h)}\right] \tag{10}$$

$$z = 3i.(x+y) \tag{11}$$

When $h < \frac{2\pi}{3}$, $b = x$; $r = y$ and $g = z$

When $\frac{2\pi}{3} \leq h < \frac{4\pi}{3}$, $h = h - \frac{2\pi}{3}$ and $r = x$; $g = y$ and $b = z$

When $\frac{4\pi}{3} \leq h < 2\pi$, $h = h - \frac{4\pi}{3}$ and $g = x$; $b = y$ and $r = z$

Regarding the texture, statistical methods of 1st and 2nd order of the co-occurrence matrix of gray levels were applied, where of the multiple characteristics analyzed, 6 of them showed in all the images of the DataSet an efficiency in the results presented in the tests. With this it is possible to find the texture indexes that allow segmenting the image according to the criteria provided by the co-occurrence matrix [18, 19]. The above was established by:

- The peculiarities presented in the fruit skin (softness, fineness, roughness, among others).
- The spatial level of the degree of intensity.
- The positive response of different statistical methods.

In Eq. 12, the probability of occurrence of a reference pixel i followed by a neighbor j is determined where $V_{i,j}$ is the value of the image window cell, N is the number of records and columns, and $P_{i,j}$ is the probability of the cells i and j.

$$P_{i,j} = \frac{V_{i,j}}{\sum_{i,j=1}^{N} V_{i,j}} \tag{12}$$

The following are the properties applied for the texture:

1. **Dissimilarity**: Increases weights linearly.

$$\sum_{i=1}^{N} \sum_{j=1}^{M} P_{I,J} |i,j| \tag{13}$$

2. **Homogeneity**: Weights values by the inverse of the contrast weighting, with weights decreasing exponentially away from the diagonal.

$$\sum_{i,j=0}^{N-1} \frac{P_{i-j}}{1 + (i - j)^2} \tag{14}$$

3. **Energy**: Returns the sum of the squared elements in the GLCM. Energy is 1 for a constant image.

$$\sqrt{ASM} \tag{15}$$

4. **Correlation**: Existence of a linear and predictable relationship between the two neighboring pixels within the window.

$$\sum_{i,j=0}^{N-1} P_{i,j} \left[\frac{(i - \mu_i)(j - \mu_j)}{\sqrt{(\sigma_i^2)(\sigma_j^2)}} \right] \tag{16}$$

5. **Contrast**: Number of local variations in shades of gray of the image.

$$\sum_{i,j=0}^{N-1} P_{i,j}(i-j)^2 \tag{17}$$

6. **ASM**: The higher the ASM, the greater the uniformity (less variation in gray levels).

$$ASM = \sum_{i,j=0}^{N-1} P_{i,j}^2 \tag{18}$$

4.5 Classification

Once the necessary features for classification were obtained, it was decided to implement the SVM (Support Vector Machine) classifier, an artificial intelligence algorithm that uses supervised learning techniques and returns optimal values, even with a limited number of data [33].

The optimal solution (the one sought) is the one that provides a maximum edge (implying the importance of only those support vectors and treating the rest of the training as irrelevant) between the elements of the categories Table 1.

The following is the algorithm used for the classification of Manila mangoes:

Table 1. Algorithm for the classification of the Manila mango.

Begin
1.   Library import.
2.   Loading images and their current mask.
3.   Unique names are extracted from the tag vector.
4.   Tags are coded according to the type they belong to.
5.   The data vector is divided into "data".
6.   The "trainingSet" and the "dataSet" are constructed.
7.   Classifier training with "trainData" and their respective "trainTarget" tags.
8.   Evaluation of the classifier through a test report of the "testSet".
9.   Test of the images of the classifier.
10.   A Load test addresses and masks.
11.   Load images and test mask.
12.   Feature extraction from the masked image to be predicted.
13.   Application of the mango type predictor.
14. Print the results.
End

First, the SVM algorithm was trained using a Dataset of 45 images, of which 15 images belong to the manila mango in the "Size" or class 0 stage; 15 images in the "Color" or class 1 stage; and 15 images in class 2 or "Semi".

5 Results

The images of the Dataset were obtained using a cell phone with 48 megapixel (Mpx) triple camera with AI of the Xiaomi POCO M3 cell phone and 4 gigabytes (GB) of memory, for the development was used in an ASUS LAPTOP-UIP1QDOM laptop with a 64-bit operating system, Windows 10 Pro, 1. 8 gigahertz (GHz), Intel Core i7 and 8 gigabytes (GB) of memory, using code in the Python programming language version 3.9, handling OpenCv, NumPy, Matplotlib libraries, among others.

For the validation of the system, 3 experiments were carried out: a) Class 0; b) Class 1; and c) Class 2; each experiment was carried out with 30 samples, where 50% of the fruits were considered with damage or with a non-ideal state of maturity and the remaining 50% without damage and in an ideal state of maturity.

Table 2 shows the percentage of Accuracy of the model, the "Precision" value defines the percentage of positive predictions correctly, and "Recall" represents the percentage of positive cases detected.

Table 2. Accuracy percentage.

Class	Recall	Precision	Accuracy
0	0.86	0.86	0.86
1	0.93	0.86	0.86
2	0.93	0.87	0.90

Class 0 are mangoes that have an ideal skin tone (green color) and no imperfections, class 1 represents mangoes classified as "Color" (this determines the state of maturity), and class 2 "Semi" are fruits with damage to the skin. For the case of maturity stage classification (class 0), the values obtained by the system were: Positive identified = 14, False positives = 3, Negative identified = 12, False negatives = 1, so when calculating the Accuracy of the system, 86% was obtained. The value obtained from the calculation of Recall was 0.93%, and the value of Precision was 86%.

6 Discussions and Conclusions

The study, research and testing of different methods related to fruit classification and the documentation obtained from field observation greatly influenced the determination of the methods to be applied, which together result in the characteristics to be extracted from the mango. In this work, a methodology has been planned for the realization of an algorithm that categorizes Manila mangoes in a controlled environment, which, as a result of its implementation, facilitates the classifiers to sort the fruit and the farmer to obtain the profit according to the harvested product.

Despite the satisfactory results where mangoes were classified and labeled in the "Color" and "Semi" stages, 86 - 90% Accuracy in classification was obtained, it is necessary to test the algorithm in different environments and increase the training of the classifier to improve its efficiency and in the future offer SMEs in the industry a robust system with a low error rate.

7 Future Work

Due to the growth and demand for mango fruit, the state of Guerrero is becoming a significant exporter of mangos, the application of technology is inexistent in the region, it is necessary to develop a viable technological proposal for an automated grading system that offers an acceptable level of efficiency. This work is one of the first in this area of Mexico. It is planned in a second stage to cover a nonlinear SVM with a nonlinear dividing plane. The experiments carried out were developed in a controlled environment, as a next phase we will experiment in real environments, using automated processing line.

References

1. Rocha, A., Hauagge, D.C., Wainer, J., Goldenstein, S.: Automatic fruit and vegetable classification from images. Comput. Electron. Agric. **70**(1), 96–104 (2010)
2. Wajid, A., Singh, N.K.: Recognition of ripe, unripe and scaled condition of orange citrus based on decisión tree classification. In: International Conference on Computing, Mathematics and Engineering Technologies (iCoMET) (2018).
3. Aguirre Radilla, J., De La Cruz Gámez, E., Hernández Hernández, J. L., Carranza Gómez, J.: Clasificación del Mango Manila Aplicando. RVP-AI/ROC&C'2021 (2021)
4. Aguirre Radilla, J., De La Cruz Gámez, E., Hernández Hernández, J., Carranza Gómez, J., Montero Valverde, J., Martinez Arroyo, M.: Clasificación por Color y Textura del Mango Manila Aplicando. III Convención Científica Internacional (2021)
5. Albera, S.: Vehicle logo recognition using image. Atilim University, The Department of Software Engineering (2017)
6. Bhargava, A.: Fruits and vegetables quality evaluation using computer vision. J. King Saud Univ. **33**(3), 243–257 (2018)
7. Bravo-Reyna, J.L., Montero-Valverde, J.A., Martínez-Arroyo, M., Hernández-Hernández, J.L.: Recognition of the damage caused by the cogollero worm to the corn plant, using artificial vision. In: Valencia-García, R., Alcaraz-Marmol, G., Del Cioppo-Morstadt, J., Vera-Lucio, N., Bucaram-Leverone, M. (eds.) CITI 2020. CCIS, vol. 1309, pp. 111–122. Springer, Cham (2020). https://doi.org/10.1007/978-3-030-62015-8_9
8. Burger, W., Burge, M.J.: Digital Image Processing: An Algorithmic Introduction Using Java. Springer London, London (2016)
9. Cavanillas, B.: (10 de Marzo de 2015). Láser para comprobar la madurez de la fruta sin estropearla. Obtenido de smartlighting: https://smart-lighting.es/laser-para-comprobar-la-madurez-de-la-fruta-sin-estropearla/
10. Dadwal, M.: Color image segmentation for fruit ripeness detection. a review. Singapore (2012)
11. Dwairi, A.A.: Optimized True-Color Image Processing (2010). Recuperado de: https://www.researchgate.net/publication/260402622_Optimized_True-Color_Image_Processing
12. Yossy, E.H., Pranata, J., Wijaya, T., Hermawan, H., Budiharto, W.: Mango fruit sortation system using neural network and computer vision. In: 2nd International Conference on Computer Science and Computational Intelligence, pp. 596–603 (2017)
13. Escobar, M.: Determinación del estado de madurez del aguacate mediante procesamiento de imágenes con la raspberry pi. Programa de Ingeniería Eléctrica (2018)

14. Forsyth, D.: Probability and Statistics for Computer Science. Springer International Publishing, Cham (2018). https://doi.org/10.1007/978-3-319-64410-3
15. Geografía, I.N.: El mango en Guerrero: Censo Agropecuario 2007. Instituto Nacional de Estadística y Geografía (2007)
16. Choi, H.S., Cho, J.B.:A real-time Smart fruit quality grading system classi-fying by external appearence and internal flavor factors. In: IEEE International Conference on Industrial Technology (ICIT) (2018)
17. Hague, A.R.: Color segmentation in the HSI color space using the K-means algorithm. In: Proceedings of the SPIE 3026, Nonlinear Image Processing VIII (1997)
18. Hall-Beyer, M.: GLCM texture: a tutorial (2017)
19. Haralick, R.M., Shanmugam, K., Dinstein, I.: Textural features for image classification. IEEE Trans. Syst. Man Cybern. **SMC-3**(6), 610–621 (1973). https://doi.org/10.1109/TSMC.1973.4309314
20. Herrera, J.M.: Clasificación de los frutos de café según su estado de maduración y detección de la broca mediante técnicas de procesamiento de imágenes.Prospectiva, pp. 15–22 (2016)
21. Hu, M.D.: The potential of double K-means clustering for banana image segmentation. J. Food Process, **37**(1), 10–18 (2013)
22. La Serna, N.C.: Procesamiento Digital de textura: Téc-nicas utilizadas en aplicaciones actuales de CBIR. Revista de investigación de sistemas e informática, **7**(1), 57–64 (2010)
23. Leal., A. C.: Segmentación de imágenes por textura. Universidad de Concepción. Facultad de Ingeniería, Departamento de Ingeniería Eléctrica (2006)
24. Pham, V.H., Lee, B.R.: An image segmentation approach for fruit defect detection using k-means clustering and graph-based algorithm. Vietnam J. Comput. Sci. **2**(1), 25–33 (2014). https://doi.org/10.1007/s40595-014-0028-3
25. Majed, O., Al-Dwairi, Z.A.: Optimized true-color image processing. World Appl. Sci. J. **8**(10), 1175–1182 (2010)
26. Megha, P.A.: Computer vision based fruit grading system for quality evaluation of tomato in agriculture industry. In: 7th International Conference on Communication, Computing and Virtualization (2016)
27. Meruliya, T., Dhamcliya, P., Patel, J., Panchal, D., Kadam, P., Naik, S.: Image processing for fruit shape and texture feature extraction - review. Int. J. Comput. Appl. **129**(8), 30–33 (2015). https://doi.org/10.5120/ijca2015907000
28. Otsu, N.: A treshold selection method from Gary level histograms. IEEE Trans. Syst. Man Cybern. **9**(1), 62–66 (1979)
29. Patel, H.J.: Fruit detection using improved multiple features based algorithm. Int. J. Comput. Appl. **13**(2), 1–5(2011).
30. Sahu, D., Potdar, R.M.: Defect identification and maturity detection of mango fruits using image analysis. Am. J. Artif. Intell. **1**(1), 5–14 (2017). http://www.sciencepublishinggroup.com/j/ajai
31. Rural, Planeación Agrícola Nacional 17–30.Secretaría de Cultura y Desarrollo Social (2017)
32. Rios-Diaz, J., Javier Martinez-Paya, J., del Bano Aledo, M.E.:Textural analysis by means of a grey level co-occurrence matrix method on patellar tendon ultrasonography is useful for the detection of histological changes after whole-body vibration training. Cultura, Ciencia y Deporte, **4**(11), 91–102 (2009)
33. Mustafa, S., Dauda, A.B., Dauda, M.: Image processing and SVM classification for melanoma detection. In: International Conference on Computing Networking and Informatics (ICCNI), pp. 1–5 (2017)
34. Behera, S.K., Sangita, S., Rath, A.K., Sethy, P.K.: Automatic classification of mango using statistical feature and SVM. In: Biswas, U., Banerjee, A., Pal, S., Biswas, A., Sarkar, D., Haldar, S. (eds.) Advances in Computer, Communication and Control: Proceedings of ETES

2018, pp. 469–475. Springer Singapore, Singapore (2019). https://doi.org/10.1007/978-981-13-3122-0_47

35. Subey, S.A.: Adapted Approach for Fruit Disease Identification us-ing Images. Int. J. Comput. Vis. Image Process. 44–58 (2012)

36. Zha, H., Chen, X., Wang, L., Miao, Q. (eds.): CCCV 2015. CCIS, vol. 546. Springer, Heidelberg (2015). https://doi.org/10.1007/978-3-662-48558-3

37. Long, N.T.M., Thinh, N.T.: Using machine learning to grade the mango's quality based on external features captured by vision system. Appl. Sci. **10**(17), 5775 (2020). https://doi.org/10.3390/app10175775

38. Zhang, Y., Lian, J., Fan, M., Zheng, Y.: Deep indicator for fine-grained classification of banana's ripening stages. EURASIP J. Image Video Process. **2018**(1), 1–10 (2018). https://doi.org/10.1186/s13640-018-0284-8

Detection of Motorcyclists Without a Safety Helmet Through YOLO: Support for Road Safety

Oscar J. M. Peña Cáceres[1]([envelope]) [iD], Manuel A. More-More[1] [iD],
Jorge F. Yáñez-Palacios[2] [iD], Teresa Samaniego-Cobo[3] [iD],
and Jimmy Vargas-Vargas[4] [iD]

[1] Universidad Nacional de Piura, Piura, Perú
{openaca,mmorem}@unp.edu.pe
[2] Universidad de Guayaquil, Guayaquil, Ecuador
jorge.yanezp@ug.edu.ec
[3] Universidad Agraria del Ecuador, Guayaquil, Ecuador
tsamaniego@uagraria.edu.ec
[4] Universidad Espíritu Santo, Guayaquil, Ecuador
javargasv@uees.edu.ec

Abstract. In this research, the YOLOv4 algorithm based on deep learning was
used, with the objective of detecting people who wear a safety helmet while driving a motorcycle, as well as those who do not use it while moving around the
city, violating road safety regulations. In this context, the proposed methodology
consisted of seven phases that go from the determination of the data source to
the validation and deployment, in which the Labellmg tool and the Google Colab
online platform are used due to their capacity and flexibility in the work environment. The model was developed using 287 images, of which 60% correspond to
training images, 35% to validation and 5% to perform the tests. In addition, 30
additional photographic shots are available at different times of the day to determine the model's behaviour and precision. The results show that the trained model
has a detection efficiency of 88.65% and that sing YOLOv5x could improve the
detection quality by having a more significant number of layers.

Keywords: Road Safety · Algorithm · YOLOv4 · Model

1 Introduction

In recent decades, human beings have managed to strengthen their capacities and adapt
their different skills in the use of vehicles that allow them to be transported from one
place to another immediately, which is why at the moment, the use of two-wheeled
vehicles (motorcycles) has been recognized as an affordable means of transportation.
However, the human being is subject to compliance and respect for road safety regulations, failing to comply with these guidelines impacts directly on the accident rate and

© The Author(s), under exclusive license to Springer Nature Switzerland AG 2022
R. Valencia-García et al. (Eds.): CITI 2022, CCIS 1658, pp. 107–122, 2022.
https://doi.org/10.1007/978-3-031-19961-5_8

the number of people killed for not respecting road safety regulations [1]. Another reason that impacts negatively on the accident rate is believing that this type of vehicle has been designed to work as a transportation service for passengers, as is currently the case in South American countries, particularly Perú. Nowadays, road safety in business and educational environments is the object of study, due to the impacts it has on fundamental pillars such as human behavior, institutional management, infrastructure, vehicles, and care for victims [2].

That is why, in recent decades, Traffic Accidents (TA) have been one of the ten causes of death worldwide, generating millions of deaths; without a doubt, the most predominant reasons for traffic accidents fall on vehicular congestion, inefficient use of the safety helmet, invasion of restricted lanes, maneuvers not allowed and speeding [3]. On the other hand, no less important, but of great consideration, is that the occurrence of a traffic accident often leads to the generation of road violence, characterizing it as another public health problem. In 2016, low -and middle-income countries accounted for approximately 93% of all road traffic deaths worldwide, the risks of which impacted on injuries and deaths, particularly in male adolescents and young adults [4].

Definitely, traffic accidents have a negative impact on society, the economy and the quality of people's life. Each year, 1.23 million people die, and this type of events injures more than 50 million. Trends show that these figures may increase over the next 20 years if preventive measures are not taken. In Latin America and the Caribbean, collisions cause approximately 100,000 deaths per year [5], which generates a worldwide social phenomenon due to the high rates of morbidity and mortality that cause premature death due to different injuries and often leave the victims with consequences that temporarily or permanently interrupt their normal life. In this scenario, the occurrence of traffic accidents on motorcycles has stood out in relation to accidents that occur with other types of vehicles, where one of the characteristics with the highest occurrence index is traffic congestion and the inappropriate use of security helmets. Nowadays the number of motorcycles on the street is increasing because it is considered an alternative to fast transport and a means of greater ease of use and displacement. In addition to this, the economic terms have to be considered, its costs of acquisition and maintenance are low. The facts that directly affect the motorcycle fleet are the high accident rates in this type of transport, and the high mortality and morbidity rates that are considerable due to the weak protection mechanisms that the human being adopts while using it. This scenario represents a disadvantage for the motorcycle driver compared to the population that uses four-wheel vehicles, where a better characteristic of protection and integrity of the driver and passengers is expected. Finally, a great impact of two-wheeled vehicles could be capable of generating polytraumatized mirrors, a fact observed from the assistance to motorcyclists in emergency units [6].

It is essential to point out that this problem is highly impacted due to the lack of people awareness and authorities executing a poor application of good practices in road safety or not fully fulfilling their supervisory role. The production of motorcycles has been increasing more and more due to the great demand of South American countries, particularly Perú, Colombia and Ecuador, a situation that leads to proposing new strategies that contribute and enrich the knowledge of the driver in road safety, encouraging the driver to respect the rules, make proper use of a safety helmet and above all to understand that this type of vehicle should not be used as a means of public transport.

Information Technology (IT) must be an integrating link that articulates available means, such as Artificial Intelligence (AI). The application developed makes use of the OpenCV free artificial vision library and the learning algorithm called LinearSVC [7], achieving a globalized labelling in the entire object of a cyclist, both in the bicycle and in the person. The label of the cyclist should define if he wears a safety helmet or not, but this is a contribution that is limited to the current reality of the confluence of users who travel on motorcycles, therefore it is required a greater precision and mastery of the problem. In auditing activities mainly, IT can help to generate a higher rate of awareness in population.

These new challenges of the described reality are closely related to the development of an intelligent system that allows taking advantage of the available data and information sources. Classical statistical models, which were useful for making predictions a few decades ago, have limitations in this new context. Computational intelligence methods have shown excellent prediction accuracy in different areas in recent years. [8]. These methods are robust and tolerant to uncertainty, and can learn the most relevant features of the considered data to provide an accurate forecast, thus providing excellent results by excluding non-relevant information and focusing on the most useful data [9]. Currently there are security cameras that perform easy recognition and even reading of the license plates of vehicles that circulate through the streets of a city, however, it has not been seen this strategy used on the motorcycle driver to determine if he carries or makes proper use of a safety helmet, allowing the user to analyze, evaluate and determine clearer and more specific factors on the increase in accidents or people killed by driving this type of vehicle.

The identification of motorcycle drivers who make adequate and inappropriate use of safety helmets will contribute to propose new educational strategies in road safety, as well as carrying out immediate control through the detection of offenders who drive motorcycles without a safety helmet. However, the educational institutions must help to generate better habits of commitment and safe behavior on the road, because road safety is transversal in any sociocultural context. The detection of objects that contribute to road safety has become increasingly popular, however, images with visible light require stable lighting conditions to guarantee good performance, on the contrary, night images can represent certain limitations as well as long-distance detection, so we believe that YOLOv4 could fill these gaps and have effective results [10].

This research aims to make use of artificial intelligence through YOLO (You Only Look Once), an emerging image detection algorithm [11] through which motorcycle drivers who drive with and without a safety helmet will be identified. YOLO can be considered a fast, modern and economical tool [12] with a technological impact that contributes to society and particularly to public and private institutions that promote road safety and carry out inspections for identifying people who doesn't comply with the regulations established.

2 Related Work

Previous research has been carried out with the purpose of identifying offenders who don't comply road safety regulations, by using deep learning algorithms and in their context, applying artificial intelligence.

Valencia et al. developed a study whose purpose was the detection of infractions and license plates on motorcycles, through artificial vision, with the purpose of providing a tool for traffic officers in the detection of three types of infractions by motorcyclists: not wearing a helmet of protection; circulate in prohibited areas; and using racks in places where it is not allowed. The results expressed an accuracy of 87.5%, in addition to proposing for future work the creation of a classifier using YOLO for the detection of helmets, seeking to train the algorithm so that it can identify them and thus optimize the detection method by mean of [13].

Espinosa et al. designed EspiNet V2: a deep learning model, which is also used for the detection of motorcycles in urban environments, where there is some level of occlusion. EspiNet V2 outperforms popular models like YOLO V3 and Faster R-CNN. However, it is vital to keep in mind that YOLO has evolved with new performance patterns, so it is necessary to carry out tests on versions higher than YOLO V3 in order to know the response capacity in this type of scenario [14].

Zheng et al. conducted a research called an approach to moving vehicle counting and short-term traffic prediction from video images based on deep learning. The results express that the activation function of YOLOv4 demonstrates smooth, non-monotonic characteristics and no upper limit, considering that the computational complexity is higher than the complexity of ReLu in YOLOv3, its detection effect is improved [15].

Rodriguez et al. evaluated the analysis of statistical and artificial intelligence algorithms for real-time speed estimation based on vehicle detection with YOLO, which has proven to be part of the machine learning methods with acceptable performance compared to statistical algorithms [16].

Previous work show that the YOLO v4 application provides reliable application characteristics for this type of study and for the various scenarios that are linked to road safety.

3 Methodology

For the identification of motorcycle drivers who drive with and without a safety helmet, seven phases have been proposed, as shown in Fig. 1.

3.1 Determine the Data Source

In recent years, humanity has witnessed the great proportionality of data that travels through the network, where many of them are usually effective and helpful, especially for the development of applied and basic research that contributes to the knowledge management. However, there is a piece of information known as infotrash, which generally produces biases in the great diversity of research work. The abilities of the human being have been strengthened every time better, that in principle it has been possible to learn

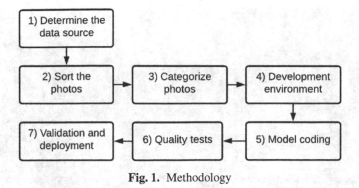

Fig. 1. Methodology

to discern and value the information that surrounds us, however, to determine the source of data, a slow and permanent search was carried out through different search engines, particularly Google, where photographs of people who are driving a motorcycle have been identified and among them the state of use of the safety helmet can be differentiated. In addition to this, photographic shots have been taken in the region, province and district of Piura in Perú, with the aim of strengthening the data source and being able to effectively and accurately detect people who drive a motorcycle with or without a helmet.

3.2 Photos Sorting

In this section, it was carried out the classification of the photographs obtained through field trips in the district of Piura, Perú and it was complemented with photo-graphs located in search engines and social networks. Criteria such as 1) adequate approach, 2) visibility of the safety helmet, 3) schedule and 4) traveling through streets or avenues have been taken into account. This classification will make it possible to carry out a first test on the identification of motorcycle drivers at peak hours in the city, taking as a reference the peak hour of the motorized flow that normally occurs in the hours from 07:00 to 07:30, 12:30 to 2:00 p.m., 3:30 p.m. to 4:30 p.m. and 6:00 p.m. to 8:00 p.m.

3.3 Photos Categorization

The categorization of the photographs is one of the fundamental phases, because at this point the manual, visual and own criterion identification is carried out through the LabelImg tool, as it is considered as the means of graphic annotation that allows labeling delimited boxes of an element or object. Therefore, LabelImg will contribute to the categorization of the images that will be used in the YOLO model, as shown in Fig. 2.

Figure 2, through segment (a), represents the categorization of motorcycle drivers who use safety helmets, while segment (b) characterizes two people who do not use safety helmets, activity that has had to be carried out continuously and according to criteria in the evaluation process of each of the photographs available for this investigation.

112 O. J. M. Peña Cáceres et al.

Fig. 2. Image categorization

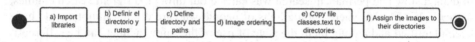

Fig. 3. Coding phases for image segmentation

After the categorization of the images, the coding of a Python script was devised, whose stages are represented in Fig. 3.

The stages defined in Fig. 3 allow for a segmentation of 287 images whose characteristics are represented in Table 1.

Table 1. Characteristics of the images

Description	Number of images
Images where only one person has a safety helmet	107
Images where only one person has a safety helmet and the passenger does not have a safety helmet	33
Images of only safety helmets	104
Images where they do not use a safety helmet	43

60% of the images were for training, 35% for validation and 5% for testing, as shown in the script in Fig. 4.

It is essential to make use of programming techniques to be able to segment the data [17], taking into consideration that, if this activity would be carried out manually, there would be no impartiality, being judge and party in the ordering of the data, that is why it was believed convenient that this action be carried out through computational methods, the same ones that they are described in Table 2, on the interpretation of Fig. 4, for a better reason on the use and application.

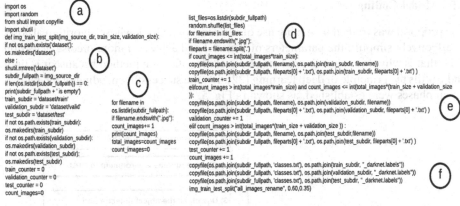

```
import os
import random                   (a)
from shutil import copyfile
import shutil
def img_train_test_split(img_source_dir, train_size, validation_size):
if not os.path.exists('dataset'):
os.makedirs('dataset')
else :                           (b)
shutil.rmtree('dataset')
subdir_fullpath = img_source_dir
if len(os.listdir(subdir_fullpath)) == 0:
print(subdir_fullpath + ' is empty')                    (c)
train_subdir = 'dataset/train'
validation_subdir = 'dataset/valid'
test_subdir = 'dataset/test'
if not os.path.exists(train_subdir):
os.makedirs(train_subdir)
if not os.path.exists(validation_subdir):
os.makedirs(validation_subdir)
if not os.path.exists(test_subdir):
os.makedirs(test_subdir)
train_counter = 0
validation_counter = 0
test_counter = 0
count_images=0

for filename in
os.listdir(subdir_fullpath):
if filename.endswith('.jpg'):
count_images+= 1
print(count_images)
total_images=count_images
count_images=0

list_files=os.listdir(subdir_fullpath)
random.shuffle(list_files)
for filename in list_files:
if filename.endswith('.jpg'):       (d)
fileparts = filename.split('.')
if count_images <= int(total_images*train_size):
copyfile(os.path.join(subdir_fullpath, filename), os.path.join(train_subdir, filename))
copyfile(os.path.join(subdir_fullpath, fileparts[0] + '.txt'), os.path.join(train_subdir, fileparts[0] + '.txt') )
train_counter += 1
elif count_images > int(total_images*train_size) and count_images <= int(total_images*(train_size + validation_size
)):
copyfile(os.path.join(subdir_fullpath, filename), os.path.join(validation_subdir, filename))
copyfile(os.path.join(subdir_fullpath, fileparts[0] + '.txt'), os.path.join(validation_subdir, fileparts[0] + '.txt') )    (e)
validation_counter += 1
elif count_images > int(total_images*(train_size + validation_size )) :
copyfile(os.path.join(subdir_fullpath, filename), os.path.join(test_subdir, filename))
copyfile(os.path.join(subdir_fullpath, fileparts[0] + '.txt'), os.path.join(test_subdir, fileparts[0] + '.txt') )
test_counter += 1
count_images += 1
copyfile(os.path.join(subdir_fullpath, 'classes.txt'), os.path.join(train_subdir, '_darknet.labels'))
copyfile(os.path.join(subdir_fullpath, 'classes.txt'), os.path.join(validation_subdir, '_darknet.labels'))
copyfile(os.path.join(subdir_fullpath, 'classes.txt'), os.path.join(test_subdir, '_darknet.labels'))     (f)
img_train_test_split("all_images_rename", 0.60,0.35)
```

Fig. 4. Python script to segment data

Table 2. Interpreting the image segmentation script flags

Interpretation criteria	Description
a	The libraries for file management are defined and continue with the coding in the image segmentation process
b	Configure the structure of empty folders if it does not exist, in addition to creating the subdirectories putting training, validation and test folder names
c	Through the count instruction, the number of images housed in the folder named "all_images_rename" was counted
d	The ordering of the images is performed randomly
e	Copy the file classes.txt to the different directories, but with another name
f	Execution of the img_train_test_split function, considering the location criteria of the images and the weights

3.4 Development Environment

As a development environment, it was determined to use the Google Colab online plat-form, due to its accessibility and ease of writing Python code through the web browser [18], being the only requirement to have a gmail email account.

In this context, it is important to mention that other features that enrich this plat-form is that it is possible to analyze, visualize and import a data set in real time in order to train the classifier and evaluate the model. Colab notebooks run code on Google cloud servers, this means that regardless of the capacity of the computer, the power of Google hardware can be used, including Graphics Processing Units [19] and Tensor Processing Units (TPU), in order to perform various activities through a simple browser [20].

3.5 Model Coding

The proposal was framed in making use of version 4 of YOLO, whose algorithm al-lows to effectively simplify the parameters of a model and achieve a more precise detection [21], that is why this research proposes a novel identification method because it is light and fulfills the principle of deep learning [22]. For the successful encoding of the model, seven phases were established, as shown in Fig. 5.

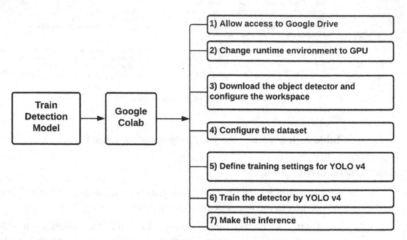

Fig. 5. Phases for model coding

The execution of Fig. 5, starts by accessing the Google Colab platform and then establish the permissions so that the Notebook created in Colab can access the data source that is stored in Google Drive, the space where the segment was made according to Fig. 4. The execution environment was in GPU mode, a special feature for graphic purposes and that contributes to the process of downloading and configuring the objects that will allow the detection of the established symbology and the identification of motorcycle drivers who use the safety helmet correctly and incorrectly, as shown in Fig. 6.

In the fifth phase, the configuration of the environment for the execution of YOLO was carried out, a characteristic that must be established in a uniform way, knowing how to assess the patterns of the GPU for a standardized training execution. For this reason, in the sixth phase, the model was trained and according to the number of images it consecutively generated a series of interactions, which took from 6 to 8 h to have an effectively trained model. For this study, the waiting time demand was 4 h and 49 min, reaching 3,200 thousand interactions and a training exchange of 17,200 images.

Hosting the images through Google Drive has been fundamental for the training of the model, due to its easy access and fast start-up and execution process, considering that stable and permanent access to the internet service must be available to channel a successful training. In addition to this, it is important to note that the Google Colab platform has free access for daily handling that goes from 6 to 12 h, so it is necessary to take into account that if we have a large volume of data (images) to carry out the

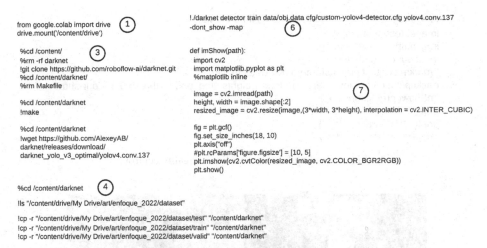

```
from google.colab import drive          (1)
drive.mount('/content/drive')
```

```
%cd /content/                    (3)
%rm -rf darknet
!git clone https://github.com/roboflow-ai/darknet.git
%cd /content/darknet/
%rm Makefile
```

```
%cd /content/darknet
!make
```

```
%cd /content/darknet
!wget https://github.com/AlexeyAB/
darknet/releases/download/
darknet_yolo_v3_optimal/yolov4.conv.137
```

```
%cd /content/darknet          (4)

!ls "/content/drive/My Drive/art/enfoque_2022/dataset"

!cp -r "/content/drive/My Drive/art/enfoque_2022/dataset/test" "/content/darknet"
!cp -r "/content/drive/My Drive/art/enfoque_2022/dataset/train" "/content/darknet"
!cp -r "/content/drive/My Drive/art/enfoque_2022/dataset/valid" "/content/darknet"
```

```
!./darknet detector train data/obj.data cfg/custom-yolov4-detector.cfg yolov4.conv.137
-dont_show -map          (6)
```

```
def imShow(path):
    import cv2
    import matplotlib.pyplot as plt
    %matplotlib inline

    image = cv2.imread(path)          (7)
    height, width = image.shape[:2]
    resized_image = cv2.resize(image,(3*width, 3*height), interpolation = cv2.INTER_CUBIC)

    fig = plt.gcf()
    fig.set_size_inches(18, 10)
    plt.axis("off")
    #plt.rcParams['figure.figsize'] = [10, 5]
    plt.imshow(cv2.cvtColor(resized_image, cv2.COLOR_BGR2RGB))
    plt.show()
```

Fig. 6. Coding of the key phases of the model

training, we must anticipate that the execution time does not exceed the time provided, otherwise a Google Colab Pro package must be obtained, in order to access to a greater execution capacity and a better time for the development of this type of activities related to computational vision. YOLO v4 has shown to have the capacity to develop this type of activities, particularly about the training of the model that has a fast recognition speed in initial tests and a high accuracy [23].

As it is known there are different versions of YOLO, but in this context YOLO v4, shows an excellent role compared to YOLO-D model which also has great potential for accurate detection, but the speed is slightly slower than YOLOv3, YOLOv4 and YOLOv5 [24].

3.6 Quality Control

To determine the efficiency of the model, quality control was carried out where the information scenario corresponds to 5% of the images used as a test, characterized in 14 images. However, 30 additional images were considered, the same ones that have been considered as "foreign" because they were obtained through field activities, which allowed reaching a total of 44 images evaluated through the script encoded in Fig. 7.

This activity allows us to know a certain degree of efficiency of the model, in this specific research with the 44 images has provided very promising results. However, the sharpness of the images plays a fundamental role for the model to make the appropriate identification and do not confuse objects that might look similar to a safety helmet, such as hats. In Fig. 8, we observe some of the images evaluated with results that demonstrate a high coincidence and efficiency index of the trained model, this can still be improved in order to perform remote or real-time detections through digital media connectivity as video surveillance cameras that are installed in the most transitable areas of a city [25], knowing that YOLO is a scalable single-stage object detection algorithm and has good real-time performance [26].

```
test_images = [f for f in os.listdir('test') if f.endswith('.jpg')]
image=test_images[3]
img_path = "test/" + image;
#test out our detector!
!./darknet detect cfg/custom-yolov4-detector.cfg
backup/custom-yolov4-detector_best.weights {img_path}  -thresh 0.3 -dont-show
imShow('predictions.jpg')
print("********************")
print("*****",image,"*****")
print("********************")
```

Fig. 7. Coding for the execution of quality control

Fig. 8. Quality control results

3.7 Validation and Deployment

In this last phase, 44 images were validated, taking into account that 14 of them are motorcycle drivers who are not wearing a safety helmet, 18 with a safety helmet and 12 with mixed qualities, where the pilot wears a safety helmet and the passenger does not have the aforementioned accessory. Figure 9 expresses an average precision of 89.88%, Fig. 10 of 90.5% and Fig. 11 of 90.87%.

In this context, the validated images have showed satisfactory results; however, Fig. 12 has an accuracy of 89.5% because in the recognition of the image, it is possible to detect a person who uses a green cap green and there is also agglomeration by people, resulting as dispersion that weakens the results of the model.

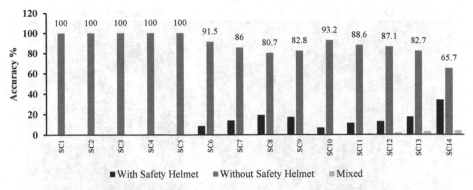

Fig. 9. Accuracy of 14 images validated without a safety helmet

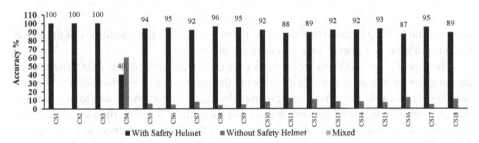

Fig. 10. Accuracy of 18 validated images that have a safety helmet

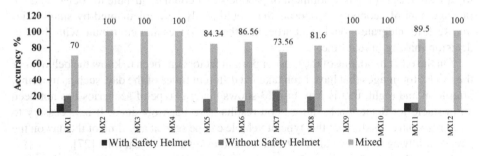

Fig. 11. Accuracy of 12 mixed images with and without safety helmet

4 Results

As part of the main training results, it is demonstrated that the model has an accuracy of 89.5% for the detection of motorcycle drivers who wear the safety helmet correctly. Nevertheless, the model's accuracy for the detection of drivers who do not use a safety helmet while riding a motorcycle is 87.8%. In this context, the model ex-presses an average accuracy of 88.65% regarding the efficiency on the identification of motorcycle drivers who make or not an adequate use of safety helmets while moving around a city. It

Fig. 12. Comparative on the result of a validated image

is important to keep in mind that the author seek to improve the conditions of the model not only in time, but also in more accurate results,

The OpenCV and sklearn technologies have showed good results in similar investigations; however, one of the shortcomings is the precision in identification of elements and objects, because if we need to recognize the face of a person we would need images that only involve this type of composition, yet through YOLO and the use of the LabelImg tool, it is carried out the label and framing of the object or element to be classified, which demonstrates a better dosage of time and optimization of resources. For this reason, this research seeks to demonstrate that there are new technologies as alternatives to local resources for the development of products that could contribute to society and the management of economic proposals that could easily be implemented by small cities that seek to integrate models that articulate their ser-vices and contribute with them to decision making in real time.

On the other hand, one of the most important factors has been to know the behavior of the model for images that have been taken at different times of the day, such as morning, afternoon and night, that is why Fig. 13 shows that this type of scenarios has not been an obstacle for detection because good results have been obtained. It is necessary to recognize and consider that this type of vehicle can be seen at any time of the day on the streets, allowing to project an identification and evaluation in real time [27].

The method used in this study was able to obtain a better balance between detection performance and detection speed, by making use of platform services with greater hardware capacity such as Google Colab Pro [28]. In addition, the classification accuracy on the correct use of the safety helmet can be greatly improved with the help of transfer learning [29].

The identification proposed in this research is key to reduce the risk of death by accidents caused while motorcycle driving, as reflected in the country of Thailand which permanently monitors trafficability on the roads of the city as an essential process for the intelligent management and control of highway traffic. With the wide-spread use of surveillance cameras, it is possible to strengthen a wide library of images not only

Fig. 13. Results of photographs at different times of the day

referring to the subject addressed, but also to monitor the possible behavior of the driver [30].

In recent years, with the rapid development of deep learning, computer vision (CV) has been widely used in facial expression recognition, disease diagnosis [31] and even in cattle counting by making use of unmanned aerial vehicles However, deep learning has not been immersed in the development of capacities that promote road safety and good information technology practices that will generously contribute to strengthening a city's transit system. At the same time, it is important to note that CV techniques have boomed and many classic object detection methods have emerged, including one-stage, two-stage, and non-anchoring algorithms such as Faster RCNN [32], RetinaNet, YOLOv3, YOLOv4, YOLOv5 and YOLOv5x. Still, we should know that the existing algorithms for detection are divided into two classes, where one is the real-time detection method that pursues fast inference speed, and the other is the high-performance detection method that prioritizes accuracy of the image or video [33].

After having experimented with YOLOv4, the author is working on new proposals in order to seek the safety and precision of the model, being the main reason why the use of the YOLO-V5x version has the highest average detection per image among the models before mentioned by having a greater number of layers in its network model [34].

5   Conclusions

In the present research, the YOLOv4 algorithm was used to detect motorcycle drivers who wear a safety helmet and those who do not use a safety helmet while traveling in their vehicle. The results show us that the trained model has a detection efficiency of 88.65%.

Regarding the use of images used for model training, it is emphasized that, in order to strengthen the model, it is necessary to train the model with a greater number of images, taking into account that in this research it was carried out with 287 images, where 60% of the images have been for training, 35% for validation, 5% for tests and additionally 30 images were considered as part of the foreign tests, having a total of 331 images that allowed knowing the development of the model in its precisions and inaccuracies.

The 44 test images have represented a greater precision and approach in their results, which allows to know more closely the behavior of the model, especially when images are available at different times of the day, particularly at night where it evades the use of a safety helmet, due to the limited visibility of the human being. It is necessary that, during the process of categorizing the images, those people who use caps and hoods that can limit the veracity and precision of the model are also valued.

YOLOv4, responds very well in the detection of objects on images that are taken at different times of the day, an achievement that favors the authorities and above all to promote the use of these computer vision techniques, strengthening through information technologies the compliance with safety standards that allow guidance and supervision of motorcycle drivers who make inappropriate use of this means of personal transportation.

Future research related to road safety are invited to make use of YOLOv5x, as it is a more flexible version and allows integration with technologies that lead to the development of an online platform that integrates the inspection service for bad drivers and this is one of the main factors to the development of smart city, improving the cultural habits and quality of life of the population that resides in a geographic space. The management of new methods and strategies that exploit local technology and that contribute to the road safety sector should be promoted, which by lukewarm measures, daily impacts people's lives who don't respect the rules and laws established by the authorities.

References

1. Berrones-Sanz, L.D.: Análisis de los accidentes y las lesiones de los motociclistas en México. Gac. Med. Mex. **153**, 662–671 (2017). https://doi.org/10.24875/GMM017002812
2. Torres, D.F.M., Pérez, G.L., De Segura, B.E.: Analysis of road safety in educational institutions with multiple sites, cartagena de indias, colombia. Prod. y Limpia. **14**, 93–107 (2020). https://doi.org/10.22507/PML.V14N2A7
3. Torres, F.T., Baltazar, J.Y., Vargas, D.P.: Physical and operational replantation of an urban roundabout of five interior rails in congestion situation to improve its road efficiency and safety. In: Proceedings of the LACCEI international Multi-conference for Engineering, Education and Technology. Latin American and Caribbean Consortium of Engineering Institutions (2020). https://doi.org/10.18687/LACCEI2020.1.1.385
4. de Sousa, R.A., et al.: Tendência temporal e distribuição espacial da mortalidade por acidentes de trânsito no Piauí, 2000-2017. Epidemiologia e Serviços de Saúde **29**(5), e2019558 (2020). https://doi.org/10.1590/s1679-49742020000500005
5. Valencia-Alaix, V.G., Betancur, B.R., Jimenez, C.L., Mendez, R.: Estimation of safety performance functions (SPF) at signalized intersections in Medellín Colombia. DYNA **87**(214), 215–220 (2020). https://doi.org/10.15446/dyna.v87n214.83880
6. Freitas, E.B. da S., de França, I.S.X.: Motor deficiencies and trauma severity in motorcyclist victims of road traffic accidents. Cogitare Enferm. **23**, 1–9 (2018). https://doi.org/10.5380/ce.v23i4.57751

7. Padmini, V.L., Kishore, G.K., Durgamalleswarao, P., Sree, P.T.: Real time automatic detection of motorcyclists with and without a safety helmet. In: Proceedings - International Conference Smart Electronics Communication ICOSEC 2020, pp. 1251–1256 (2020). https://doi.org/10.1109/ICOSEC49089.2020.9215415

8. Fracarolli, J.A., Adimari Pavarin, F.F., Castro, W., Blasco, J.: Computer vision applied to food and agricultural products. Rev. Cienc. Agron. **51**, 1–20 (2020). https://doi.org/10.5935/1806-6690.20200087

9. Porteiro, R., Hernández-Callejo, L., Nesmachnow, S.: Electricity demand forecasting in industrial and residential facilities using ensemble machine learning. Rev. Fac. Ing. **102**, 9–25 (2022). https://doi.org/10.17533/UDEA.REDIN.20200584

10. Sun, M., Zhang, H., Huang, Z., Luo, Y., Li, Y.: Road infrared target detection with I-YOLO. IET Image Process. **16**, 92–101 (2022). https://doi.org/10.1049/IPR2.12331

11. Lu, Y., Yang, B., Gao, Y., Xu, Z.: An automatic sorting system for electronic components detached from waste printed circuit boards. Waste Manag. **137**, 1–8 (2022). https://doi.org/10.1016/J.WASMAN.2021.10.016

12. Mancin, W.R., Pereira, L.E.T., Carvalho, R.S.B., Shi, Y., Silupu, W.M.C., Tech, A.R.B.: The use of computer vision to classify Xaraés grass according to nutritional status in nitrogen. Rev. Ciência Agronômica. **53**, 1–12 (2022). https://doi.org/10.5935/1806-6690.20220006

13. Valencia, J., Ramirez-Guerrero, T., Castañeda, L., Toro, M.: Detección de infracciones y matrículas en motocicletas, mediante visión artificial, aplicado a Sistemas Inteligentes de Transporte. RISTI - Revista Ibérica de Sistemas e Tecnologias de Informação **37**, 1–15 (2020). https://doi.org/10.17013/risti.37.1-15

14. Oviedo, J.E.E., Velastín, S.A., Bedoya, J.W.B.: Espinet v2: a region based deep learning model for detecting motorcycles in urban scenarios. DYNA **86**(211), 317–326 (2019). https://doi.org/10.15446/dyna.v86n211.81639

15. Zheng, Y., Li, X., Xu, L.C., Wen, N.: A deep learning-based approach for moving vehicle counting and short-term traffic prediction from video images. Front. Environ. Sci. **10**, 905433 (2022). https://doi.org/10.3389/FENVS.2022.905443

16. Rodríguez-Rangel, H., Morales-Rosales, L.A., Imperial-Rojo, R., Roman-Garay, M.A., Peralta-Peñuñuri, G.E., Lobato-Báez, M.: Analysis of statistical and artificial intelligence algorithms for real-time speed estimation based on vehicle detection with YOLO. Appl. Sci. **12**(6), 2907 (2022). https://doi.org/10.3390/app12062907

17. Rajpal, R., Yadav, V, Tomar, R.: Applying computation intelligence for improved computer vision capabilities. In: Tomar, R., Hina, M.D., Zitouni, R., Ramdane-Cherif, A. (eds.) Innovative Trends in Computational Intelligence. EICC, pp. 143–176. Springer, Cham (2022). https://doi.org/10.1007/978-3-030-78284-9_7

18. Kuroki, M.: Using Python and Google Colab to teach undergraduate microeconomic theory. Int. Rev. Econ. Educ. **38**, 100225 (2021). https://doi.org/10.1016/j.iree.2021.100225

19. Sadakatul Bari, S.M., Islam, R., Mardia, S.R.: Performance evaluation of convolution neural network based object detection model for Bangladeshi traffic vehicle detection. In: Arefin, M.S., Kaiser, M.S., Bandyopadhyay, A., Ahad, M.A.R., Ray, K. (eds.) Proceedings of the International Conference on Big Data, IoT, and Machine Learning. LNDECT, vol. 95, pp. 115–128. Springer, Singapore (2022). https://doi.org/10.1007/978-981-16-6636-0_10

20. Ray, S., Alshouiliy, K., Agrawal, D.P.: Dimensionality reduction for human activity recognition using google colab. Information **12**, 1–23 (2021). https://doi.org/10.3390/info12010006

21. Zhuxi, M.A., Li, Y., Huang, M., Huang, Q., Cheng, J., Tang, S.: A lightweight detector based on attention mechanism for aluminum strip surface defect detection. Comput. Ind. **136**, 103585 (2022). https://doi.org/10.1016/j.compind.2021.103585

22. Zhang, Y.: Application and analysis of psychological scale based on genetic algorithm in sports psychology. Rev. Bras. Med. do Esporte. **27**, 31–34 (2021). https://doi.org/10.1590/1517-8692202127022021_0017

23. Wang, J., Gao, Z., Zhang, Y., Zhou, J., Wu, J., Li, P.: Real-time detection and location of potted flowers based on a ZED camera and a YOLO V4-tiny deep learning algorithm. Horticulturae **8**, 21 (2021). https://doi.org/10.3390/horticulturae8010021

24. Wang, Z., Zhang, X., Li, J., Luan, K.: A yolo-based target detection model for offshore unmanned aerial vehicle data. Sustainability **13**(23), 12980 (2021). https://doi.org/10.3390/su132312980

25. Li, X., Deng, J., Fang, Y.: Few-shot object detection on remote sensing images. IEEE Trans. Geosci. Remote Sensing **60**, 1–14 (2022). https://doi.org/10.1109/TGRS.2021.3051383

26. Wang, G., Ding, H., Li, B., Nie, R., Zhao, Y.: Trident-YOLO: Improving the precision and speed of mobile device object detection. IET Image Process. **16**, 145–157 (2022). https://doi.org/10.1049/IPR2.12340

27. Guo, F., Wang, Y., Qian, Y.: Computer vision-based approach for smart traffic condition assessment at the railroad grade crossing. Adv. Eng. Inform. **51**, 101456 (2022). https://doi.org/10.1016/j.aei.2021.101456

28. Wang, Z., Jin, L., Wang, S., Xu, H.: Apple stem/calyx real-time recognition using YOLO-v5 algorithm for fruit automatic loading system. Postharvest Biol. Technol. **185**, 111808 (2022). https://doi.org/10.1016/j.postharvbio.2021.111808

29. Wan, L., Liu, R., Sun, L., Nie, H., Wang, X.: UAV swarm based radar signal sorting via multi-source data fusion: A deep transfer learning framework. Inf. Fusion. **78**, 90–101 (2022). https://doi.org/10.1016/j.inffus.2021.09.007

30. Panboonyuen, T., Thongbai, S., Wongweeranimit, W., Santitamnont, P., Suphan, K., Charoenphon, C.: Object detection of road assets using transformer-based yolox with feature pyramid decoder on Thai highway panorama. Information **13**, 5 (2021). https://doi.org/10.3390/INFO13010005

31. López, M.A., Gutiérrez, E.C.: Implementation of a model based on deep learning techniques applied to computer vision in the classification of x-ray images, for the support of the diagnosis of traumatological injuries of the pelvic structure. In: Proceedings of the LACCEI International Multi-conference Engineering Education Technology (2019). https://doi.org/10.18687/LACCEI2019.1.1.395

32. Francies, M.L., Ata, M.M., Mohamed, M.A.: A robust multiclass 3D object recognition based on modern YOLO deep learning algorithms. Concurr. Comput. Pract. Exp. **34**, e6517 (2022). https://doi.org/10.1002/CPE.6517

33. Peishu, W., Li, H., Zeng, N., Li, F.: FMD-Yolo: An efficient face mask detection method for COVID-19 prevention and control in public. Image Vis. Comput. **117**, 104341 (2022). https://doi.org/10.1016/j.imavis.2021.104341

34. Jintasuttisak, T., Edirisinghe, E., Elbattay, A.: Deep neural network based date palm tree detection in drone imagery. Comput. Electron. Agr. **192**, 106560 (2022). https://doi.org/10.1016/j.compag.2021.106560

Computer Vision-Based Ovitrap for Dengue Control

Jesús Emmanuel Abad-Salinas[1] , José Antonio Montero-Valverde[1(✉)] ,
José Luis Hernández-Hernández[2,4(✉)] , Virgilio Cruz-Guzmán[3] ,
Miriam Martínez-Arroyo[1] , Eduardo de la Cruz-Gámez[1] ,
and Mario Hernández-Hernández[2,4]

[1] Tecnológico Nacional de México/IT de Acapulco, Acapulco, Mexico
{mm20320001,jose.mv,miriam.ma,eduardo.dg}@acapulco.tecnm.mx
[2] Tecnológico Nacional de México/IT de Chilpancingo, Chilpancingo, Mexico
joseluis.hh@chilpancingo.tecnm.mx
[3] Facultad de Matemáticas extensión Acapulco, Universidad Autónoma de Guerrero, Acapulco,
Mexico
vguzman@uagro.mx
[4] Facultad de Ingeniería, Universidad Autónoma de Guerrero, Chilpancingo, Mexico
mhernandezh@uagro.mx

Abstract. According to information from health institutions, the deadliest animal
in the world is the Aedes aegypti mosquito. Regarding Mexico, in 2020, 9,000
infections and 580 deaths caused by dengue were registered. Veracruz, Tabasco,
Guerrero, Nayarit and Tamaulipas are the states that represent 61% of the infections. Currently, one of the ways to combat it is to identify the areas with the highest
risk of contagion by installing and reviewing ovitraps. The review and counting
process is carried out manually by specialised personnel, every week. This leads to
generating a certain degree of uncertainty in the information collected, in addition
to the excessive consumption of resources. In some countries, such as Malaysia,
Indonesia, Brazil, among others, attempts have already been made to automate the
process of collecting and counting eggs. Some have used embedded systems, while
others have focused on the implementation of techniques derived from artificial
intelligence. However, the results presented are around controlled environments
(laboratories). In this work, an ovitrap prototype is presented that uses Raspberry
Pi technology, integrated with software based on artificial vision techniques, which
allows the images obtained from inside the ovitrap to be analyzed, this by means
of segmentation and a simple counting of the eggs deposited by the Aedes aegypti
mosquito. At the moment, preliminary results are satisfactory, since they are based
on more than a hundred images in real environmental conditions.

Keywords: Aedes aegypti · Intelligent ovitrap · Digital image processing ·
Computer vision · Raspberry Pi · Python

1 Introduction

The mosquito of the genus Aedes aegypti (Ae. Aegypti) is responsible for transmitting
vector-borne diseases such as dengue, yellow fever, chikungunya fever and zika virus

[1]. These diseases have a high mortality rate in the world. World Health Organization (WHO) points out, than the method commonly used to limit the transmission of dengue, is to control mosquitoes and protect against their bites [2, 18].

A simple an economic method used for surveillance and control of populations of Ae. Aegypti are the ovitraps. This device consists of a 500 ml plastic container with oviposition support (repository of the eggs of the female mosquito Ae. Aegypti). These traps are installed in strategic places in urban areas, whose incidence of contagion is moderate or high. Once installed, they remain for a time to sample populations of Ae. Aegypti by the trained personnel of the Secretariat of Health and Assistance (SHA). However, this method for control appears to be inadequate to meet the needs of vector entomological surveillance, since the SHA personnel must carry out reviews and on-site data removal every week [3] (see Fig. 1), In fact, this problem has been the object of study by some researchers [4–7, 9] because, this process has the risk of losing information or inconsistency in the data collected, this is due to the time that elapses between one revision and another, since in this period the mosquitoes can lay more eggs or eclosionar [5] which generates a certain degree of uncertainty in the statistical analysis and consequently in the decision-making of the distribution of health personnel. Therefore, the incorporation of emerging technologies that include a mechanism, that automate measurement processes and mosquito population density control Ae. Aegypti in an embryonic state, will help by providing useful and timely information for the decision-making process by the health sector.

The authors Gaburro et al. [8] designed a built-in vision based system that allows automatic egg counting of the Aedes aegypti mosquito. They indicated that egg estimation realized by the system is statistically equivalent compared to manual counting. However, currently their software has been tested under controlled environmental conditions using different egg densities.

In another work realized by Santana et al. [9] the authors, present a hardware and software vision-based system that automatizes the counting Aedes aegypti eggs applying deep learning techniques. Results reported by authors indicate a confidence interval of 95% applying the Wilcoxon test. They use reeds to simulate the real world conditions, however, the images are not captured under real environmental conditions. A recent review shows that machine learning techniques have gained a lot of attention for mosquito control in urban environments [10]. In this sense, the authors of [11] address the detection of potential mosquito breeding grounds using an unmanable aerial vehicle. They aim to detect water tanks as well as scenarios containing objects that can hold stagnant water. The work in [12] proposes a neural network-based model to extract features from the images of mosquitoes to automate the classification among the *Aedes aegypti*, *Aedes albopictus*, and *Culex quinquefasciatus* species. In [13], the authors propose a system to identify potential mosquito breeding sites in geotagged images received from the population. In this work, the images are converted into feature vectors using the bag of visual words model through the scale- invariant feature transform (SIFT) descriptor to train a support vector machine (SVM) classifier. According to classification, the system outputs a heat map highlighting the regions with the highest risk of having mosquito habitats. The work in [14] uses a bag of naive Bayes classifiers with speeded-up robust features (SURF) extracted from thermal and gray level images to detect stagnant water.

Their approach only classify the images as to whether containing or not potential breeding grounds. The authors of [15] use images from Google Street View, Google image search, and Common Objects in Context (COCO) dataset to train and test the Faster R-CNN to detect several objects like as tires, buckets, potted plants, vases, bowls, and cups. They use the detected objects to compose a dashboard showing the risk areas.

In this work we present preliminary results of a prototype of an intelligent ovitrap whose function is to capture, count and report Ae. Aegypti mosquito populations in real time. However, in this first part of the ongoing research, the objective is to present a first version of the developed algorithm, based on artificial vision techniques, obtaining satisfactory results from the segmentation process of the region of interest, to a simple count of Ae. Aegypti populations.

2 Materials and Methods

The methodology used in this ongoing research consists of 4 phases, of which the first two, explain the design and development of the ovitrap prototype as shown in Fig. 1. These phases are listed below:

- Phase 1. Hardware Design and Construction
- Phase 2: Algorithm Development
- Phase 3: Ovitrap site selection and Dataset Collection
- Phase 4: Testing and Results

The explanation of the phases one, two and three are described below.

2.1 Phase 1. Design and Construction of the Prototype

2.1.1 Selection of Materials

In the process of designing the ovitrap, we do a review of the most widely used technologies in the development of smart ovitraps and technologies used to combat the mosquito Ae. Aegypti in Mexico and the world, however no many work have been developed in this regard, in the research work [6], an analysis and selection of a technology for the development of an intelligent ovitrap was carried out, in this work the conclusion is reached to implement the NodeMCU ESP8266 technology, considering some criteria such as: WiFi connectivity, operational voltage, clock speed, system memory, flash memory, etc. In another approach [16] authors, it is proposed to perform the task of counting the eggs deposited in the ovitraps in an automated way through Deep Learning algorithms, in order to avoid counting errors and reduce the time consumed in this activity. For the design of ovitrap we select as the main electronic device the Raspberry Pi Model B+ with camera NoIR Raspberry V2. This device has the following features: It has a microprocessor with Greater capacity in RAM memory, GPIO pins for connecting actuators and sensors, USB ports to connect peripherals, Capable of running LINUX based operating systems, Capable of processing computer vision algorithms, It's really a mini computer, Supports different programming languages such as Python, Java, C,

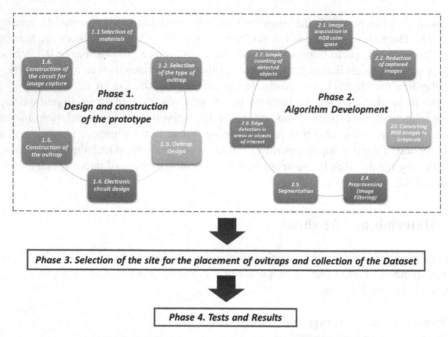

Fig. 1. Methodology used for ovitrap dengue control.

C++, among others. Also we decided is to use Raspberry Pi technology, due to its capacity to process Artificial Vision algorithms, execute tasks corresponding to digital image processing, flexibility, portability and in general for being the technology that covers the highest percentage of the technological needs of the proposed prototype [17, 19]. Table 1 shows some aspects (advantages and disadvantages) of the main electronic devices used in the reviewed works).

We decided is to use Raspberry Pi technology, due to its capacity to process Artificial Vision algorithms, execute tasks corresponding to digital image processing, flexibility, portability and in general for being the technology that covers the highest percentage of the technological needs of the proposed prototype.

2.1.2 Selection of the Type of Ovitrap

According to the World Health Organization (WHO) [10] there are 3 types of ovitraps:

- **Lethal**: These have been used to a limited extent and employ an oviposition substrate impregnated with insecticide.
- **Autodrops**: They are those that allow oviposition, but prevent the eggs from hatching, preventing the formation of adult mosquitoes.
- **Adhesive/tracking**: These are those that capture the mosquito at the moment it lands or the eggs that oviposit inside them for analysis and counting.

Table 1. Comparison of embedded technologies.

Technology	Advantage	Disadvantages
Arduino ONE + Camera VGA OV7670	• Wide use worldwide • Great compatibility with sensors and actuators • High flexibility • Shield compatibility • Low cost development board • Average cost camera • Many applications and uses • High availability in the market	• Does not have a microprocessor • Has no memory RAM/FLASH • Does not have a graphical user interface (GUI) • Does not integrate connectivity WiFi/Bluetooth • Camera compatibility issues • Does not have the ability to process artificial vision algorithms by computer
NodeMCU ESP-32CAM + Camera OV2640	• Medium flexibility • Powerful for IOT projects, Robotics and more • Compatible with a wide variety of sensors and actuators • Economic • 2 MP on-board camera with flash light • Integrated Wi-Fi and Bluetooth connectivity • Integrated compartment for external Micro SD storage	• Low availability in the market • Little development worldwide • Does not have a graphical interface (GUI) • Low RAM capacity • Does not have the ability to process artificial vision algorithms by computer
Raspberry Pi 3 Model B+ Camera NoIR Raspberry V2	• It has a microprocessor • Greater capacity in RAM memory • GPIO pins for connecting actuators and sensors • USB ports to connect peripherals • Capable of running LINUX based operating systems • Capable of processing computer vision algorithms • It's a mini computer • Supports different programming languages such as Python, Java, C, C++, among others	• High availability in the market • Top cost vs Arduino ONE and Esp-32CAM

According to the needs of the prototype, we selected ovitraps of the adhesive type, this model has adequate characteristics for the development of the project. The design of this type consists of a dark container with water inside up to half of its storage capacity, F – 1600 fleece fabric placed inside for the oviposition of the female Ae. Aegypti, since it prefers to oviposit on a rough surface, this type of material despite absorbing liquids remains rigid [3]. In addition, this type of ovitrap is the most common and recommended by the scientific community [11].

2.1.3 Design of the Ovitrap

The material used for the production of the ovitraps is recycled, based on cans of disposable supplies, which are normally considered polluting to the environment.

2.1.4 Design of the Electronic Circuit Inside the Ovitrap

Once the technology that will be used to capture images of the eggs that the female Ae. Aegypti oviposits inside the ovitrap is chosen, the next step is to design the electronic circuit that integrates all the selected components (to obtain and analize the images).

The Open Source CAD software called Fritzing is used to design the circuit. The pictorial diagram is shown in Fig. 2.

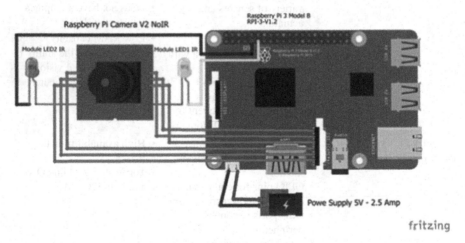

Fig. 2. Pictorial diagram of the ovitrap circuit with the technology selected.

2.1.5 Construction of the Ovitrap

We currently have a prototype of an ideal ovitrap (see Fig. 3), made of the material described in Sect. 2.1.3, on which we have carried out some tests and captured images of its inside.

2.1.6 Simple Counting of Detected Objects

After the circuit design is made (Sect. 2.1.4), it is physically built with the selected components. After an improvement is made to the Raspberry Pi V2 camera, adding to

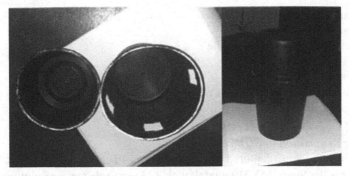

Fig. 3. Prototype of the ideal ovitrap.

the camera 2 infrared (IR) LED modules that incorporate light sensors (LDR), these sensors help the lights to be activated only in the dark as shown in Fig. 4b, this provides greater visibility inside the ovitrap when capturing images. A macro type lens was also adapted to capture macroscopic objects inside the prototype, whose approximate size is 1 mm, with greater definition.

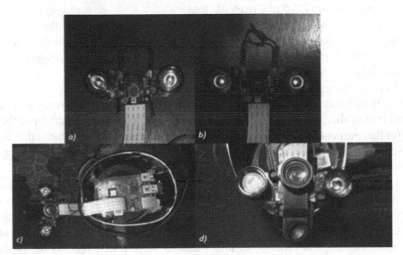

Fig. 4. a) Camera with IR LED modules. b) IR LED modules activated. c) Electronic circuit built. d) Raspberry Pi camera with Macro lens adaptation.

Subsequently, the camera is connected to the Raspberry Pi board, configured for use in the Raspberry Pi OS operating system and the algorithm developed in Sect. 2.2 (explained below) is implemented for image capture and processing.

2.2 Phase 2. Algorithm Development

Methodology for the treatment of the images obtained consists of the following stages:

- Image acquisition in RGB color space
- Reduction of captured images
- Conversion from RGB to greyscale
- Preprocessing (Image filtering)
- Segmentation
- Edge detection in areas or objects of interest
- Simple count of detected objects

(i) *Image acquisition in RGB color space*

The images are captured using a Raspberry Pi camera model NoIR V2, whose sensor is the Sony IMX219 model, with 8 Megapixels and a resolution of 3280×2464 pixels. The images are captured in the RGB color space (See Fig. 5a, Fig. 6 left). Once captured, they are stored in a repository stored in the Raspberry Pi's memory system where they are ready for preprocessing [6, 7].

(ii) *Reduction of captured images*

In this phase, the images are resized, reducing each image to the size of a resolution of 400×400 pixels, in order to facilitate their analysis and interpretation in real time, without any loss of information affecting the search for the objects of interest.

(iii) *Conversion from RGB to Grayscale images*

Because the objective of the project is to detect and count the Ae. Aegypti mosquito population in its incubation stage (eggs), in this phase the images are converted to grayscale (see Fig. 5b–c) for greater efficiency in the image processing techniques used and also to support the analysis in real time.

(iv) *Preprocessing (Image filtering)*

In this stage, the aim is to eliminate the imperfections of the captured images caused by dust from the photographic lens, noise or any error captured by the lens, for this purpose, we applied a median filter with a 3×3 size of mask, this process resulted in the smoothing of the images and the reduction of noise (see Fig. 5d).

(v) *Segmentation*

In the segmentation task, the purpose consists in detect and isolate the regions and objects of interest (eggs of the mosquitoes in our case). For this work, a simple segmentation approach known as thresholding was applied. Thresholding technique helps to separate greyscale image pixels based on a threshold intensity value. During this process, various methods were tested such as the procedure proposed by Otsu and the Gaussian approach among others. The best results were obtained using inverted binary thresholding method (see Fig. 5e, Fig. 6).

(vi) *Edge detection in areas or objects of interest*

Prior to counting the objects of interest, it is necessary to detect the edges of the segmented objects.

For this purpose, we applied an edge detection algorithm, the best option was the Canny edge detector, because this algorithm is considered one of the best operators for the detection of contours or edges on objects in digital images, using convolution masks (see Fig. 5e and Fig. 6 right).

Once this operator has been applied to the image, the contours of the Ae. Aegypti eggs found in the resulting segmented image are highlighted.

(vii) *Simple count of detected objects*
    Finally, once the edges of the objects found in the image have been detected, the search for the contours of the Ae. Aegypti eggs is started using two functions from the OpenCV (Open Source Computer Vision) library: findContours and drawContours.

The findContours technique is used under binary images where the Canny edge detector operator has been applied to count all the objects found within the image through the edges found, and drawContours allows to highlight all the edges or contours found in the image with black color. Next, the objects detected are counted using findCountours library. Figure 6 shows the results obtained for each phase of the algorithm.

Fig. 5. The figure shows the results of each stage of preprocessing. a) Original image. b) Reduction of the original image with edges found from segmentation. c) Conversion to greyscale. d) Application of the filter from the Median. e) Segmentation and counting of the elements of interest found.

2.3   Phase 3. Site Selection for Ovitrap Placement and Dataset Collection

In this section we explain the criteria followed to select the places where to ovitraps were put. The selection mode was carried out as described below: In the first instance, the distribution by zones in the city of Acapulco is considered, and subsequently, based on the entomological methodological guide of the Ministry of Health SHA [3], considering the following criteria: risk indices, degree of safeguarding of the ovitrap, accessibility and population concentration. That is, the sites to place the ovitraps were selected manually at the suggestion of the health personnel.
    Table 2 shows the sites for the installation of the ovitraps. Carrying out the installation of the ovitraps also is necessary, as it is necessary to build a dataset, which to have the available dataset to realize the corresponding tests.

Table 2. Ovitraps emplacement matrix.

Zone	Coordinates (latitude-longitude)	ID-ovitrap	State
Center	16.872548, −99.884960	A-001	Activates
Northwest	16.878188, −99.871392	A-002	Activates
West	16.910547, −99.983791	A-003	Activates
East	16.816742, −99.797888	A-004	Activates
Southeast	16.851483, −99.846560	A-005	Activates
Center	16.871692, −99.885076	A-006	Activates
Northwest	16.880380, −99.878271	A-007	Activates
West	16.914390, −99.993940	A-008	Activates
East	16.817204, −99.797832	A-009	Activates
Southeast	16.850502, −99.847372	A-010	Activates

3   Results

Unlike most of the works reported in the literature, where the tests are carried out with various restrictions or in labs conditions, the preliminary results that we are presenting were carried out in real environmental conditions. Following we explain this results:

- 10 samples of Ae. Aegypti mosquito populations were collected with the help of ovitraps deployed at different points in the municipality of Acapulco, over a period of two weeks of 15 days, allowing for the collection of a Dataset composed of more than a hundred images, with this data we realize the preliminary tests of the proposed prototype.
- Next and with the contribution of the adaptation of the Macro lens to the Raspberry camera, it was possible to capture images with greater definition of the Ae. Aegypti mosquito eggs, which is an advantage in the image segmentation process.
- Figure 6 shows some images processed and segmented with computer vision algorithm described in previous section and stored in the Raspberry Pi board.
- The developed algorithm performs a reliable count of mosquito eggs as long as they are isolated, when the eggs are crowded the counting procedure fails, this is a task that will be solved soon.

From the above tests we conclude the following: the technology selected for the construction of the prototype hardware is functional and meets the required needs, therefore, Raspberry Pi can be suggested as a useful technology for this purpose.

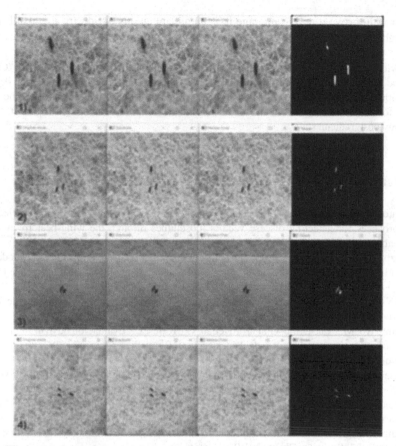

Fig. 6. The image shows the various ways in which eggs are deposited in the ovitraps, all of which have a low egg density, which allows to perform a better segmentation. In results 1), 2) and 4) an exact density matching was obtained, on the contrary, in result 3) there is a small cluster made up of 2 eggs, so the algorithm counts it as a single element found.

4 Conclusions

The work presented shows that the use of an intelligent ovitrap automates, performing in situ the tasks currently carried out by health personnel, this clearly presents advantages over the current conventional process of information collection, impacting positively on technical, economic and even environmental aspects. This device, equipped with emerging technology and processing capacity, is capable of providing real-time information related to the population density of the Ae. Aegypti mosquito, which allows for timely planning of the SHA's health brigades. This prototype is placed inside the houses since, according with information of the health secretary, Aedes aegypti mosquitoes generally live in these places, so these devices will be powered by household electricity.

For the time being, preliminary results of the prototype has been presented, showing results that are considered satisfactory to date. However, work continues on this prototype in order to improve it and to manage it as an advantageous option for the health sector in its fight against diseases caused by the Ae. Aegypti mosquito.

Acknowledgements. I would like to thank the Consejo Nacional de Ciencia y Tecnología (CONA-CyT) and the Postgraduate Program in Computer Systems of the Tecnológico Nacional de México/Campus Acapulco (TecNM/ITA) for providing me with their support and the scholarship granted to be able to carry out the research on this project and continue developing it. I work during my postgraduate stay.

References

1. Santos, D.A., Rodrigues, J.J., Furtado, V., Saleem, K., Korotaev, V.: Automated electronic approaches for detecting disease vectors mosquitoes through the wing-beat frequency. J. Cleaner Prod. **217**, 767–775 (2019). https://doi.org/10.1016/j.jclepro.2019.01.187
2. Guzmán, V.C., Pelta, D.A., Verdegay, J.L.: Fuzzy maximal covering location models for fighting dengue. In: 2016 IEEE Symposium Series on Computational Intelligence (SSCI), pp. 1–7, Dec, IEEE. https://doi.org/10.1109/SSCI.2016.7850139
3. CENAPRECE (Centro Nacional de Programas Preventivos y Control de Enfermedades): Guía metodológica para la vigilancia entomológica con ovitrampas (2015)
4. Quimbayo, M., Rúa-Uribe, G., Parra-Henao, G., Torres, C.: Evaluación de ovitrampas letales como estrategia para el control de Aedes aegypti. Biomedica **34**(3), 473–482 (2014). https://doi.org/10.7705/biomedica.v34i3.2146
5. Balladares Orellana, M.P.: Diseño de ovitrampa para el diagnóstico y control de vectores Aedes aegypti. Caso de estudio Instituto Nacional de Investigación en Salud Pública (2018)
6. Hernández-Hernández, J.L., Hernández-Hernández, M., Feliciano-Morales, S., Álvarez-Hilario, V., Herrera-Miranda, I.: Search for optimum color space for the recognition of oranges in agricultural fields. In: International Conference on Technologies and Innovation, pp. 296–307. Springer, Cham (2017)
7. García-Mateos, G., Hernández-Hernández, J.L., Escarabajal-Henarejos, D., Jaén-Terrones, S., Molina-Martínez, J.M.: Study and comparison of color models for automatic image analysis in irrigation management applications. Agric. Water Manag. **151**, 158–166 (2015)
8. Gaburro, J., Duchemin, J.-B., Paradkar, P., Nahavandi, N., Batti, A.: Assessment of ICount software, a precise and fast egg counting tool for the mosquito vector Aedes aegypti. Parasit. Vectors **9**, 590 (2016). https://doi.org/10.1186/s13071-016-1870-1
9. Santana, C., Firmo, A., Oliveira, R., Buarque, P., Alves, G., Lima, R.: A solution for counting Aedes aegypti and Aedes albopictus eggs in paddles from ovitraps using deep learning. IEEE Latin Amer. Trans. **17**(12), 1987–1994 (2019)
10. Joshi, A., Miller, C.: Review of machine learning techniques for mosquito control in urban environments. Ecol. Inf. **61**, 101241 (2021)
11. Bravo, D.T.: Automatic detection of potential mosquito breeding sites from aerial images acquired by unmanned aerial vehicles. Comp. Environ. Urban Syst. **90**(9), 1–13 (2021)
12. D. Motta, et al.: Optimization of convolutional neural network hyperparameters for automatic classification of adult mosquitoes. PLOS One **15**(7), 1–30 (2020)
13. Agarwal, A., Chaudhuri, U., Chaudhuri, S., Seetharaman, G.: Detection of potential mosquito breeding sites based on community sourced geotagged images. In: Geospatial InfoFusion and Video Analytics IV; and Motion Imagery for ISR and Situational Awareness II, p. 90890M. Baltimore, USA (2014)

14. Mehra, M., Bagri, A., Jiang, X., Ortiz, J.: Image analysis for identifying mosquito breeding grounds. In: IEEE International Conference on Sensing, Communication and Networking, pp. 1–6, London, UK, Jun 2016
15. Haddawy, P., et al.: Large scale detailed mapping of dengue vector breeding sites using street view images. PLOS Neg. Trop. **13**(7), 1–27 (2019)
16. Howse, J., Minichino, J.: Learning OpenCV 4 Computer Vision with Python 3: Get to Grips with Tools, Techniques, and Algorithms for Computer Vision and Machine Learning. Packt Publishing Ltd (2020)
17. Isa, I., Ishak, A.R., Dom, N.C., Mohamed, Z., Anuar, M.A.: An IoT-based ovitrap system applied for aedes mosquito surveillance. Int. J. Eng. Adv. Technol. **9**(1), 5752–5758 (2019). https://doi.org/10.35940/ijeat.A3058.109119
18. World Health Organization: Dengue guias para el diagnóstico, tratamiento, prevención y control: nueva edición (No. WHO/HTM/NTD/DEN/2009.1). Organización Mundial de la Salud, Ginebra (2009)
19. Lenhart, A.E., Walle, M., Cedillo, H., Kroeger, A.: Building a better ovitrap for detecting Aedes aegypti oviposition. Acta Trop. **96**(1), 56–59 (2005). https://doi.org/10.1016/j.actatropica.2005.06.020

Networks, Monitoring
and Collaborative Systems

Performance Analysis of Multipath TCP Congestion Control Variants

Jenny Elizabeth Arizaga-Gamboa[✉] and Eduardo Antonio Alvarado-Unamuno

Universidad de Guayaquil, Cdla. Universitaria Salvador Allende, Guayaquil, Ecuador
{jenny.arizagag,eduardo.alvaradou}@ug.edu.ec

Abstract. The multiple interfaces in today's modern devices hold great promise for improving the delivery of network services over wired or wireless networks. However, the IP-coupled nature of the TCP protocol inhibits the simultaneous use of these interfaces. Multipath TCP (MPTCP) has been developed to use multiple interfaces simultaneously to provide services over the Internet. MPTCP has been implemented on systems based on Linux distributions that can be compiled and installed for use in both live and experimental scenarios. In the present work, its performance was experimentally evaluated on a real environment in the TEMONET platform, the coupled congestion control algorithms available in the Linux kernel such as LIA, OLIA, BALIA, and wVEGAS were compared, in previous work good results were obtained results in its use, but the same was obtained on symmetric paths, it has been shown that low latency communication is difficult to achieve when a device has network interfaces with asymmetric capacity and delay. Despite these results, MPTCP is still a good alternative to optimize performance through load balancing and resilience to coverage drops and link failures.

Keywords: Coupled congestion control · TCP · Multipath TCP

1 Introduction

The Internet follows the conceptual design of a protocol suite where the main components are the network layer Internet Protocol (IP) and the connection-based reliable transport protocol TCP, which popularly form the TCP/IP protocol suite. TCP has continually evolved since the earliest experiments in research networks.

TCP and IP are separate protocols, but the separation between network and transport protocols is not complete, to differentiate individual data streams between incoming packets the receiving end host demultiplexes the packets based on IP addresses, port numbers, and protocol identifiers. This implies that a TCP connection is bound to the IP addresses used on the client and server at the time of connection establishment.

Today we find that a device can have more than one network interface for example a laptop can have an Ethernet interface and a Wi-Fi interface, when the computer changes from Ethernet to Wi-Fi, it gets another IP address, which produces that all existing TCP connections must be killed and new connections restarted one of the problems is that TCP connections cannot pass from one IP address to another.

© The Author(s), under exclusive license to Springer Nature Switzerland AG 2022
R. Valencia-García et al. (Eds.): CITI 2022, CCIS 1658, pp. 139–150, 2022.
https://doi.org/10.1007/978-3-031-19961-5_10

Recent studies show that an incredibly large portion of the data traffic that passes through the Internet depends on the use of TCP [1], in addition, future M2M and IoT network applications require reliable transmission of a large volume of data which requires the use of the TCP protocol. However, the currently available version is designed to run on a single path, consequently the networking community has explored end-to-end protocols to support new functionality such as multipathing, MPTCP has been developed for this purpose, where the connection between a sender and a receiver is established through multiple paths through multiple interfaces, MPTCP is the most widely explored alternative to TCP providing reliability and congestion control features for end-to-end connection [2]. MPTCP is a fully backward compatible extension to TCP, to guarantee the transparency of applications it is necessary to implement MPTCP in the kernel of the operating system [3].

The implementation of MPTCP in the Linux kernel [4] is the most complete, it includes several algorithms that are not part of the protocol specification [5], but that influence its performance and packet transmission. There are three main modular components that affect the performance of the Linux implementation: (i) the route manager, (ii) the congestion control scheme, and (iii) the scheduler.

The route manager defines the strategy that the MPTCP stack uses to create sub flows. Two route managers are included in the Linux implementation: full-mesh and f find ports, they decide when and how sub flows are created, sub flows are only created by clients, the server does not attempt to create sub flows. In full-mesh, the route manager creates a sub flow from each address owned by the client to each address advertised by the server. In find -ports, an MPTCP connection is made up of n sub flows that use different source ports. The full-mesh route manager is the default route manager in the Linux implementation.

In congestion controller, various congestion control algorithms have been proposed for MPTCP. This congestion control schemes couples the congestion windows of the different sub flows, four of them are included in the Linux kernel implementation: LIA, OLIA, BALIA and wVegas. LIA is the default congestion control scheme.

The third is the packet scheduler, it is used every time a data segment needs to be sent, it selects among the active sub flows that have an open congestion window, the sub flow that will be used to send the data. The default scheduler tries to send data through the sub flow that has the lowest round trip time.

In the present work, the content download times of the TEMONET platform will be experimentally evaluated, which offers audiovisual content of medical therapies, the files generated on the platform are approximately 200 MB, which are downloaded by users, the architecture of the platform is made up of a cloud computing service as an online server and a client, in this case the TEMONET Edge server, which is connected to two networks of different service providers, will analyze the use of the protocol MPTCP and varying the congestion control algorithms, the latency in the transfer of files through the Internet will be measured, with the aim of determining which would be the best configuration to reduce latency in the TEMONET platform. The main contribution of this work is to analyze the performance in a real environment of production to MPTCP, in therapy support applications in the health domain.

2 Related Work

In [6] an empirical study of the effectiveness and viability of MPTCP for data center and cloud applications is presented, under different network conditions, the results show that, although MPTCP provides aggregation of useful bandwidth, it avoids congestion, and improves resiliency for some cloud applications, these benefits are not applied uniformly across applications, especially in cloud settings.

In [7] an application of MPTCP in data center networks (DCN) is carried out, since these networks have many flows between two nodes (servers), TCP does not fully use the bandwidth of the network, due to its limitations. Therefore, MPTCP is used to consume maximum network bandwidth smoothly by using numbers of streams simultaneously. MPTCP improves performance and provides greater fairness in many topologies over DCN. In this work, the congestion control algorithms LIA, OLIA, and BALIA are compared in terms of performance and link utilization.

In [8] the article, provides a performance analysis for MPTCP with a laptop connected to a WiFi hotspot and 3G cellular network at the same time. MPTCP was experimentally proven to outperform regular TCP for WiFi or 3G interfaces. Four types of congestion control algorithms for MPTCP that are also implemented in the Linux Kernel were also compared. The results show that LIA increases congestion control, this algorithm outperforms the others in normal traffic load, while the BALIA algorithm outperforms the rest when routes are shared with heavy.

In [9], a study is done with a field of evidence using a bank of proof based in communication MPTCP among operators in a mobil network that proportions sub flows in different performances. Considering that the MPTCP conventional implementation it not adequate for a heterogenous network due to that it doesn't have into account the sub flows in different performances, the MPTCP implementations improve due to the updated algorithms in control about routing management and plan. The results about the performance evidence of the prior links and the time of commuting suggest that a combination of algorithms of control congestion and route programming achieve an excellent performance of low lactency.

In [10], Multipath TCP is applied in an IoT system. In this terms, the communication between machines are the key to allow that this gadgets (such as sensors, updaters, smart meters) recollect data for a remote server using a port that TCP of multiple routers connected to multiple cellular networks download data flow, show the capacity of the MPTCP transport as key facilitators for the IoT download flow from sites.

In [11], Multipath TCP utilizes satellites for such satellite communication with multiple satellites orbiting the low Earth orbit (LEO). This technology offers a mayor band width and lots of reliability since users can connect to multiple satellites simultaneously. The MPTCP performance is studied with many configurations simulating it with Mininet, the results show that it works properly when using all the links available at any moment.

3 TCP and MPTCP Congestion Control

Congestion is an omnipresent problem in all data packet networks in general and in the Internet in particular, it does not provide an end-to-end information service on the state of network congestion, it is the transport layer together with the TCP protocol that implements this end-to-end congestion control mechanism between two processes running on different computers. Congestion is considered one of the main problems faced by data transmission, saturating network resources and degrading their use.

It should be noted that congestion has two effects [12]: first, when congestion begins to occur, the transmission time through the network increases. Second, as congestion becomes more severe, network nodes drop packets.

Therefore, we must control this congestion to improve the quality of network service, the window-based congestion control technique used by TCP regulates the data sending rate by adjusting the window size to avoid network congestion, network while providing a fair share of network bandwidth to all connections. TCP defines an internal parameter called CWND in this document it is referred to as W, based on which congestion control is implemented. Depending on the value that W takes, the source host will be able to estimate the number of packets, for which an acknowledgment has not been received, that they can have in transit at a given time without causing congestion. TCP assumes that there is congestion when a packet is lost.

Similar to TCP, also MPTCP needs congestion control to adapt transmission rates on each path according to changing network and congestion conditions, congestion control strategies for multipath transport can be classified into two groups: coupled and decoupled strategies [13].

Decoupled Congestion Control
Decoupled congestion control is the simplest form of congestion control for MPTCP, each sub flow is handled as an independent TCP connection, with its own instance of TCP congestion control. However, this solution is unsatisfactory, since it gives the multipath flow an unfair share [14] when the paths taken by its different sub flows share a common bottleneck, examples of this type of control we have the A variant of TCP Vegas, this control adjusts the size of its congestion window based on the value of the round trip time (RTT). Another variant is Reno, this is the most widely used congestion control algorithm but its bandwidth usage is not very high and as network link bandwidths improve this disadvantage will become more obvious, another is Cubic which aggressively increases the size of the congestion window when the window is far from the saturation point and then slowly when it is close to the saturation point. This feature allows Cubic, the default TCP algorithm in GNU/Linux, to be very scalable when the network bandwidth-delay product is large, while still being very stable and fair for standard TCP.

Coupled Congestion Control
The basic idea to solve the unfairness problem of decoupled congestion control on shared bottlenecks [14] is to couple the congestion windows of all sub flows of an MPTCP connection with the resource pooling principle, bottleneck detection Sharing bottles reliably is difficult, but it's only part of a larger problem. The bigger question is how much bandwidth should a multipath user use in total, even if there is no shared bottleneck. The main idea is that by using a coupled congestion control method, the transport protocol can change the congestion window of each sub flow and ensure bottleneck fairness and fairness in the broadest sense of the network. There are several approaches available to handle this problem, for example LIA (Linked Augmentation

Algorithm), OLIA (Opportunistic LIA), Balia (Balanced LIA), and wVegas (Weighted Vegas). These MPTCP algorithms avoid congestion in the congestion avoidance phase and satisfy IETF Objectives 1–3 [15], ie improve performance, do no harm, and balance congestion. For this work we will carry out the tests with the coupled congestion control algorithms supported by the Linux Kernel, and then a brief description of the operation of the three algorithms is presented.

LIA

LIA couples the additive increase functions of sub flows LIA [16], for each ACK received in sub flow i, LIA increases its congestion window by the following amount.

$$min\left(\alpha L\frac{MSS_i}{W_{sum}}, L\frac{MSS_i}{W_i}\right) \tag{1}$$

The boost formula (1) takes the minimum between the boost calculated for the multipath subflow (first argument to min), and the boost that TCP would get in the same scenario (the second argument). In this way, we ensure that any multipath subflow cannot be more aggressive than a TCP flow under the same circumstances.

Where alpha" is a parameter of the algorithm that describes the aggressiveness of the multipath flow, to meet the goal of improving performance, the value of alpha is chosen such that the performance of the multipath flow aggregate is equal to the performance of a TCP flow will be executed in the best way.

$$\alpha = W_{sum}\frac{max\left(\frac{W_i}{Rtt_i^2}\right)}{\left(\sum_{i=1}^{N}\frac{W_i}{Rtt_i}\right)^2} \tag{2}$$

In (1), L is the number of recognized bytes, Mss_i is the maximum segment size of i, W_i is the congestion window of subflow i, N is the number of subflows, Wsum is the sum of the congestion window of all subflows and Rtt_i, es el Round-Trip Time (RTT) of subflow i.

LIA utiliza un comportamiento TCP estándar sin modificar en caso de pérdida de un paquete. El algoritmo está diseñado para aumentar el rendimiento y la compatibilidad con otros flujos TCP coexistentes.

OLIA

Like LIA, OLIA couples the function of additively increasing the size of the congestion window of the MPTCP subflows, while using an unmodified standard TCP behavior in the event of a segment loss event. When a subflow i receives an ACK, its congestion window is increased by the following amount [17].

$$\left(\frac{\frac{W_i}{Rtt_i^2}}{\left(\sum_{k=1}^{N}\frac{W_k}{Rtt_k^2}\right)^2} + \frac{\alpha_i}{W_i}\right)L\,MSS_i \tag{3}$$

The first term is an optimal congestion balance defined by $\frac{W_i}{Rtt_i^2} / \left(\sum_{k=1}^{N} \frac{W_k}{Rtt_k^2} \right)^2$, where Rtt is the round trip time observed in subflow i, the second term is added by α_i / W_i, which guarantees the responsiveness to react to changes in the current congestion window, where α_i is calculated based on in the number of bytes transmitted since the last loss.

Balanced Linked Adaptation (BALIA)

BALIA [18, 19] is a multipath congestion control alternative that allows oscillation to an ideal level to provide a good balance between friendliness and responsiveness. For the subflow on the best path or for a single path MPTCP connection ($|R|=1$), we have $\alpha_i = 1$. This causes both the increment and decrement of W_i to be reduced to the same as in the TCP standard.

When a subflow receives an Ack, its congestion window is increased by

$$Wi = Wi + \left[\frac{X_i}{Rtt_i x_k} \left(\frac{1+\alpha_i}{2} \right) \left(\frac{4+\alpha_i}{5} \right) \right] \tag{4}$$

where

$$X_i = \frac{W_i}{Rtt_i} \quad y \quad \alpha_i = \max\{X_k\}/X_i \tag{5}$$

wVEGAS

Weighted Vegas (wVegas) [20],], is a delay-based algorithm for multipath congestion control, which uses delays in the packet queue as congestion signals, thus achieving load balancing. wVegas assigns a weight P_i to each subflow and adjusts it adaptively according to the congestion equality principle, the weight quantifies the aggressiveness of the competition for bandwidth. Therefore, the underflow on less congested routes may carry a higher weight and therefore compete more aggressively, which in turn will lead to an increase in the extent of congestion on the corresponding route and vice versa. This cycle is repeated until all the paths used by each flow in the network are equally congested. At the balance point, network resources will be shared fairly and efficiently by all flows.

For each subflow i, calculate the difference between the expected sending rate and the actual sending rate.

$$dif \ f_i = \left(\frac{W_i}{base_{Rtt_i}} - \frac{W_i}{Rtt_i} \right) * base_{Rtt_i} \tag{6}$$

where Rtt_i is the average Rtt in the last round in subflow i, and $base\_Rtt_i$ is the Rtt of a subflow i when the route is not congested.

If the subflow is in the slow start phase and the difference is greater than a threshold called gamma, the algorithm must enter the congestion avoidance phase.

In the congestion avoidance phase, if the difference is not less than the injustice a_i, then the tariff must be updated.

$$rate = \frac{W_i}{Rtt_i} \tag{7}$$

$$P_i = \frac{rate_i}{Total \ rate \ of \ all_i} \tag{8}$$

$$a_i = P_i * total_a \tag{9}$$

4 Scenario and Test Results

In this work, it is proposed to analyze and implement the Multipath TCP protocol in end devices (Raspberry Pi) and in a cloud server, Fig. 1 shows the proposed topology for the tests for the TEMONET platform, which consists of a cloud computing service as an online server and a client, in this case, TEMONET Edge connected to two provider networks different, one LTE cellular network connection (ISP 1) and the other GPON network connection (ISP 2).

It shows the diagram of the test platform for client-server end-to-end communication. The server is a virtual machine with the RHEL 8 operating system running the MPTCP kernel compiled for its architecture. The Raspberry Pi 4 acts as an edge device (TEMONET Edge) with the Ubuntu operating system running the MPTCP kernel that simultaneously connects to different Internet providers through its ports.

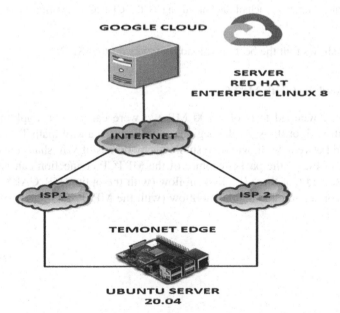

Fig. 1. Proposed topology

4.1 Download Test with TCP

Download tests were carried out using CUBIC as a TCP congestion control algorithm, the downloads were carried out using the FTP utility, the file size was 200 MB, the download was made using each of the connections to the service providers, obtaining the following results.

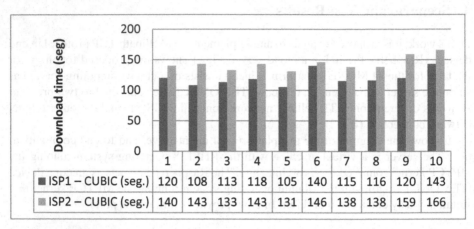

Fig. 2. Download times in each of the links using TCP – CUBIC congestion control algorithm.

Figure 2 shows that the best download time was on the ISP 2.

4.2 Download Test with MPTCP

In this stage, download tests of a 200 MB file were carried out, applying different MPTCP control algorithms. At the beginning of the tests, a Multipath TCP connection is established between both, with two subflows, by means of Wireshark the connection is validated, in Fig. 2 the packet capture of the MPTCP connection can be observed, it can be observed that there is a first subflow (with the option MP_CAPABLE) when starting the connection and another subflow (with the MP_JOIN option) subsequently established (Fig. 3).

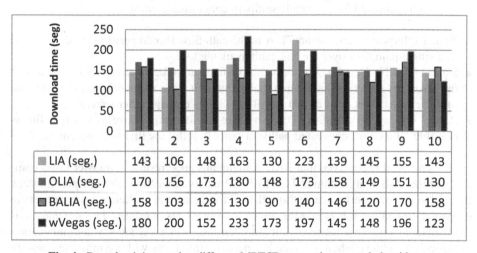

Source	Destination	Protocol	Length	Info
192.168.100.64	34.148.122.13	MPTCP	88 44832 → 80	[SYN] Seq=0 Win=64240 Len=0 MSS=1460 SACK_PERM=1 TSval=2541833421 TSecr=0 WS=128
34.148.122.13	192.168.100.64	MPTCP	88 80 → 44832	[SYN, ACK] Seq=0 Ack=1 Win=65236 Len=0 MSS=1412 SACK_PERM=1 TSval=3632950775 TSecr=2541833421 WS=128
192.168.100.64	34.148.122.13	MPTCP	96 44832 → 80	[ACK] Seq=1 Ack=1 Win=64256 Len=0 TSval=2541833502 TSecr=3632950775
192.168.100.64	34.148.122.13	MPTCP	84 [TCP Dup ACK 3#1] 44832 → 80 [ACK] Seq=1 Ack=1 Win=64256 Len=0 TSval=2541833502 TSecr=3632950775	
192.168.100.64	34.148.122.13	HTTP	525 GET / HTTP/1.1	
34.148.122.13	192.168.100.64	MPTCP	76 80 → 44832	[ACK] Seq=1 Ack=438 Win=64896 Len=0 TSval=3632950856 TSecr=2541833503
34.148.122.13	192.168.100.64	HTTP	287 HTTP/1.1 304 Not Modified	
192.168.42.113	34.148.122.13	MPTCP	88 36197 → 80	[SYN] Seq=0 Win=64248 Len=0 MSS=1460 SACK_PERM=1 TSval=3676377586 TSecr=0 WS=128
192.168.100.64	34.148.122.13	MPTCP	76 44832 → 80	[ACK] Seq=438 Ack=288 Win=64128 Len=0 TSval=2541833504 TSecr=3632950857
34.148.122.13	192.168.42.113	MPTCP	92 80 → 36197	[SYN, ACK] Seq=0 Ack=1 Win=65230 Len=0 MSS=1412 SACK_PERM=1 TSval=3632950957 TSecr=3676377586 WS=128
192.168.42.113	34.148.122.13	MPTCP	92 36197 → 80	[ACK] Seq=1 Ack=1 Win=128256 Len=0 TSval=3676377695 TSecr=3632950957
34.148.122.13	192.168.42.113	MPTCP	76 [TCP Window Update] 80 → 36197 [ACK] Seq=1 Ack=1 Win=128256 Len=0 TSval=3632951849 TSecr=3676377695	
192.168.100.64	34.148.122.13	MPTCP	76 44832 → 80	[ACK] Seq=738 Ack=630 Win=128256 Len=0 TSval=2541834174 TSecr=3632951447
34.148.122.13	192.168.100.64	MPTCP	88 80 → 44832	[FIN, ACK] Seq=630 Ack=738 Win=128256 Len=0 TSval=3632956447 TSecr=2541834174
192.168.100.64	34.148.122.13	MPTCP	76 44832 → 80	[ACK] Seq=738 Ack=631 Win=128256 Len=0 TSval=2541839174 TSecr=3632956447
192.168.100.64	34.148.122.13	MPTCP	88 44832 → 80	[FIN, ACK] Seq=738 Ack=631 Win=128256 Len=0 TSval=2541839174 TSecr=3632956447
34.148.122.13	192.168.100.64	MPTCP	76 80 → 44832	[ACK] Seq=631 Ack=739 Win=128256 Len=0 TSval=3632956527 TSecr=2541839174
34.148.122.13	192.168.100.64	MPTCP	76 [TCP Dup ACK 45#1] 80 → 44832 [ACK] Seq=631 Ack=739 Win=128256 Len=0 TSval=3632956527 TSecr=2541839174	
34.148.122.13	192.168.42.113	MPTCP	76 80 → 36197	[ACK] Seq=1 Ack=1 Win=128256 Len=0 TSval=3632956527 TSecr=3676383265
192.168.42.113	34.148.122.13	MPTCP	76 36197 → 80	[FIN, ACK] Seq=1 Ack=2 Win=128256 Len=0 TSval=3676383265 TSecr=3632956527
34.148.122.13	192.168.42.113	MPTCP	76 80 → 36197	[ACK] Seq=2 Ack=2 Win=128256 Len=0 TSval=3632956617 TSecr=3676383265

Fig. 3. Wireshark capture

We proceeded to perform 10 downloads using each of the algorithms available in the Linux operating system for MPTCP.

Download time (seg)	1	2	3	4	5	6	7	8	9	10
■ LIA (seg.)	143	106	148	163	130	223	139	145	155	143
■ OLIA (seg.)	170	156	173	180	148	173	158	149	151	130
▨ BALIA (seg.)	158	103	128	130	90	140	146	120	170	158
■ wVegas (seg.)	180	200	152	233	173	197	145	148	196	123

Fig. 4. Download times using different MPTCP congestion control algorithms.

Figure 4 shows the download times obtained by applying different MPTCP control algorithms. Analyzing the data, the BALIA algorithm presents the best transfer times.

4.3 Comparisons of TCP y MPTCP Download Times

Figure 5, below is a comparison of the download times obtained between BALIA and CUBIC.

Considering that congestion control in MPTCP is used to adjust the congestion windows within subflows, in order to control the data transmission rate [16], with the

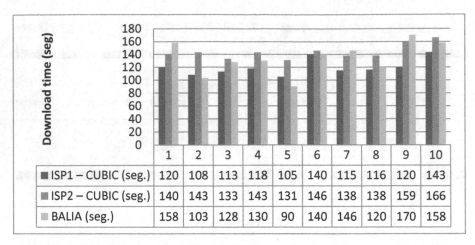

	1	2	3	4	5	6	7	8	9	10
■ ISP1 – CUBIC (seg.)	120	108	113	118	105	140	115	116	120	143
■ ISP2 – CUBIC (seg.)	140	143	133	143	131	146	138	138	159	166
■ BALIA (seg.)	158	103	128	130	90	140	146	120	170	158

Fig. 5. Download times using different MPTCP and TCP congestion control algorithms

aim of achieving a user-friendly Internet implementation TCP, the following three rules [15] must be achieved for practical multipath congestion control:

- Rule 1 ("Improve performance"): A multi-path flow should perform at least as well as a single-path flow over the best path available to it.
- Rule 2 ("Do No Harm"): A multipath flow must not take more capacity from any of the resources shared by its different paths than if it were a single flow using only one of these paths. This ensures that it will not unduly damage other streams.
- Rule 3 ("Congestion Balance"): A multi-route flow must move as much traffic as possible off its most congested paths, in order to fulfill the first two objectives.

Given this, it is observed that BALIA maintains good results in transfer times compared to the CUBIC algorithm of TCP, MPTCP and its congestion control algorithms can be used to optimize performance through load balancing and resilience against coverage drops and link failures, however the use of heterogeneous interfaces does not automatically guarantee better performance, it has been shown that low latency communication is difficult to achieve when a device has network interfaces with asymmetric capacity and delay.

Since multipath protocols like MPTCP split data between multiple paths, data is likely to arrive out of order, this is especially true if the paths are asymmetric, in terms of capacity and/or delay. When data arrives out of order, a number of performance-related issues can occur [21].

5   Conclusions

Today's networks are often multipath, meaning an end host can reach its peer via more than one network path. For example, mobile devices often have multiple interfaces, and data centers have redundant paths between servers. In view of this, several works have investigated how to exploit this increased connectivity to add capacity and improve robustness. While capacity aggregation works well for network paths with symmetric capacity and delays, it has been shown to limit performance and increase delays when using asymmetric link technologies such as LTE and LAN in this case, despite Therefore, BALIA presents a performance similar to a connection with CUBIC in this type of environment, however it should be noted that MPTCP and its congestion control algorithms can be used to optimize performance through load balancing and resilience against failures, coverage and link failures.

It is proposed as future work to work with the MPTCP data scheduler, which is essential to provide low latency in heterogeneous asymmetric environments, since it decides through which network interface to send individual data segments and combine it with congestion control to obtain a decrease in latency.

References

1. Meng, Q., Ren, F., Zhang, T.: Demystifying and Mitigating TCP Capping. In: 2022 IEEE/ACM 30. Simp. Int. sobre Calid. Serv. (2022)
2. Mondal, A., Bhattacharjee, S., Chakraborty, S.: Viscous: an end to end protocol for ubiquitous communication over internet of everything. In: Proc. – Conf. Local Comput. Networks, LCN, vol. 2017 Oct., pp. 312–320, 2017, doi: https://doi.org/10.1109/LCN.2017.79
3. Tran, V.H., De Coninck, Q., Hesmans, B., Sadre, R., Bonaventure, O.: Observing real Multipath TCP traffic. Comput. Commun. **94**, 114–122 (2016). https://doi.org/10.1016/j.comcom.2016.01.014
4. Thakur, N.R., Kunte, A.S.: Analysing schedulers of multipath TCP in diverse environment. In: Proc. – 2021 3rd Int. Conf. Adv. Comput. Commun. Control Networking, ICAC3N 2021, pp. 1337–1340. https://doi.org/10.1109/ICAC3N53548.2021.9725523
5. hjp: doc: RFC 6182: Architectural guidelines for multipath TCP development [Online]. Available: https://www.hjp.at/doc/rfc/rfc6182.html. Accessed 23 May 2022
6. Rahgozar, N., Rahgozar, N., Moghadam, A.S., Aziminejad, A.: Performance evaluation of vol. 445, pp. 1–14 (2016)
7. Chaturvedi, R.K., Chand, S.: MPTCP over datacenter networks. In: Proc. Int. Conf. Inven. Commun. Comput. Technol. ICICCT 2018, Icicct, pp. 894–898, 2018. https://doi.org/10.1109/ICICCT.2018.8473290
8. Hijawi, H.M.A., Hamarsheh, M.M.N.: Performance analysis of multi-path TCP network. Int. J. Comput. Netw. Commun. **8**(2), 145–157 (2016). https://doi.org/10.5121/ijcnc.2016.8213
9. Kawasaki, H., Ibuka, K., Kojima, F., Matsumura, T.: Field trials of link aggregation system based on multipath TCP in heterogeneous mobile network. In: Int. Symp. Wirel. Pers. Multimed. Commun. WPMC, vol. 2021, Dec 2021. https://doi.org/10.1109/WPMC52694.2021.9700462
10. Silva, C.F., Ferlin, S., Alay, O., Brunstrom, A., Kimura, B.Y.L.: IoT traffic offloading with multipath TCP. IEEE Commun. Mag. **59**(4), 51–57 (2021). https://doi.org/10.1109/MCOM.001.2000915
11. Park, C.H., Austria, P., Kim, Y., Jo, J.Y.: MPTCP performance simulation in multiple LEO satellite environment. In: 2022 IEEE 12th Annu. Comput. Commun. Work. Conf., CCWC 2022, pp. 895–899, 2022. https://doi.org/10.1109/CCWC54503.2022.9720772.
12. Kaur, H., Singh, G.: TCP congestion control and its variants. Adv. Comput. Sci. Technol. **10**(6), 1715–1723 (2017)

13. Li, W., Zhang, H., Gao, S., Xue, C., Wang, X., Lu, S.: SmartCC: a reinforcement learning approach for multipath TCP congestion control in heterogeneous networks. IEEE J. Sel. Areas Commun. **37**(11), 2621–2633 (2019). https://doi.org/10.1109/JSAC.2019.2933761
14. Becke, M., Dreibholz, T., Adhari, H., Rathgeb, E.P.: On the fairness of transport protocols in a multi-path environment. In: IEEE Int. Conf. Commun., pp. 2666–2672, 2012. https://doi.org/10.1109/ICC.2012.6363695
15. Nguyen, S.C., Nguyen, T.M.T.: Evaluation of multipath TCP load sharing with coupled congestion control option in heterogeneous networks. Glob. Inf. Infrastruct. Symp. GIIS **6**, 2011 (2011). https://doi.org/10.1109/GIIS.2011.6026698
16. RFC 6356 – Coupled congestion control for multipath transport protocols [Online]. Available: https://datatracker.ietf.org/doc/rfc6356/. Accessed 29 May 2022
17. Prakash, M., Abdrabou, A., Zhuang, W.: An Experimental study on multipath TCP congestion control with heterogeneous radio access technologies. IEEE Access **7**, 25563–25574 (2019). https://doi.org/10.1109/ACCESS.2019.2900290
18. draft-walid-mptcp-congestion-control-04: Balanced linked adaptation congestion control algorithm for MPTCP [Online]. Available: https://datatracker.ietf.org/doc/draft-walid-mptcp-congestion-control/. Accessed 30 May 2022
19. Peng, Q., Walid, A., Hwang, J., Low, S.H.: Multipath TCP: analysis, design, and implementation. IEEE/ACM Trans. Netw. **24**(1), 596–609 (2016). https://doi.org/10.1109/TNET.2014.2379698
20. Cao, Y., Xu, M., Fu, X.: Delay-based congestion control for multipath TCP. In: Proc. – Int. Conf. Netw. Protoc. ICNP, no. Jan 2015, 2012. https://doi.org/10.1109/ICNP.2012.6459978
21. Hurtig, P., Grinnemo, K.J., Brunstrom, A., Ferlin, S., Alay, Ö., Kuhn, N.: Low-latency scheduling in MPTCP. IEEE/ACM Trans. Netw. **27**(1), 302–315 (2019). https://doi.org/10.1109/TNET.2018.2884791

Data Stream Processing Method for Clustering of Trajectories

Gary Reyes[1]([envelope]) [iD], Laura Lanzarini[2] [iD], César Estrebou[2] [iD],
and Aurelio Bariviera[3] [iD]

[1] Facultad de Ciencias Matemáticas y Físicas, Universidad de Guayaquil,
Cdla. Universitaria Salvador Allende, Guayaquil 090514, Ecuador
gary.reyesz@ug.edu.ec
[2] Facultad de Informática, Instituto de Investigación en Informática LIDI (Centro CICPBA) 1900 La Plata, Universidad Nacional de La Plata, Buenos Aires, Argentina
{laural,cesarest}@lidi.info.unlp.edu.ar
[3] Department of Business, Universitat Rovira i Virgili, Reus, Spain
aurelio.fernandez@urv.cat

Abstract. The constant advances in techniques for recording and collecting GPS trajectory information, the increase in the number of devices that collect this type of information such as video cameras, traffic sensors, smart phones, etc., has resulted in a large volume of information. Being able to process this information through data streams that allow intelligent analysis of the data in real time is an area where many researchers are currently making efforts to identify solutions. GPS trajectory clustering techniques allow the identification of vehicle patterns over large volumes of data. This paper presents a method that processes data streams for dynamic clustering of vehicular GPS trajectories. The proposed method here receives a GPS data stream, processes it using a buffer memory and the creation of a grid with the use of indexes, and subsequently analyzes each cell of the grid with the use of a dynamic clustering technique that extracts the characteristics of reduced zones of the study area, visualizing common speed ranges in interactive maps. To validate the proposed method, two data sets from Rome-Italy and Guayaquil-Ecuador were used, and measurements were made of execution time, used memory and silhouette coefficient. The obtained results are satisfactory.

Keywords: Buffer memory · Clusters · Trajectories · Cells · Data stream

1 Introduction

Nowadays, the constant increase in traffic volume in large cities causes problems in vehicular flow, so the analysis of generated data by vehicle monitoring and control systems, as well as the processing of GPS trajectories, becomes relevant [29]. Its study by means of descriptive techniques allows the identification of relationships between vehicle trajectories, facilitating the analysis of vehicle flow. Currently, descriptive techniques provide solutions in a wide range of areas, such as health, finance, telecommunications, agriculture and transportation, among others [17].

Data clustering is a descriptive technique widely used in data mining to identify common characteristics between instances of the same problem [22]. Over time, researchers have proposed improvements to the identified limitations in some techniques, Bahmani et al. [6] achieved a correct initialization of the algorithm in a much shorter time, Dafir et al. [9] use parallel computing to improve the efficiency of algorithms or Han et al. [15] who use neural networks to improve the performance of the models. In other cases, techniques have been adapted to work in a specific context such as for spatial data mining [14,30,31], for GPS trajectory analysis [24] and even for real-time motion trend search [23] taking into account the dynamic nature of the data [12].

This work proposes a method that processes data streams for dynamic groupings of GPS trajectories, achieving a low memory consumption and a shorter processing time, which allows an agile analysis of the vehicular flow at a given time. A GPS trajectory is defined by a set of geographic locations, each of which is represented by its latitude and longitude, at an instant of time. As the GPS trajectory data collection progresses, the information in each cell of the grid is updated to reflect its average speed over a given period of time. These cells are delimited at the beginning of the process and their size depends on the desired accuracy of the analysis within the study area. The processing of this new representation in cells is analyzed using as a basis a dynamic clustering methodology of batch processing [26], which was adapted in this work to process data online and to which was incorporated the management of a buffer memory and the use of indexes in the creation of cells, allowing to reduce the memory consumption and the needed time to perform the calculations. As a result, areas with similar characteristics can be identified and an interactive map is generated in real time on which the speed ranges corresponding to the current vehicular flow and the areas where they occur can be observed. The comparison between the batch method and the proposed method will allow identifying the obtained differences for the memory consumption, the used execution time and the Silhouette coefficient assessment of the clusters.

This proposed method can be used, together with other tools, by traffic managers in a city to plan urban roads, detect critical points in traffic flow, identify anomalous situations, predict future mobility behavior, analyze vehicular flow, among others. The method can be used to characterize data corresponding to GPS trajectories generated by a group of students from the University of Guayaquil in Ecuador and historical cab data from the city of Rome in Italy. The obtained results allow the identification, in each city, of different time instants where vehicles have common speeds, and through the measurements of execution time, used memory and Silhoutte coefficient, a greater efficiency than the batch method is evidenced.

This article is organized as follows: Sect. 1 discusses some related works that were identified in the literature and present various solutions to the problem, Sect. 2 describes the proposed processing method used, Sect. 3 presents the obtained results and finally Sect. 4 contains the conclusions and lines of future work.

1.1 Related Work

Clustering techniques have been used in trajectory analysis for several years. They are usually adaptations of conventional algorithms using similarity metrics specially designed for trajectories [8,18,32]. Such is the case of the Enhanced DBScan algorithm [21] which improves the traditional DBScan algorithm by using a proprietary density measurement method suggesting the new concept of motion capability and the introduction of data field theory. On the other hand, Ferreira et al. [11] have presented a new trajectory clustering technique that uses vector fields to represent the cluster centers and propose a definition of similarity between trajectories. Research efforts in this area continue today, as evidenced by several research papers [16,20].

Certain treatments can be considered in trajectory clustering, such as segmentation, dynamic clustering, or online processing of data streams. An important feature that must be taken into account when performing dynamic clustering is the way in which the centers of the groups are represented [27,28]. Most of the generated data in a data stream requires real-time data analysis and the used data must manifest in the output within seconds [10,19]. The main goal of data stream clustering is to recognize patterns in data, which arrive at varying speeds and structures and evolve over time [4].

In summary, it can be stated that clustering techniques have proven to perform well in the analysis of vehicular trajectories although their parameterization remains an interesting challenge. This is related to the fact that they are unsupervised techniques that usually combine distance and density metrics to control the construction of the clusters.

In this paper we have used a dynamic clustering algorithm for data streams. This type of algorithms process data streams managing to overcome some of the limitations of traditional clustering algorithms, which usually iterate over the data set more than once, causing higher memory usage and increasing the execution time [5,13]. This is of great importance for systems that depend on accurate results especially in real-time environments [25]. As the data distribution of each stream changes continuously, it is important that these clustering algorithms that process data streams generate dynamic groups, where the number of groups will depend on the distribution of the stream data [1,2].

In particular, this work uses a variation of the DyClee algorithm defined originally by Barbosa et al. [7], a dynamic clustering algorithm for tracking evolving environments capable of adapting the clustering structure as data are processed. Dyclee uses a two-stage clustering approach based on distance and density [3]. The used methodology in this work was previously defined by Reyes et al. [26]. As an interpretation tool for the user, the use of interactive automatic maps is incorporated to facilitate the visualization of the clustering result. In the published article by Reyes et al. [26], the proposed methodology was used to analyze defined trajectories over the city of Guayaquil-Ecuador in order to automatically obtain the frequent speed ranges for different time intervals.

In this work, the batch processing [26] was adapted to work on a micro-batch basis and a method was employed to improve the performance of the process of creating cells in a grid, making use of a buffer and indexes to optimize the time and amount of memory needed.

A method is proposed that, unlike traditional methods that process trajectories [16], consolidates the information of a given area and transforms it into cells with summarized information. This information is processed by a modified clustering algorithm defined by Reyes et al. [26] to use a different dimension, obtaining clusters that reflect a different perspective of patterns. To facilitate the exploration and visualization of the results, the use of an interactive tool is proposed.

2   Proposed Method

This work proposes an adapted method for online processing or micro-batches for dynamic clustering of trajectories in large volumes of information based on batch processing, using a data buffer that reduces required memory consumption to process large amounts of GPS trajectory information. In addition, the proposed method makes use of indexes to improves the processing that transforms the GPS data into cells will be used by the clustering algorithm. The data corresponding to GPS points are presented as consecutive micro-batches of ordered data with respect to the time stamp of each record.

2.1   General Processing

Unlike batch processing, whose required data for processing are previously obtained from some repository, in online or micro-batch processing the data are received as the required time for clustering execution elapses.

The construction of the method contemplates the use of sequential processes, which are created and executed when required during processing.

The first processing step is the reception of GPS data, which are collected from the repository progressively over a certain period of time, which in this work was set at three minutes, and stored in a buffer memory. The second step is responsible for the transformation of these GPS data to summarized information in cells using indexes to improve processing performance; then in a third step the cells are clustered according to the speed ranges, generated during the clustering process. The last step is the generation of interactive maps for the visualization of clustering results. A general scheme of the micro-batch processing can be seen in Fig. 1, the processes used for the treatment of each cycle, which involves the processing of all the steps of the method for a data flow, are repeated iteratively; to process each set of data, the necessary cycles will be performed until the required period of time is covered and a real time processing will be used.

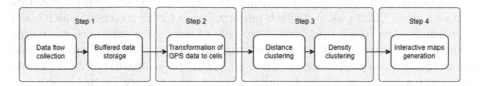

Fig. 1. General processing scheme of the micro-batch method

Step 1: Use of a Buffer. A part of the processing is in charge of storing in a temporary memory constantly GPS data collected from some repository and according to the period of time being analyzed, in order to contemplate different execution periods, use is made of a temporary storage memory that selects and stores small batches from the entire main data set; this processing called micro-batch allows the buffer of the micro-batch method does not require loading in memory the entire data, which reduces the consumption of this and allows to reduce considerably the calculations necessary for the generation of grid cells.

Each GPS data contains its respective time stamp that is not modified, which ensures that each data is allocated to a single buffer. The size of this temporary buffer can contain from one to a number n of GPS data, and this capacity will be smaller if the collection intervals of the data streams for the buffer decrease. The GPS data collected by a buffer is organized temporally in a sorted list according to the time stamp, this allows to maintain a consistency in the collection and will avoid errors in future processes.

Step 2: Use of Indexes to Create Cells with Summary Information. A cell is the representation of a data set with summarized information over a delimited area or grid.

Use of Indexes. The cell creation process makes use of indexes that are generated from single cells containing GPS information records. This process starts with the generation of indexes corresponding to the location of the cells; this generation evaluates each GPS point on the areas of the cells or grid, using the corresponding axes on the plane, so that an index for longitude and one for latitude are obtained independently of each other. Then we proceed to the extraction of these indexes and a subsequent filtering from which only a list of unique indexes containing GPS data will be obtained; one of the advantages of performing this step is to discard from the processing those cells that do not contain any GPS point assigned to them.

Shape Conformation of the Cells. The next step is to use the unique index list, which determines the cells to be processed for the transformation of the data into cells containing summary information. The cell formation consists of the classification and transformation of each GPS data into cells. During the transformation, the information in common of the GPS points is extracted and a summary of this data is obtained, which will form the contained information in each of the cells.

Unlike the cell creation process using the batch method whose representation can be seen in Fig. 2 (A), and which performs a cell to cell traversal, which is not very efficient because it evaluates all the cells of the area or grid, even evaluating cells in which there is no GPS point on that area; using the micro-batch method whose representation can be seen in Fig. 2 (B), the evaluation of cells that do not contain data is avoided, obtaining a better performance for this process.

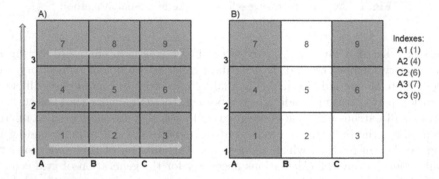

Fig. 2. Differences between the used methods in the formation of cells

Step 3: Use of a Clustering Technique. The cells are then clustered according to their velocity characteristic.

Clustering by Distance. The operation of this clustering process consists of identifying nearby clusters based on the velocity of the cells; the assignment of a cell to some group is determined by the smallest difference in velocities between the cell and the nearby clusters.

Density Clustering. In this clustering, classification of existing clusters is performed to categorize them into dense or sparse groups based on the number of GPS points contained in the cells within the clusters.

Step 4: Visualization of Results. After obtaining the clusterings of the cells, an interactive map is generated in which each resulting clustering can be visualized for each processed cycle and represented by a color scale according to the velocity of each cluster. Figure 3 shows the representation of the clusterings on an interactive map.

3   Results

3.1   Used Data

A collected dataset on the city of Guayaquil-Ecuador and a extracted dataset from a public repository belonging to the city of Rome-Italy were used to validate

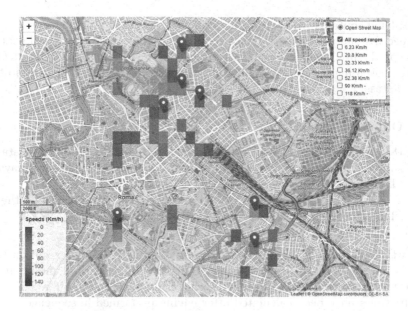

Fig. 3. Visualization of clustering results for the city of Rome in a time period of 3 min.

the micro-batch method. In the data selection process, for each of the data sets, first the day with the highest number of stored records was established and then the period of time with the highest number of vehicles circulating in the selected areas for analysis was identified (Guayaquil resulted in 30557 GPS points and Rome resulted in 33793 GPS points). A description of each dataset is presented below:

Guayaquil Dataset. It is a dataset collected by university students[1] tracing routes by means of some means of transportation such as cabs or motorcycles, the data corresponds to 218 trajectories, collected on October 28, 2017. The collection method used data collection from smartphone devices at 5-s intervals between consecutive locations. The structure of the collected records include id_trajectory, latitude, longitude, time, username, email, and transport type. The used data for this dataset comprises a time period between 16:30 and 18:30 due to the highest concentration of records. As a result of this filtering process, 30557 records were obtained, representing 206 trajectories of the entire dataset.

Rome Dataset. The data in this dataset collected over the city of Rome[2] was collected from GPS devices located in cabs corresponding to the day February

---

[1] Guayaquil dataset is available at https://github.com/gary-reyes-zambrano/Guayaquil-DataSet.

[2] Roma dataset available at https://github.com/gary-reyes-zambrano/Roma-Dataset.

12, 2014 and contains 137 trajectories with time intervals between records of 10 s. The record structure of this dataset contains id_trajectory, latitude, longitude, time, speed, direction. The analysis performed covers the time from 18:00 to 20:00 h, obtaining a total of 33793 records representing 137 trajectories of the entire dataset.

3.2   Obtained Results

Eight (8) consecutive runs were performed on the Rome and Guayaquil datasets. Each run contemplates data of 15 min duration, so for Rome and Guayaquil two(2) hours of data streams were considered for processing.

The results are presented below for the achieved measurements by the run time, silhoutte coefficient and used memory indicators.

Execution Times. During the execution of the method, the execution times required for each part of the processing of both the batch method and the micro-batch method were measured, until the clustering results were obtained.

The times have been calculated after having performed in sequence eight(8) runs containing data in periods of duration of 3 min. The results in minutes, can be observed for Rome in Table 1 and for Guayaquil in Table 2, and it is evident that the micro-batch method obtains better total times than the batch method.

The results of the average duration of the execution times of each cycle, measured in seconds for the eight (8) executions can be observed in Table 3 and show that the micro-batch method has shorter times.

Table 1. Rome execution times

	Batch method every 3 min (min)	Micro-batch method every 3 min (min)
Preprocessing	32:59	00:00
Execution 1	02:42	03:10
Execution 2	00:58	03:41
Execution 3	01:08	02:50
Execution 4	00:57	03:31
Execution 5	01:25	03:46
Execution 6	01:20	03:48
Execution 7	01:16	02:49
Execution 8	01:20	03:17
Total Time	**44:06**	**26:52**

Unlike the batch method, in which the cell conformation is a simple process that is performed separately and evaluates all the cells, the micro-batch method

Table 2. Guayaquil Execution Times

	Batch method every 3 min (min)	Micro-batch method every 3 min (min)
Preprocessing	24:59	00:00
Execution 1	00:08	01:02
Execution 2	00:10	02:07
Execution 3	00:54	01:59
Execution 4	01:09	03:13
Execution 5	00:44	01:39
Execution 6	00:19	02:13
Execution 7	00:22	01:17
Execution 8	00:09	01:19
Total Time	**28:54**	**14:48**

Table 3. Average Time per Cycle (in seconds)

	Batch method every 3 min (secs)	Micro-batch method every 3 min (secs)
Rome	59,94	13,43
Guayaquil	45,76	23,38

applies improvements to this process and performs it when the buffer is received, first identifying in each buffer only the cells that contain a GPS point through the use of indices and then performs the conformation of these cells, thus avoiding the analysis of cells that do not contain any GPS data. This is shown in Table 1 and Table 2 when observing the times in each execution, in the micro-batch method the times are higher because they are considering the conformation of cells that in the batch method was performed in a preprocessing stage, the improvement is evidenced when totaling all the times where independently of the organization of the processes the micro-batch method has required less time.

Silhouette Coefficient. To determine the quality of the formed clusters, the use of the Silhouette coefficient was considered, which establishes a scale with values from -1 indicating that the elements might not have been assigned correctly, to 1 representing better clusters. The Silhouette score is based only on the elements of dense clusterings, excluding sparse clusterings.

The obtained results of the silhouette score for the two data sets are presented in Table 4, for the results of Rome the micro-batch method has obtained a lower score, but its deviation has been reduced considerably; for the results of Guayaquil, the results of the Silhouette coefficient have been higher and its deviation has also decreased.

According to the obtained results in the Rome runs it can be observed that the results of the batch method have a high mean dispersion compared to the micro-batch method which has a lower mean dispersion, in this sense it can be stated that the results of the micro-batch method present a better allocation of the points to the groupings.

In the case of Guayaquil, the scores of the batch method have a mean dispersion similar to that of the micro-batch method; however, the silhouette scores of the micro-batch method are higher.

Table 4. Silhouette Results Summary

	Rome		Guayaquil	
	Mean Score	Desv.	Mean Score	Desv.
Batch method every 3 min	0,567	0,029	0,545	0,114
Micro-batch method every 3 min	0,565	0,018	0,556	0,111

Used Memory by GPS Data. This memory corresponds to the weight of the GPS data when received and corresponds to the information of the records of each collected point by GPS devices.

With respect to the measurement performed, whose results measured in bytes can be observed in Table 5, it is observed a larger memory space used by the batch method, this is because all GPS data are kept loaded in memory during each execution, whereas in the micro-batch method GPS data are received in different data streams during the execution of the method. In this sense, in the micro-batch method the memory space allocated is released as the different cycles are processed over time and varies depending on the volume of collected data for a cycle and the processing frequency. In addition to the above, the micro-batch method shows that the resulting weights in Guayaquil are lower than those in Rome due to the inclusion of additional filters that allow data cleaning to eliminate atypical data such as recorded data with zero velocities, resulting in a lower consumption of memory space.

Table 5. Average of Used Memory Space by GPS data (in bytes)

	Batch method every 3 min (bytes)	Micro-batch method every 3 min (bytes)
Rome	1218192	227581
Guayaquil	1309824	211865

Used Memory by Cells. This memory corresponds to the weight measured after having transformed the GPS point data into divisions of cells with fixed dimensions whose information contemplates a summary of the GPS points that are located on the areas of each cell, this causes that the memory space measured by the cells are lower if compared with the used memory by the GPS points.

The results of the measurements on the different datasets can be seen in Fig. 4, the average of used memory during the eight (8) executions and obtained after the transformation of the data into cells in the micro-batch method are lower compared to the Batch method.

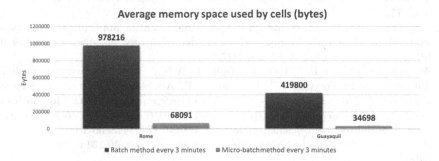

Fig. 4. Average of used memory space by cells

4 Conclusions

In this paper, a method that processes data streams for dynamic clustering of vehicular GPS trajectories has been proposed.

The proposed method receives a data stream, then by means of a buffer memory and the creation of cells with indexes it processes the stream that will be analyzed by a dynamic clustering technique; in order to do this, the trajectory information has been represented in cells and the clustering of cells by the speed dimension has been performed. Finally, the results of the clustering cells are visualized in interactive maps that allow observing the different groups, identifying common speeds at different time instants, which allows making decisions regarding the traffic of a city.

The execution time, the Silhouette coefficient, and the used memory were measured; the results are favorable for the proposed method. As lines of future work, it is proposed to analyze the implementation of the method using a platform for real-time processing and for distributed data processing through a parallel processing architecture.

Compared to traditional methods, the proposed method has advantages such as low memory consumption, low processing times, high quality clustering, the results are displayed by cells which allows reflecting the traffic status in certain areas.

On the other hand, among the disadvantages of the proposed method, it has been identified that the performance of the algorithm is relative to the amount of data being processed, the incorrect calibration of initial parameters can affect the quality of the results, and the method requires historical information, that is, for a certain number of minutes before showing optimal groupings.

References

1. Ackermann, M.R., Lammersen, C., Sohler, C., Swierkot, K., Raupach, C.: StreamKM++: a clustering algorithm for data streams. ACM J. Exp. Algorithmics **17**, 173–187 (2012)
2. Aggarwal, C.C.: Data streams: an overview and scientific applications. In: Gaber, M. (ed.) Scientific Data Mining and Knowledge Discovery. Springer, Berlin (2010). https://doi.org/10.1007/978-3-642-02788-8
3. Aggarwal, C.C., Yu, P.S., Han, J., Wang, J.: A framework for clustering evolving data streams. In: Freytag, J.C., Lockemann, P., Abiteboul, S., Carey, M., Selinger, P., Heuer, A. (eds.) Proceedings 2003 VLDB Conference, pp. 81–92. Morgan Kaufmann, San Francisco (2003). https://doi.org/10.1016/B978-012722442-8/50016-1, www.sciencedirect.com/science/article/pii/B9780127224428500161
4. Ahmed, R.: Stream clustering (2020). https://doi.org/10.13140/RG.2.2.18295.04007
5. Babcock, B., Widom, J.: Models and Issues in Data Stream Systems (2002)
6. Bahmani, B., Moseley, B., Vattani, A., Kumar, R., Vassilvitskii, S.: Scalable k-means++ (2012)
7. Barbosa Roa, N., Travé-Massuyès, L., Grisales-Palacio, V.H.: DyClee: dynamic clustering for tracking evolving environments. Pattern Recognit. **94**, 162–186 (2019). https://doi.org/10.1016/j.patcog.2019.05.024https://www.sciencedirect.com/science/article/pii/S0031320319301992
8. Choong, M.Y., Chin, R.K.Y., Yeo, K.B., Teo, K.T.K.: Trajectory pattern mining via clustering based on similarity function for transportation surveillance. Int. J. Simul.-Syst. Sci. Technol. **17**(34), 1–19 (2016)
9. Dafir, Z., Lamari, Y., Slaoui, S.C.: A survey on parallel clustering algorithms for big data. Artif. Intell. Rev. **54**(4), 2411–2443 (2021). https://doi.org/10.1007/s10462-020-09918-2
10. Ding, S., Wu, F., Qian, J., Jia, H., Jin, F.: Research on data stream clustering algorithms. Artif. Intell. Rev. **43**(4), 593–600 (2015). https://doi.org/10.1007/s10462-013-9398-7
11. Ferreira, N., Klosowski, J.T., Scheidegger, C., Silva, C.: Vector field k-means: Clustering trajectories by fitting multiple vector fields (2012)
12. Fotakis, D., Piliouras, G., Skoulakis, S.: Efficient online learning for dynamic k-clustering (2021). arXiv:2106.04336, https://doi.org/10.48550/ARXIV.2106.04336
13. Garofalakis, M., Gehrke, J., Rastogi, R.: Data Stream Management (2016)
14. Han, J., Kamber, M., Tung, A.K.: Spatial clustering methods in data mining. Geographic data mining and knowledge discovery, pp. 188–217 (2001)
15. Han, P., Wang, W., Shi, Q., Yue, J.: A combined online-learning model with k-means clustering and GRU neural networks for trajectory prediction. Ad Hoc Networks 117, 102476 (2021). https://linkinghub.elsevier.com/retrieve/pii/S1570870521000433, https://doi.org/10.1016/j.adhoc.2021.102476

16. Hu, H., Lee, G., Kim, J.H., Shin, H.: Estimating micro-level on-road vehicle emissions using the k-means clustering method with GPS big data. Electronics **9**(12), 2151 (2020)
17. Jain, A.: Data clustering: 50 years beyond k-means. 2009. Pattern Recognition Letters (2009)
18. Kim, J., Mahmassani, H.S.: Spatial and temporal characterization of travel patterns in a traffic network using vehicle trajectories. Transp. Res. Procedia **9**, 164–184 (2015)
19. Kolajo, T., Daramola, O., Adebiyi, A.: Big data stream analysis: a systematic literature review. J. Big Data **6**(1), 47 (2019). https://doi.org/10.1186/s40537-019-0210-7
20. Lou, J., Cheng, A.: Behavior from Vehicle GPS/GNSS Data. Sensors (2020)
21. Luo, T., Zheng, X., Xu, G., Fu, K., Ren, W.: An improved DBSCAN algorithm to detect stops in individual trajectories. ISPRS Int. J. Geo-Inf. **6**(3), 63 (2017). www.mdpi.com/2220-9964/6/3/63, https://doi.org/10.3390/ijgi6030063
22. Madhulatha, T.S.: An overview on clustering methods. arXiv preprint arXiv:1205.1117 (2012)
23. Mao, J., Song, Q., Jin, C., Zhang, Z., Zhou, A.: Online clustering of streaming trajectories. Front. Comput. Sci. **12**(2), 245–263 (2018). https://doi.org/10.1007/s11704-017-6325-0
24. Mazimpaka, J.D., Timpf, S.: Trajectory data mining: a review of methods and applications. J. Spat. Inf. Sci. **2016**(13), 61–99 (2016)
25. Paulino, D.C., Guimarães, L.N.F., Shiguemori, E.H.: Hybrid adaptive computational intelligence-based multisensor data fusion applied to real-time UAV autonomous navigation. Inteligencia Artif. **22**(63), 162–195 (2019). https://journal.iberamia.org/index.php/intartif/article/view/237, https://doi.org/10.4114/intartif.vol22iss63pp162-195
26. Reyes, G., Lanzarini, L., Estrebou, C., Maquilón, V.: Vehicular flow analysis using clusters, pp. 261–270 (2021)
27. Reyes, G., Lanzarini, L., Hasperué, W., Bariviera, A.F.: GPS trajectory clustering method for decision making on intelligent transportation systems. J. Intell. Fuzzy Syst. **38**(5), 5529–5535 (2020). www.medra.org/servlet/aliasResolver?alias=iospress&doi=10.3233/JIFS-179644, https://doi.org/10.3233/JIFS-179644
28. Reyes, G., Lanzarini, L., Hasperué, W., Bariviera, A.F.: Proposal for a pivot-based vehicle trajectory clustering method. Transp. Res. Rec. **2676**(4), 281–295 (2022). https://doi.org/10.1177/03611981211058429
29. Reyes, G., Maquilón, V., Estrada, V.: Relationships of compression ratio and error in trajectory simplification algorithms. In: Valencia-García, R., Bucaram-Leverone, M., Del Cioppo-Morstadt, J., Vera-Lucio, N., Jácome-Murillo, E. (eds.) Technologies and Innovation, pp. 140–155. Springer International Publishing, Cham (2021)
30. Tork, H.F.: Spatio-temporal clustering methods classification. In: Doctoral Symposium on Informatics Engineering, vol. 1, pp. 199–209. Faculdade de Engenharia da Universidade do Porto Porto, Portugal (2012)
31. Varghese, B.M., Unnikrishnan, A., Jacob, K.: Spatial clustering algorithms-an overview. Asian J. Comput. Sci. Inf. Technol. **3**(1), 1–8 (2013)
32. Wang, H., Sha, Y., Wang, D., Nazari, H.: A gene expression clustering method to extraction of cell-to-cell biological communication. Inteligencia Artif. **25**(69), 1–12 (2022). https://journal.iberamia.org/index.php/intartif/article/view/701, https://doi.org/10.4114/intartif.vol25iss69pp1-12

Low-Cost Energy Consumption Monitoring System Using NodeMCU

Manuel Ayala-Chauvín[1] (iD), Joel Andrés Acurio-Pérez[2] (iD), Genís Riba Sanmartí[3] (iD), and Jorge Buele[2,4](✉) (iD)

[1] Centro de Investigaciones de Ciencias Humanas y de la Educación CICHE, Universidad Indoa-mérica, Ambato 180103, Ecuador
mayala@uti.edu.ec
[2] Carrera de Ingeniería Industrial, Facultad de Ingeniería y Tecnologías de la Información y la Comunicación, Universidad Indoamérica, Ambato 180103, Ecuador
joelacurio@indoamerica.edu.ec, jorgebuele@uti.edu.ec
[3] Centro de Diseño de Equipos Industriales, Universidad Politécnica de Cataluña, Barcelona, Spain
genis.riba@upc.edu
[4] Department of Electronic Engineering and Communications, University of Zaragoza, 44003 Teruel, Spain

Abstract. Energy consumption in urban areas has experienced unprecedented growth. This shows the need to know the consumption in real-time to make efficient use. Therefore, this paper describes the development of a low-cost prototype for the acquisition of energy consumption data. A simple design has been proposed, using electronic components readily available in the local market. Measurements are made with an SCT013 electrical sensor placed around a conductor in the distribution box. The NodeMCU development board is a processing unit connecting several devices through data buses and WiFi. The script programming was done in c++ language using the Arduino IDE, while the mobile application for visualization was developed in Blynk. As a case study, real-time measurements and tests were carried out in a higher education center. A standard ammeter and multimeter were used for system calibration to ensure reliable and accurate results. During the experimental tests, an error of 2,839% was obtained compared to commercial equipment, which validates the use of this proposal. Linear regression is performed to propose an approximation model based on monthly consumption data for one year. With this average measurement, abnormal variations in monthly consumption can be identified, which could mean an electrical failure in the building. This type of proposal allows for better decision-making, proposes structural improvements, and is a basis for developing smarter cities.

Keywords: Power consumption · NodeMCU · Smart meter · Blynk

1 Introduction

Nowadays, the increase in the world population is generating a growth in buildings, for which the energy demand for their implementation and supply tends to grow [1,

R. Valencia-García et al. (Eds.): CITI 2022, CCIS 1658, pp. 164–177, 2022.
https://doi.org/10.1007/978-3-031-19961-5_12

2]. According to data from the European Union (EU), an increase of 130000 million square meters was determined in approximately 40 years, representing a considerable increase in CO^2 emissions [3, 4]. The imminent increase in land value makes traditional housing significantly more expensive, promoting the use of lower-cost prefabricated housing. As a sample, there are several articles in the media about the use of these living structures in Barcelona and Tokyo [5]. In 2018, approximately 9000 residences were implemented, corroborating their acceptance [6]. This measure contributes to the change of conventional energy consumption for a more sustainable one. This could be seen as a solution to the global economic crisis resulting from the COVID-19 pandemic [7, 8].

According to the World Bank report, Latin America and the Caribbean (LAC) is where the monetary situation worsened the most [9]. This region experienced an economic contraction of over 6%, producing political, social, and health changes. Initiatives such as RELAC (REnewables in Latin America and the Caribbean) arise to consolidate the energy transition's political will and channel international assistance [10]. Ecuador has a diverse energy matrix, but hydroelectric is the most developed and sustainable. There are important projects such as the "Coca Codo Sinclair" and "Sopladora" hydroelectric plants that generate clean energy from the flow of rivers. These are part of the "El Inga-Chorrillos" transmission system and supply the "Chorrillos" substation, contributing to economical and productive growth in the coastal region [9].

Therefore, it is essential to analyze the behavior of commercial and residential electricity consumption. The world average indicates that annually there is 2% in energy consumption and 5% in household expenses, with an elasticity of 0.4. While within the Ecuadorian state, energy consumption corresponds to 0.2% and 3% in family expenses, giving an elasticity of 0.08 [11]. All this is produced by a lack of energy-saving culture, which uses artificial lighting (bulbs and lamps). Electronic elements that remain active for extended periods should also be considered, which produces an unnecessary surplus of energy consumption. This shows the requirement to understand the energy consumption of each home and thus provide more benefits to the distribution networks of developing countries. To achieve more efficiency, it is necessary to incorporate more technology gradually [12].

1.1 Related Work

This problem has led to the development of several studies that seek to measure and regulate energy consumption [13]. In most European countries, the use of intelligent devices to monitor electricity consumption has already been accepted, as seen in [14]. Something similar has been evidenced in Asia [15], where demographic expansion and the world crisis demand better use of resources and care for the environment. Population surveys show their approval and the need for this type of proposal to be implemented on a massive scale. In studies such as [16], intelligent control algorithms are proposed to identify faults in the electrical grid to improve the service provided to the user. Electricity consumption monitoring systems are being used all over the world. In Italy, Buono et al. [17] proposed the development of an energy consumption measurement device for domestic use, a home automation proposal. Something similar is presented in [18], where a low-cost home meter is developed remotely and in real-time. In Latin America, real-time monitoring systems are already being developed, as shown in [19]. This system, which uses low-cost elements, is applied in domestic environments and performs well at a reduced cost.

The prototype of [20] stands out in the industrial part, which measures the power consumption in a building. This distributed system application performs well, even though it cannot monitor over a considerable distance. Mataloto et al. [21] proposes a complete measurement system to know an institution's energy consumption. Additionally, ambient temperature, illumination, and humidity are measured, making it an entire device. In [22], an Electric Consumption Monitoring System using IoT and Blockchain in China is proposed.

The sleep mode of electronic equipment such as computers, display screens, and other devices generates consumption, even if not in use [23]. According to the equipment, these devices require electrical energy to avoid losing data or configurations [24]. In addition, there are energy leaks due to problems in the sizing of the distribution network or wiring in poor condition. All these incidents are reflected in the increase in the electric energy bill issued by the local electric utility company. In this context, the present research proposes implementing data acquisition and energy monitoring systems. These elements are essential for the optimization of consumption and increased performance. To validate the proposed system, a comparison is made with commercial equipment, whose error is less than 3%. In this way, a low-cost, high-performance system is presented.

This document has five sections, including the introduction in Sect. 1. The materials and methods used and the development of the proposal are described in Sect. 2 and Sect. 3, respectively. The results are shown in Sect. 4, while Sect. 5 presents the discussion and conclusions.

2 Methods and Materials

2.1 Methodology

This is applied research since a practical problem of economic and social importance has been identified, and a solution has been found. An empirical methodology was chosen based on experimentation, considering it is an engineering study. A quantitative approach was also defined since the data processes are numerical only. First, a field investigation is performed to identify the parameters and technical requirements of the building. The state of the load centers is also examined to determine the current state of the electrical networks and installed equipment and thus determine the power generated by each floor. Afterward, measuring equipment is built, the general diagram shown in Fig. 1. It is placed in the two buildings, on each of the five floors that comprise them, to obtain values and calibrate them. This is a quantitative study since numerical data are obtained on daily and monthly energy consumption.

2.2 Data Processing

The quantification of these data will provide the energy consumption curve to compare it with a commercial device. It allows corrections at various points and through

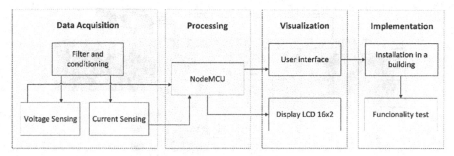

Fig. 1. System block diagram.

subsequent evaluations to establish the final version of the prototype. The active power is the multiplication of instantaneous voltages and current; in the same way, it works independently of the reactive power so that they can be treated as different quantities in electrical connections.

2.3 Case Study

Este estudio se desarrolló en la Universidad Tecnológica Indoamérica de la ciudad de Ambato, Ecuador. The main economic activity is training undergraduate and graduate students in various areas of knowledge. There are several academic days where administrative personnel, teachers, students, and support staff interact. Considering the institution's line of business, potable water, electricity, and internet facilities and services are constantly used. However, this study focuses only on energy consumption by the university community. Thus, it is possible to define the demand for this resource inside and outside working hours.

3 Proposal Development

3.1 Electronics Design

After the initial observation, it is identified that this system should be applied on each floor. Given the magnitude of the building, we started with the electronic design of the equipment. Figure 2 shows the circuit developed in the Fritzing software, which served as the basis for the respective simulation. The SCT-013 clamp-type electric current sensor is used for data acquisition, coupling a filter and some resistors for signal conditioning. This non-invasive device calculates the current crossing a conductor without interrupting the circuit or cutting the conductor. This is achieved by the magnetic induction produced in the internal current transformers, which provides a voltage signal at its output. The central processing unit is the NodeMCU development board, based on the ESP8266 microcontroller. This device is easy to implement and can easily connect to various external plug-ins and modules. A 16x2 LCD (liquid crystal display) with its respective serial communication bus (LCM1602) is used for the local display of the data. The cost of the required hardware is $30.40, not including the PLA printed protection structure.

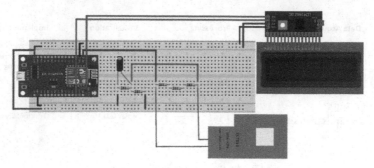

Fig. 2. Prototype electronic design.

3.2 Script Development

Given the limited space, the code used is available at the following link: https://drive.goo gle.com/file/d/12f0dzs8efzl5OwO9ThUfmfj2h3sDEi6I/view?usp=sharing. High-level c++ programming is used to develop the script, using the IDE (integrated development environment) of the Arduino board, which is compatible with the NodeMCU board. The code uses the Emonlib libraries, which facilitate mathematical calculations. We start by defining the variable "gridVoltage" as a float, which enables the use of decimals for the acquisition of data from the power grid. The void setup () is defined and the function Serial.begin(9600) is used to configure the communication at 9600 baud between the Arduino IDE software (in the serial plotter section) and the NodeMCU board. Then an object of the energyMonitor class is initialized with the current function, representing the analog pin A0 (correction factor).

Finally, the RMS current is obtained within the void loop () function by calling the calcIrms function (number of samples). For this, the technical requirements of the Latin American electrical network, which are 120VAC and 60 Hz, must be considered. Using Eq. (1), we determine the cycle period, divided by the data transport time of port A0, which is 0.000189 s in Eq. (2). This calculation defines that 88 samples will be taken in a 60 Hz signal cycle. The data acquired and printed in the variable T.KW by Arduino is sent every 500 ms.

$$T = \frac{1}{f} \tag{1}$$

$$T = \frac{1}{60} = 0,01666\hat{6} \, [s]$$

$$n = \frac{0,01666\hat{6} \, [s]}{0,000189 \, [s]} = 88 \tag{2}$$

To achieve a better resolution, the number of cycles is increased; OpenEnergyMonitor[1] recommends using 14 cycles, and with this, 1232 samples are obtained. This number of samples makes it possible to get the RMS current value. Using an ammeter clamp,

---

[1] https://openenergymonitor.org/.

current measurements are taken to calibrate the prototype (Fig. 3 (a)). Similarly, the voltage is measured using a multimeter, as shown in Fig. 3 (b), and the product is used to obtain the power. Finally, we check that all our libraries are working correctly by performing the respective simulation in Fritzing.

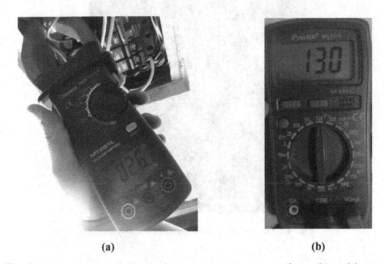

(a)   (b)

Fig. 3. Measurement of electrical parameters: (a) current clamp (b) multimeter.

Taking advantage of the use of the NodeMCU board, which is based on the ESP8266, we have the necessary hardware to create a mobile application. The blynk library is used in the development environment, and the visualized data is written. This is achieved using the virtual pins that the Blynk application has. Figure 4 shows the developed interface and the successful reception of data within a local network.

3.3 Structural Design

After the prototype's initial testing, the components' size for the protective cover design is measured. As shown in Fig. 5 (a), a three-dimensional model of three independent pieces is obtained using SolidWorks software, forming a box with certain modifications. This model is suitable for printing using PLA due to its low cost and good performance. With this, greater robustness is obtained when using the equipment, unifying it in a single piece, as shown in Fig. 5 (b). This equipment can be placed in different places without the risk of damage or false contact with the internal elements, and the visualization is done exclusively using the LCD screen.

4   Results

4.1 Diagrams and Power

After observing the buildings, AutoCAD software is used to draw the floor plans for each floor. Figure 6 shows the first floor's distribution of outlets, lighting, electrical

Fig. 4. Remote monitoring using the Blynk app.

(a)   (b)

Fig. 5. Equipment protection cover: (a) design; (b) printed structure.

equipment, pumps, and motors. All the drawings are available for better visualization at the following link: https://drive.google.com/file/d/1-Nu2qMI7FkKR5JYMZ6Iu7fxGn cqs69E-/view?usp=sharing. Subsequently, all the electrical elements available on the drawings are quantified on each floor. In this way, it will be easier to identify the power independently to have the total value of the building. Figure 7 shows the summary of the calculation of the electrical installations of the basement. Accordingly, the prototype should be placed independently in the distribution box on each floor. This is because the power can be higher than 100A, the limit of the sensor's operating range. All calculations and diagrams describing this section are uploaded in the same link.

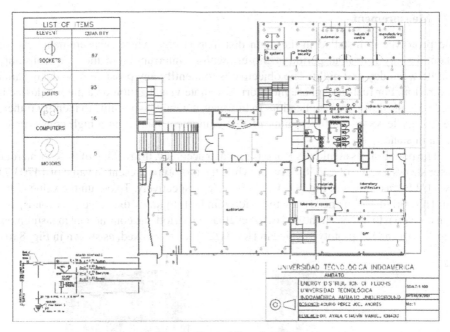

Fig. 6. Ground floor layout.

# CIRCUIT (IPs)N	LIGHTING CIRCUIT [W]			CURRENT COLLECTOR		SPECIAL LOADS OR MACHINERY CIRCUIT [W]						POWER FACTOR	TOTAL POWER [W]	VOLTAGE [V]	INTENSITY [A]	POWER PER LINE		
	SAVER	FLUORECENT	INCANDESENT	TYPE CHARGES 1	TYPE CHARGES 2	COMPUTERS	TWO-PHASE MOTOR 1	TWO-PHASE MOTOR 2	SINGLE-PHASE MOTOR	TWO-PHASE MOTOR 4	THREE-PHASE MOTOR					LINE 1 A	LINE 2 B	LINE 3 C
	30	100	150	200	500	600	2000	3000	500	2000	1000							
C1 (1,2)N				60	0							0,9	12000	220	34,99	6000	6000	
C2(2,3)N	45	3	1									0,55	1800	220	12,94		400	1400
C3(1,3)N						9						0,9	5400	220	23,72	700		4700
POWER OF THE LIGHTING CIRCUIT [W]	1800															6700	6400	6100
POWER OF THE TAP CIRCUIT [W]	12000												P[W]	I[A]				
POWER OF THE SPECIAL LOADS OR MACHINERY CIRCUIT [W]						5400							19200	56,05				
MAXIMUM ADMISSIBLE POWER	3240		12000			4725							MAXIMUM TOTAL POWER ICP	19965				
													INTENSITY ICP	0,000				

CALCULATION OF THE FIFTH FLOOR INDUSTRIAL INSTALLATIONS

Fig. 7. Underground industrial installations.

4.2 Measurement

The prototype is installed in the main distribution box, where measurements can be taken. Twenty-four-hour period is chosen, without interruption of the daily consumption between day and night. The objective is to identify any possible time delays after calibration. For real-time phase monitoring, remote visualization on a mobile device is used with the developed application. In this way, it would be possible to identify if there are energy leaks or malfunctioning of that equipment that show a high consumption while in standby status.

The period starts at midnight, and for greater accuracy, the reading of the commercial meter shows a value of 14178,7 Kw*h, while the prototype presents a value of 14703,71 Kw*1/2 [s], as shown in Fig. 8 (a) and Fig. 8 (c) respectively. To obtain the value in the unit [Kw*h], it will be necessary to divide it in half, to know the value in seconds, and then convert it to hours. At the end of the evaluation period, the commercial measurement (Fig. 8 (b)) and the prototype value in [Kw*1/2 s] are rechecked, as shown in Fig. 8 (d).

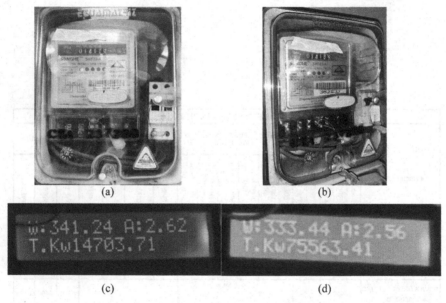

Fig. 8. Functional tests: (a) a commercial meter at start-up. (b) a commercial meter at completion. (c) Prototype at start-up. (d) Prototype at completion.

According to the data collected, the daily energy consumption measured by the prototype is determined using Eq. (3). Similarly, the consumption indicated by the conventional meter belonging to the local distribution company is analyzed with Eq. (4).

$$C_p = (M_2 - M_1)\frac{1}{2*3600} \tag{3}$$

$$C_p = \frac{(75563,41 - 14703,71)}{2*3600}$$

$$C_p = 8,453 \, [\text{Kw} * \text{h}]$$

$$C_c = M_2 - M_1 \tag{4}$$

$$C_c = 14187, 4 - 14178, 7$$

$$C_c = 8, 7 \, [\text{Kw*h}]$$

In Eq. (5), the relative error with the above data is shown. With this low error, it is estimated that the readings of the prototype are 97% effective. The 1% increase or decrease must be considered since the relation for the calibration is performed visually inside the meter.

$$\text{Relative error} = \frac{|C_p - C_c|}{C_c} * 100\% \tag{5}$$

$$\text{Relative error} = \frac{|8, 453 - 8, 7|}{8, 7} * 100\%$$

$$\text{Relative error} = 2, 839\%$$

Finally, a mathematical model is proposed to predict the institution's electricity consumption. Since 2020 and 2021 have had a virtual and hybrid education, the monthly invoices for 2019 will be considered. Using this information, we determine the equation of a line that summarizes the linear regression performed, shown in Fig. 9. To validate the model's efficiency obtained, we calculate the area under the curve of this function using Eq. (6). The sum of the monthly billing values gives a total of 142384.55 [Kw*h], which is compared with that obtained (141209.85 [Kw*h]). Using (5), we calculate the model's error about the actual measurement, and as can be seen, it is less than 1%.

$$C_a = \int_0^{12} 540, 43 \ln(x) dx + \int_0^{12} 10965 dx \tag{6}$$

$$C_a = 141209, 85 \, [\text{Kw} * \text{h}]$$

$$\text{Relative error} = \frac{|141209, 85 - 142384, 55|}{142384, 55} * 100\%$$

$$\text{Relative error} = 0, 825\%$$

The coefficient of determination (R-squared) is obtained to evaluate the linear regression. Equation (7) is used, which involves the sum of the square of the errors and the sum of the value of Y minus the average of the squared values of Y. This coefficient will enable us to see the proportion in which the independent variable explains the dependent variable. According to the calculations, a value of 0.09 was obtained, which shows a

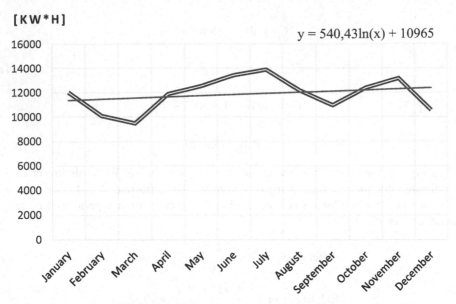

Fig. 9. Monthly energy consumption in 2019.

low explanation and a clear interpretation. The independent variable is the months of the year; there is no relationship between these and the increase or decrease in energy consumption. Therefore, it is estimated that the regression is only a measure to know an average consumption value but not to predict its behavior. However, Fig. 9 shows that there is a considerable reduction in the total value of energy consumed in the vacation months.

$$R^2 = 1 - \frac{\sum e^2}{\sum (Y - \bar{y})^2} \tag{7}$$

$$R^2 = 1 - \frac{18512870,3}{20348267,3}$$

$$R^2 = 0,09$$

5   Discussion and Conclusions

Monitoring systems are undergoing significant changes, enhanced by the interconnection through the Internet. The development of new electronic components, intelligent cell phones, and devices dedicated to home automation and industry makes new applications like this one possible. The internet is reinventing systems that for many years have been dedicated to large enterprises, monitoring complex systems and industrial areas in general. Home automation and the creation of new commercial PnP (Plug and Play) devices allow for greater control. Devices from retail brands such as Amazon use applications or voice commands to turn lights on and off through intelligent switches and outlets and other internet-connected devices. Small, high-performance, high-interconnectivity development boards have also been developed.

Intelligent devices allowed us to propose a low-cost prototype that performs local energy consumption monitoring and has remote visualization. Although our proposal does not incorporate a control system that blocks the current flow as in [19], the performance is very similar, and even the percentage of error in the measurements is slightly lower. This energy data acquisition system is a recommendable alternative that will establish a better basis for establishing smart cities. Thus, it will be possible to analyze daily consumption curves, identify the hours of highest demand, and even analyze the consumption of equipment during nighttime periods when they are not being used. With this, it will be possible to identify possible energy leaks due to the poor state of the connections or to define excessive consumption in the month and propose measures to optimize resources.

The difference between Buono et al. [17] and Buele et al. [19] is that the tests were done in a house. Therefore, their resistance to higher loads (industrial environment) cannot be correctly estimated. Jebroni et al. [18] also present a device used in homes, but they have good performance; the difference with our proposal is that they use more expensive sensors and therefore have a better resolution. In [22], they used blockchain, a technology that has had its boom in the last decades; however, based on their findings, it is still not a robust tool and needs to be improved. Although in [20] they make an industrial proposal, their disadvantage is that they use ZigBee technology and therefore have the range and remote connection problems, which are inferior to our design. In the paper by Mataloto et al. [21], an industrial and integral design has also been made that includes other variables such as temperature and humidity. Still, it has a high cost, unlike our proposal, which is lower cost.

Preliminary to the design, it is recommended to carry out an on-site observation to identify the technical requirements of the building. This made it possible to develop the electrical drawings, which show the layout of the electrical points and the average consumption per floor. In this case, the consumption invoices were used as a reference, allowing the equipment to be calibrated. The presented design is simple and replicable, whose electrical components are easy to acquire in the local market since they are mass-produced. The code used is also included for a better understanding by the reader. This preliminary study corroborated the excellent performance of this device, with an error of 2.839%, which means a low level of failure in the readings obtained.

It also confirms that it is a low-cost proposal, with an average value of $30. This is very low compared to proposals such as [16] and [19], where the investment is over $100. Within the characterization of the energy consumption of this building, it can be highlighted that the annual value is high (142384,55 [Kw * h]), being July the highest month with 13865,35 [Kw * h]. For this reason, progressive corrective actions are proposed, such as the wiring analysis, in search of electrical leaks and other elements that could be generating problems that are not visible. It is also proposed to implement awareness campaigns since the services are used by the entire university community, which cannot be monitored individually.

The authors of this study propose future work to improve this prototype using the Raspberry Pi since it has a higher processing speed and robustness. In addition, we propose to extend this study with the development of energy audits that analyze the current state of the infrastructure (energy sources and use of the facilities). This will also make it possible to propose improvements and modifications at the structural and administrative levels to optimize resources.

The supplementary material that allows the replication of this proposal is found in the following online folder: https://drive.google.com/drive/folders/1i7tgQBrc050Jmf FHOldCG_5DEIIbxsef?usp=sharing.

Acknowledgments. Universidad Tecnológica Indoamérica for its support and financing under the "Big data analysis and its impact on society, education and industry" project.

References

1. Vo, D.H., Vo, A.T.: Renewable energy and population growth for sustainable development in the Southeast Asian countries. Energy Sustain. Soc. **11**(1), 1–15 (2021). https://doi.org/10. 1186/s13705-021-00304-6
2. Ayala, M., Huaraca, D., Varela-Aldás, J., Ordóñez, A., Riba, G.: Anthropization and growth of the electricity grid as variables for the analysis of urban infrastructure. Sustain (2020). https://doi.org/10.3390/su12041486
3. Altıntaş, H., Kassouri, Y.: Is the environmental Kuznets Curve in Europe related to the per-capita ecological footprint or CO2 emissions? Ecol. Indic. **113**, 106187 (2020). https://doi. org/10.1016/j.ecolind.2020.106187
4. Guáitara, B., Buele, J., Salazar, F.W., Varela-Aldás, J.: Prototype of a low cost turbine for the generation of clean energy in the Ecuadorian Amazon. In: Rodriguez Morales, G., Fonseca C., E.R., Salgado, J.P., Pérez-Gosende, P., Orellana Cordero, M., Berrezueta, S. (eds.) TICEC 2020. CCIS, vol. 1307, pp. 564–571. Springer, Cham (2020). https://doi.org/10.1007/978-3-030-62833-8_41
5. Radmehr, R., Henneberry, S.R., Shayanmehr, S.: Renewable energy consumption, CO2 Emissions, and economic growth nexus: a simultaneity spatial modeling analysis of EU countries. Struct. Chang. Econ. Dyn. **57**, 13–27 (2021). https://doi.org/10.1016/j.strueco.2021.01.006
6. Pérez Aranda, A., Arco Díaz, J., Hidalgo García, D.: Energy study of the envelope in metal containers for building. Build. Manag. **3**, 36 (2019). https://doi.org/10.20868/bma.2019.1. 3875
7. Varela-Aldás, J., Buele, J., Lorente, P.R., García-Magariño, I., Palacios-Navarro, G.: A virtual reality-based cognitive telerehabilitation system for use in the covid-19 pandemic. Sustain **13**, 1–24 (2021). https://doi.org/10.3390/su13042183
8. Talahua, J.S., Buele, J., Calvopina, P., Varela-Aldas, J.: Facial recognition system for people with and without face mask in times of the covid-19 pandemic. Sustain **13**, 6900 (2021). https://doi.org/10.3390/su13126900
9. Organización Latinoamericana de Energía: Panorama energético de América Latina y el Caribe 2018. INDIGO EXPRESS, Quito (2018)
10. Rodríguez-Bello, L.A., Estupiñán-Escalante, E.: The impact of waste of electrical and electronic equipment public police in Latin America: analysis of the physical, economical, and information flow. In: Handbook of Electronic Waste Management, pp. 397–419. Elsevier (2020). https://doi.org/10.1016/B978-0-12-817030-4.00010-3
11. Forero, C.I.A., Molina, M.A.M., Benítez, P.B., Álvarez, G.P., Wilches, K.V.E., Muñoz, A.C.P.: Conclusiones y recomendaciones. In: Forero, C.I.A., Molina, M.A.M., Benítez, P.B., Álvarez, G.P., Wilches, K.V.E., Muñoz, A.C.P. (eds.) Adultos mayores privados de la libertad en

Colombia, pp. 250–260. Editorial Universidad del Rosario (2014). https://doi.org/10.7476/9789587385328.0011

12. Murshed, M.: An empirical analysis of the non-linear impacts of ICT-trade openness on renewable energy transition, energy efficiency, clean cooking fuel access and environmental sustainability in South Asia. Environ. Sci. Pollut. Res. **27**(29), 36254–36281 (2020). https://doi.org/10.1007/s11356-020-09497-3

13. Ayala-Chauvin, M., Kavrakov, B.S., Buele, J., Varela-Aldás, J.: Static reactive power compensator design, based on three-phase voltage converter. Energies **14**, 2198 (2021). https://doi.org/10.3390/en14082198

14. Rausser, G., Strielkowski, W., Štreimikienė, D.: Smart meters and household electricity consumption: a case study in Ireland. Energy Environ. **29**, 131–146 (2018). https://doi.org/10.1177/0958305X17741385

15. Alkawsi, G.A., Ali, N., Baashar, Y.: An Empirical study of the acceptance of IoT-based smart meter in Malaysia: the effect of electricity-saving knowledge and environmental awareness. IEEE Access **8**, 42794–42804 (2020). https://doi.org/10.1109/ACCESS.2020.2977060

16. Buzau, M.M., Tejedor-Aguilera, J., Cruz-Romero, P., Gómez-Expósito, A.: Hybrid deep neural networks for detection of non-technical losses in electricity smart meters. IEEE Trans. Power Syst. **35**, 1254–1263 (2020). https://doi.org/10.1109/TPWRS.2019.2943115

17. Buono, P., Balducci, F., Cassano, F., Piccinno, A.: EnergyAware: A non-intrusive load monitoring system to improve the domestic energy consumption awareness. In: EnSEmble 2019 - Proc. 2nd ACM SIGSOFT Int. Work. Ensemble-Based Softw. Eng. Mod. Comput. Platforms, co-located with ESEC/FSE 2019, pp. 1–8 (2019). https://doi.org/10.1145/3340436.3342726

18. Jebroni, Z., Afonso, J.A., Tidhaf, B.: Home energy monitoring system towards smart control of energy consumption. In: Afonso, J.L., Monteiro, V., Pinto, J.G. (eds.) GreeNets 2018. LNICSSITE, vol. 269, pp. 40–53. Springer, Cham (2019). https://doi.org/10.1007/978-3-030-12950-7_4

19. Buele, J., Morales-Sánchez, J.C., Varela-Aldás, J., Palacios-Navarro, G., Ayala-Chauvin, M.: Electric monitoring system for residential customers using wireless technology. Lect. Notes Comput. Sci. (including Subser. Lect. Notes Artif. Intell. Lect. Notes Bioinformatics). **13381**, 123–136 (2022)

20. Chen, Y., Mu, X., Zhang, J., Lu, Z.: Development of monitoring system of building energy consumption. IFCSTA 2009 Proc. - 2009 Int. Forum Comput. Sci. Appl. **2**, 363–366 (2009). https://doi.org/10.1109/IFCSTA.2009.211

21. Mataloto, B., Calé, D., Carimo, K., Ferreira, J.C., Resende, R.: 3D Iot system for environmental and energy consumption monitoring system. Sustain. **13**, 1–19 (2021). https://doi.org/10.3390/su13031495

22. Qi, Y., Wang, X., Zhou, Q., Mu, S.: Research of energy consumption monitoring system based on IoT and blockchain technology. J. Phys. Conf. Ser. **1757**, 012154 (2021). https://doi.org/10.1088/1742-6596/1757/1/012154

23. García-Magariño, I., Gonzalez Bedia, M., Palacios-Navarro, G.: FAMAP: a framework for developing m-health apps. In: Advances in Intelligent Systems and Computing, pp. 850–859. Springer Verlag (2018). https://doi.org/10.1007/978-3-319-77703-0_83/COVER/

24. Sutton-Parker, J.: Can analytics software measure end user computing electricity consumption? Clean Technol. Environ. Policy. **1**, 1–18 (2022). https://doi.org/10.1007/s10098-022-02325-x

Trend of the Use and Investment of Blockchain Technology in the Banking Sector in Ecuador

Mayra Garzón-Goya[1]([⊠]) [iD], Carlota Delgado-Vera[2] [iD], Katty Lagos-Ortiz[2] [iD],
and Fabricio Jurado-Larrea[3] [iD]

[1] Facultad de Economía Agrícola, Universidad Agraria del Ecuador, Av. 25 de Julio, Guayaquil,
Ecuador
mgarzon@uagraria.edu.ec
[2] Facultad de Ciencias Agrarias, Universidad Agraria del Ecuador, Av. 25 de Julio, Guayaquil,
Ecuador
{rdelgado,klagos}@uagraria.edu.ec
[3] 7CargoCorp, Guayaquil, Ecuador
fjurado@7cargo.com

Abstract. Technological advances used in the banking sector have allowed the
coupling of various technological and computer tools, giving rise to Blockchain.
This research presents a vision of the components, the architecture, the platforms,
and the algorithms used and finally the frequency of their use. This research
highlights the evolution of Fintech in Latin America, and links up these statistics
to the reality of the banking sector in Ecuador; it is also described the performance
indicator of the investment made in three of the main banks in this country and
the amounts invested in technology are shown as evidence that they are also part
of the digitalization process of the financial industry.

Keywords: Blockchain · Financial industry · Architecture fintech · Applications

1 Introduction

In recent years, global and multidisciplinary interest in Blockchain (BC) technology
has grown exponentially since it was adopted by the Bitcoin cryptocurrency in 2008. In
effect, Blockchain refers to a distributed database that keeps a continuously growing list
of blockchains, and data records that are protected from tampering and review, including
by data warehouse node operators. In its context, blockchain provides multiple benefits
to financial institutions such as reduced costs related to IT infrastructure by replacing
the back office with blockchain, reduced costs of interbank payments, improved security
of bank data, and more efficient transaction processing, smart contracts will help avoid
mistakes and provide quality financial services [1].

The United Nations, the International Monetary Fund, and many governments have
issued a series of reports on blockchain technology, actively promoting the application
of the technology in the finance industry [2]. This technology has several basic elements
such as: nodes, standard protocols, peer-to-peer network, and the decentralized system;

it means that they are a set of computers called nodes, which interconnected in the network use the same communication system whose objective is to verify and store the information registered in the network [3]. According to [4] mentions that it is divided into three categories: Blockchain 1.0 which refers to currency as a means of payment, also called cryptocurrency, Blockchain 2.0 are smart contracts used in stocks, bonds, loans, mortgages and titles; and Blockchain 3.0 are the different applications that go beyond finance. This study presents the trend of use in banking systems along with the investment analysis involved in using them as a technological tool.

2   Blockchain Technology in the Banking Sector

Blockchain technology is constantly evolving, so to address the problem in the best possible way, studies are described on everything that this technology entails, its opportunities and also the investment needed.

2.1   Technology Components and Architecture

The basic elements of the Blockchain are summarized, being the main ones:

- Node: Commonly known as computers or supercomputers, are responsible for verifying transactions; and this varies depending on the network, for it to work correctly it must have the same protocol installed, that is, a specific computer software to communicate with each other with the network.
- Protocol: These are the criteria to validate the block and continue with the emission between the nodes.
- Decentralized system: It is the counterpart of a centralized system; it is a system that allows all the information to be controlled by all the computers connected to the network. If the network is public, all the computers are equal, there is no hierarchy, but if it is private, there can exist hierarchy.
- Peer-to-peer network o P2P: It is a nodes network connected to the same network. For example, the BitTorrent.

Figure 1 shows how transactions are carried out using Blockchain, using each of the elements described above.

The Blockchain architecture is composed of the data layer, the network layer, the consensus layer, an incentive layer, a contract layer and an application layer, as presented in Fig. 1. The first layer is the information layer, which includes the underlying data block, the data structure, and the encryption and authentication algorithms. The second layer is the network, which mainly includes distributed networks, technology, data transmission and verification mechanism and other technologies between the nodes of the blockchain system [5]. The third layer is the consensus layer, which mainly includes various types of consensus mechanisms between network nodes, such as the workload proof mechanism and the fairness proof mechanism. The fourth layer is the incentive layer, which mainly includes various economic rewards and distribution systems and other economic incentive mechanisms. The fifth layer is the contract layer, which is the concrete business logic in the blockchain system, it mainly includes smart contracts and algorithms. The sixth layer is the application layer, where the blockchain application scenarios such as finance, services, supply chain management and manufacturing are located.

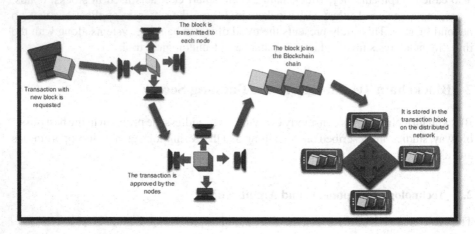

Fig. 1. Sequence of transactions in the BlockChain

2.2   Classification of the Blockchain System

As mentioned, blockchain is managed by means of a computer network in a decentralized and distributed way. Regarding the type of Blockchain according to the participating nodes in the maintenance of the blockchain network, public, private and consortium chains are defined [6]. The public Blockchain is a platform that allows access to any node in the validation process of the block chain, it means, it can consult and access the transactions. In addition, they are totally decentralized and their security includes Work of Proof (WoP) or Work of Stake (WoS) mathematical algorithms. Network users have a virtual signature to carry out their operations anonymously [7]. Blockchain is private, access permissions are only for the participating nodes of the network; specifically, only they can verify the executed operations. It is characterized by having a company as a centralizing unit, which is essential for transactions involving confidential data [8]. The Blockchain consortium access to network resources is limited to some of the participants and controlled by one or more entities. Table 1 shows a comparison of the differences between the different platforms.

Table 1. Difference of the types of platforms

Charateristic	Public	Private	Consortium
Any node can participate	X	–	–
Transparency	X	Partially	Partially
A single administrator	–	X	–
Multiple administrators	X	X	–
No admin	X	–	–
No participant has more rights than other	X	–	–
Fix reliability issues	–	X	Partially
Security base don consensus algorithm	X	–	Partially
Provide cloud services	–	–	–

2.3 Consensus Algorithms

The dimensions that this technology contributes to in the financial sector are: access to infrastructure, use of financial products and services, quality of services [1]; supply, demand and the regulatory framework where the variables regarding the use of products and financial services must be identified [3]; the services provided are grouped into credit, savings, insurance, payment and transfer categories [7]. Figure 2 shows a model of two financial entities providing tokenized money for their clients in a blockchain network developed by the authors Allende Marcos and Antonio Leas [2].

A consensus algorithm in Blockchain is the mechanism used to select the correct state of a record after the transaction is made, validating many times the transactions that occur in it and defining which ones are legitimate to add to the main chain [9, 10]. The main ones are detailed below:

- Proof-of-Work (PoW): It is the first blockchain consensus algorithm proposed by Nakamoto [7] and was first used by Bitcoin, the leading cryptocurrency in the market today. In PoW mining, miners solve complex math puzzles that require a lot of computational power. In PoW mining, miners solve complex math puzzles that require a lot of computational power, the first miner to solve the puzzle creates a block and receives a reward for it. The PoW algorithm makes sure that miners can only validate a new transaction block and add it to the chain if the distributed nodes of the network reach consensus and accept the hash found by the miner as valid [9].
- Proof-of-State (POS): This consensus algorithm was born as an alternative to PoW and aims to achieve a distributed consensus. Its operation differs a lot from the previous algorithm, it requires a person to bet, hold or block coins and validate the ownership. It uses a mechanism where the blocks are validated according to the 'participation' of those involved [11].
- Delegated Proof of Stake (DeS): It is a very fast consensus mechanism and is known as digital democracy, its operation is that each component of the network can become

a delegate who is allowed to make profits by running a full node. This method is more efficient and protects users from unwanted regulatory interference.

2.4 Blockchain in the Industry 4.0

Smart applications developed that include blockchain in the context of Industry 4.0, present various characteristics and capabilities, such as:

- Digital identities which is a feature of Blockchain that allows to authenticate the identities of people or entities involved in some commercial activity through a public network [12].
- Distributed security is another key factor because it includes high levels of replication and multiple chained encryptions that make it impossible to alter any record added to the chain [3]. Avoiding the risk of data exposure and higher level of confidence in the process of validation of transactions [13].
- Smart contracts through a public network without third parties reducing administrative costs and providing an efficient model to initiate, negotiate and finalize contracts between suppliers, service providers, distributors and subcontractors [14].
- The last feature that Blockchain provides are the microcontrols that facilitate quality controls and measurements of activities and processes, facilitating the audit and evaluation of activities, position in the market, among others [15].

3 Blockchain Usage/Investment Performance Measures for the Banking Sector

One of the information sources used is the one provided by Blockchain.com, which shows the main statistics on the use of applications based on blockchain worldwide in all industries or sectors, the indicators showed have information from the year 2009 to the present. Regarding the investment in technology of the main financial entities (banking system) of Ecuador, the information on Investment in Technology published on the page of the Superintendence of Banks of Ecuador from the years 2018 to 2021 was used, considering the amounts invested in hardware and software, as well as the Return on Assesment (ROA) of each of the periods of the selected financial entities. For this purpose, the selection criteria of the three financial entities was based on the profits earned by the institutions in the study period, so the analysis will be limited to these three entities which are: Pichincha Bank, Guayaquil Bank and Pacific Bank.

It has been demonstrated that the automation of transactions in the financial system supported by the blockchain application has multiple benefits, among them the simplification of activities and tasks, offering a rapid response to user requirements, applying more control measures and cost savings within the operations in the organizations that decide to implement it. On the other hand, one of the most outstanding characteristics is the confidence in the use of services through digital platforms, [16] indicator that reflects a constant growth since the last years, according to data published on the Blockchain website[1] there is a significant increase associated with an exponential distribution of the

---

[1] https://www.blockchain.com/.

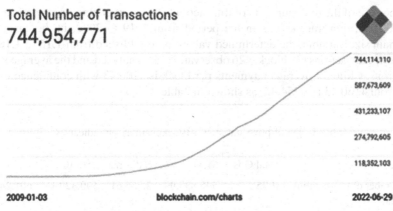

Fig. 2. Total number of transactions

number of blockchain-based transactions in the last thirteen years in various sectors, this can be seen in Fig. 2. Currently, an average of 1,586 transactions per block is estimated to date considering the activity of the last year, as shown in Table 2, according to the same data source, 745 million daily transactions are made based on blockchain applications.

Table 2. Usage statistics, main Blockchain indicators 2022

Use statistics	Description	Total
Total number of transactions	The total number of transactions on the blockchain	745 approx million
Blockchain size	The average block size over the past 24 h in megabytes	1.22 MB
Average transactions per block	The average number of transactions per block over the past 24 h	1,586
Average payments per block	The average number of payments per block over the past 24 h	4,170

The descriptive statistics for the use of applications based on blockchain worldwide in various sectors of the industry are shown in the following table for each of the variables previously defined, among the calculated measures, it is included the number of observations that have been analyzed in the last three years, the mean, the standard error and the confidence interval with an assumed level of 95% for the mean of each of the measurements.

In the case of the total numbers of transactions, the interval obtained is defined from 590 to 601 million transactions in the period from 2019 to 2022, in the case of the Blockchain size variable, the determined values are established from 1.16 to 1.18 MB, for average transactions per block, 426 observations are analyzed and the average is 2037 transactions, while for average payments per block is 4206.43 with confidence interval values from 4160.43 to 4254.42, as shown in Table 3.

Table 3. Descriptive statistics – Blockchain usage indicators

Variable	Total Obs.	Mean	Std. Err.	95% IC	
Total number of transactions (millions)	1095	595,837.99	2,756.61	590,429.16	601,246.83
Blockchain size	1095	1.17	0.01	1.16	1.183
Average transactions per block	426	2037.34	15.50	2006.88	2067.81
Average payments per block	1094	4206.42	23.44	4160.43	4252.42

According to a report about the distribution of blockchain market value worldwide in 2020 (Statista), 29.27% is associated with banking activities, so it is also estimated that global spending on blockchain solutions has grown significantly from 2017 to 2021 in 595% approximately, going from 0.95 billion dollars to 6.6 billion dollars, with the solutions being implemented not only in the financial sector– Block 1.0, but also in logistics and health administration areas – Block 3.0, evidencing the evolution of generations and the application of their development towards other sectors of the industry [4].

On the other hand, the use of Blockchain services cannot be analyzed without highlighting the significant increase in financial applications, which according to the report [17], the United States occupies the first place with the highest participation in the development of Fintech startups, followed by United Kingdom and Israel, reflecting among these three the highest score in terms of Fintech investment supported by Blockchain; while the same report shows that in Latin American region, among the countries that occupy the first positions we find Brazil, Uruguay, Mexico, Colombia and Chile, and regarding to Ecuador it occupies the 69th position in the ranking with companies dedicated to business financial management, digital payments, crowdfunding, loans, personal financial management, and other activities, where according to a report published in [18] there are already 63 startups categorized as Fintech, of which it is estimated that 46% are located in Quito, Ecuador.

For Ecuador, as well as the rest of the countries worldwide, as an effect of the pandemic due to COVID-19, there has been a decrease in the gap towards the digitalization of services and transactions within this field, still, it is necessary to consider that the limited access to financial services for a certain population group means that the development and application of this type of technology to make payments is still in a slow rise, this and other factors such as monetary policy, financial stability, and payment systems [19] can influence or affect the adaptation of this technology mainly in Latin America, while a different scenario is presented in developed countries. In Ecuador, although this scenario seems unfavourable and there is little information about the use and application of blockchain in the financial system, it has been decided to compare the indicator of Returns on Assets (ROA) for the three largest banking entities in Ecuador for the period 2019–2021 so the information can be compared with banks in countries with applied blockchain technologies, taking into account the behavior of the ratio by month/year and by institution, identifying the variation rate and the average of the ratio of the period. On the other hand, it is expected to demonstrate that there is a significant difference in the variance of the ratios analyzed for each bank in the period by Levene's Test.

Figure 3 shows the variation of the ROA for each of the banking institutions from January 2018 to December 2020, evidencing a negative variation of -93% of the indicator for March 2020 in relation to February of the same year, due to the COVID-19 pandemic, where it is observed that the most significant is the ROA associated with Guayaquil Bank (Roa_bgye), for the other entities a variation of the indicator is reflected in the same period of -16% for Pichincha Bank (Roa_bpich) and -30% for Pacific Bank (Roa_bpacif). The behaviour of this indicator tends to be similar to banks of the United States, which is the country that leads the ranking of Fintech development, thus it is also observed that the average ROA of the American banks showed a decrease between the months of the global pandemic; for this group of banks, the data is shown in quarterly periods from the second quarter of 2019 to the fourth quarter of 2021, and it can be seen in Fig. 4 a decrease of 68% affecting this return on investment in financial institutions worldwide.

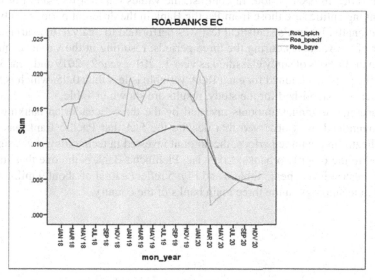

Fig. 3. Return on Assets – Ecuadorian banks

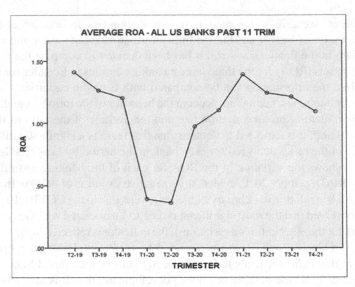

Fig. 4. Average ROA – US Banks.

The descriptive statistics of the ROA (Return on Assets) indicators at the level of the Ecuadorian banks are shown in Table 4, it can be observed that the average of the indicator varies in each period. In contrast, the values that mostly stand out from the three banking entities are those from Pacific Bank in the different periods analyzed.

Additionally, Levene's statistical test was performed to analyze the variance of the behavior of the variables during the three periods, resulting in the variances not being similar in the periods of study classified as year 1 - 2018, year 2 - 2019 and year 3 – 2020, because the p-value obtained for each ROA variable is less than 0.05, which is the level of significance established for the study, results are shown in Table 5.

Regarding the annual amounts invested by the three Ecuadorian banking entities before mentioned, it is observed that despite the fact that Pacific Bank has a better ROA indicator in the three periods, the amount invested in technology is not significant compared to the other two banks. Likewise, Pichincha Bank is the one that stands out with the greatest investment. Table 6 and Fig. 5 reflect a total of about 9 million dollars invested in technology in the three main banks of the country.

Table 4. Descriptive Statistics – ROA Ecuadorian Banks

Year	Statistics		Pichincha Bank ROA_bpich		Pacific Bank ROA_bpacif		Guayaquil Bank ROA_bgye	
			Statistic	Std. Error	Statistic	Std. Error	Statistic	Std. Error
2018	Mean		0.0108	0.0002	0.0180	0.0006	0.0139	0.0002
	95% Confidence	0.0103			0.0168		0.0133	
	Interval for Mean	0.0112			0.0193		0.0144	
	Std. Deviation		0.0007		0.0019		0.0008	
	Minimum		0.0096		0.0152		0.0121	
	Maximum		0.0116		0.0201		0.0157	
2019	Mean		0.0115	0.0003	0.0181	0.0002	0.0176	0.0003
	95% Confidence	0.0109			0.0176		0.0169	
	Interval for Mean	0.0120			0.0185		0.0182	
	Std. Deviation		0.0009		0.0007		0.0010	
	Minimum		0.0098		0.0165		0.0158	
	Maximum		0.0125		0.0191		0.0194	
2020	Mean		0.0064	0.0007	0.0071	0.0011	0.0066	0.0018
	95% Confidence	0.0048			0.0047		0.0026	
	Interval for Mean	0.0079			0.0095		0.0107	
	Std. Deviation		0.0024		0.0038		0.0063	
	Minimum		0.0040		0.0042		0.0013	
	Maximum		0.0106		0.0148		0.0206	

Table 5. Levene's statistical test

Test of homogeneity of variance		Levene statistic	df1	df2	Sig
Roa_bpich	Based on mean	10.01	2	33	.000
	Based on median	4.82	2	33	.015
Roa_bpacif	Based on mean	8.38	2	33	.001
	Based on median	2.83	2	33	.073
Roa_bgye	Based on mean	8.73	2	33	.001
	Based on median	3.55	2	33	.040

Table 6. Hardware-Software Investment

Year	Pichincha bank BPICH	Pacific bank BPACIF	Guayaquil bank BG
2018	$ 1,293,034,030.56	$ 466,634,944.29	$ 1,055,402,352.05
2019	$ 1,440,779,265.59	$ 583,340,395.12	$ 1,094,603,108.39
2020	$ 1,497,972,826.24	$ 653,893,901.90	$ 1,110,752,606.70
Total	$ 4,231,786,122.39	$ 1,703,869,241.31	$ 3,260,758,067.14

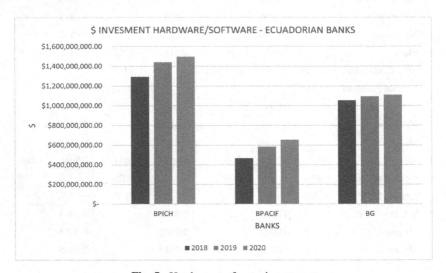

Fig. 5. Hardware-software investment

4 Conclusions and Future Work

The trend in the applications developed in Blockchain have evolved towards various sectors such as logistics, health administration, government entities, among other fields. Although the application in the financial sector has advantages in terms of time, it faces challenges such as monetary policies and access to financial services, which can make a difference mainly in Latin Americans countries in relation to developed countries. The use of technology based on blockchain in the financial sector represents approximately 29% of the entire application by the industry worldwide; however, it evolves rapidly with proposals that guarantee security and trust to organizations and customers due to its dynamism. The worldwide resurgence of Fintech is associated with countries with more developed technologies such as the United States, the United Kingdom, and Israel. In Latin America, countries that are best positioned in this field are Brazil, Uruguay, and Mexico. In Ecuador, a trend has been evidenced towards the generation of Fintech startups, and approximately 50% of these companies are located in the capital city of the country. There is no specific information available on the application of blockchain in the Ecuadorian financial sector, still, amounts invested in hardware and software for three years are shown and it is compared with the indicator of return on investment of each of the banking institutions, from which it was concluded that not necessarily who has invested more economic resources reflects a better indicator of performance.

The application of Blockchain at the level of the financial industry points to characteristics such as decentralization mainly at the level of its databases, security and agility in transactions, among the benefits to be obtained are cost reduction, and risks control in transactions/operations making it more efficient and being reflected as an increase in profits for the sector. In short, the application of Blockchain leads to a change in the business model of financial entities aiming at improving the experience in the service as a user of technological banking.

Other researchers include as a disadvantage for the use of this technology, the accelerated growth of carbon footprint values due to its relation to an excessive increase in the use of electrical energy by requiring technological equipment which consumes enormous amounts of energy that comes mostly from fossil fuels, having for example indices associated with the energy consumption of Bitcoin, which hopes to raise awareness about the unsustainability of the algorithm. Due to the emergence of new generations of blockchain, it is convenient to carry out a study about blockchain-based applications oriented towards other sectors of the industry, such as logistics and distribution, health administration, or in the government sector.

References

1. Krylov, G.O., Seleznev, V.M.: Current state and development trends of blockchain technology in the financial sector. Finance: Theory and Practice **23**(6), 26–35 (2019). https://doi.org/10.26794/2587-5671-2019-23-6-26-35
2. Zheng, X., Zhu, Y., Si, X.: A survey on challenges and progresses in blockchain technologies: a performance and security perspective. Appl. Sci. (Switzerland) **9**, 1–24 (2019). https://doi.org/10.3390/app9224731
3. Frizzo-Barker, J., Chow-White, P.A., Adams, P.R., Mentanko, J., Ha, D., Green, S.: Blockchain as a disruptive technology for business: a systematic review. Int. J. Inf. Manage. **51**, 0–1 (2020). https://doi.org/10.1016/j.ijinfomgt.2019.10.014
4. Swan, M.: Blockchain: Blueprint for a new economy. "O'Reilly Media, Inc." (2015)
5. Abbas, Q.E., Sung-Bong, J.: A survey of blockchain and its applications. In: 2019 International Conference on Artificial Intelligence in Information and Communication (ICAIIC), pp. 1–3 (2019). https://doi.org/10.1109/ICAIIC.2019.8669067
6. Chang, S.E., Chen, Y.-C., Wu, T.-C.: Exploring blockchain technology in international trade. Ind. Manag. Data Syst. **119**, 1712–1733 (2019). https://doi.org/10.1108/IMDS-12-2018-0568
7. Puthal, D., Malik, N., Mohanty, S.P., Kougianos, E., Das, G.: Everything you wanted to know about the blockchain: its promise, components, processes, and problems. IEEE Consum. Electron. Mag. **7**, 6–14 (2018). https://doi.org/10.1109/MCE.2018.2816299
8. Tasca, P., Tessone, C.J.: A taxonomy of blockchain technologies: principles of identification and classification. Ledger. **4**, 1–39 (2019). https://doi.org/10.5195/ledger.2019.140
9. Chaudhry, N., Yousaf, M.M.: consensus algorithms in blockchain: comparative analysis, challenges and opportunities. In: ICOSST 2018 - 2018 International Conference on Open Source Systems and Technologies, Proceedings, pp. 54–63 (2019). https://doi.org/10.1109/ICOSST.2018.8632190

10. Notheisen, B., Hawlitschek, F., Weinhardt, C.: Breaking down the blockchain hype – Towards a blockchain market engineering approach. In: ECIS 2017 Proceedings. 2017, pp. 1062–1080 (2017)
11. Ribera, E.G.: Design and implementation of a proof-of-stake consensus algorithm for blockchain (2018)
12. Onename Launches Blockchain Identity Product Passcard - Bitcoin Magazine - Bitcoin News, Articles and Expert Insights. https://bitcoinmagazine.com/business/onename-launches-blockchain-identity-product-passcard-1431548450. Last Accessed 13 Aug 2022
13. UnderwoodSarah: Blockchain beyond bitcoin. Communications of the ACM. **59**, 15–17 (2016). https://doi.org/10.1145/2994581
14. Luu, L., Chu, D.H., Olickel, H., Saxena, P., Hobor, A.: Making smart contracts smarter. In: Proceedings of the ACM Conference on Computer and Communications Security, pp. 254–269 (2016). https://doi.org/10.1145/2976749.2978309
15. Takahashi, R.: How can creative industries benefit from blockchain?. https://www.mckinsey.com/industries/technology-media-and-telecommunications/our-insights/how-can-creative-industries-benefit-from-blockchain. Last Accessed 13 Aug 2022
16. Chang, V., Baudier, P., Zhang, H., Xu, Q., Zhang, J., Arami, M.: How Blockchain can impact financial services – the overview, challenges and recommendations from expert interviewees. Technol. Forecast. Soc. Chang. **158**, 120166 (2020). https://doi.org/10.1016/J.TECHFORE.2020.120166
17. Findexable: The global fintech index ecosystem ranking of countries, https://mauritiusfintech.org/blog/2021-global-fintech-rankings-report-findexable/. Last Accessed 14 Aug 2022
18. Dashboard Startups Ecuatorianas. https://www.buentriphub.com/startups-ecuatorianas. Last Accessed 02 Jul 2022
19. Acosta Castro, D.: Un panorama de las fintech en américa latina y el ecuador. Quito (2022)

Effectiveness of Monitoring Indicators in the Architecture of a Collaborative System

Mitchell Vásquez-Bermúdez[1,2](✉) (iD), Jorge Hidalgo-Larrea[1] (iD),
Fausto Orozco Lara[2] (iD), and Stiven Segura Santana[1] (iD)

[1] Escuela de Ingeniería en Computación e Informática, Facultad de Ciencias Agrarias,
Universidad Agraria del Ecuador, Av. 25 de Julio y Pio Jaramillo, Guayaquil, Ecuador
{mvasquez,jhidalgo}@uagraria.edu.ec, mitchell.vasquezb@ug.edu.ec
[2] Universidad de Guayaquil. Cdla. Universitaria Salvador Allende, Guayaquil, Ecuador
fausto.orozcol@ug.edu.ec

Abstract. Collaborative work is increasingly essential in today's virtual classrooms, especially with the use of technology that facilitates collaborative interaction in the educational system and improves the time teachers spend checking if students have done the assigned activity and measuring their participation. Through dynamic statistical graphs, a collaborative system is presented based on monitoring indicators and a set of rules related to keywords that allow determining student participation. The system was evaluated to measure its effectiveness in displaying participation indicators using the Recall and F-Measure precision metrics, obtaining encouraging results in terms of the performance of the collaborative activity monitoring system.

Keywords: Collaborative activities · Effectiveness evaluation · Visualization

1 Introduction

Digital technology is rapidly changing the way students learn and participate in learning activities. In this way, virtual learning platforms allow online learning management to complement the teaching and learning process. Collaborative learning is increasingly important in today's virtual classrooms [1]. The authors [2] highlight the collaborative learning process with the use of technology that includes communication, editing, and collaboration, among other activities, which give rise to online interactions. At the same time, a massive amount of data generated by users is becoming available [3]. The data generated by the interactions of the students are often used to visualize the current state of the activity, and the results are reflected in a virtual class through the work and student performance [4]. However, most educational systems still have doubts about what constitutes relevant data and do not consider the user's perspective, nor do they involve users in the design and development of learning experiences [3]. Furthermore, most studies focus on data extraction from the flow of learning management systems rather than the learning process [5]. Likewise, it is impossible to determine the level of

© The Author(s), under exclusive license to Springer Nature Switzerland AG 2022
R. Valencia-García et al. (Eds.): CITI 2022, CCIS 1658, pp. 191–202, 2022.
https://doi.org/10.1007/978-3-031-19961-5_14

participation of each student in a group work or the level of development of a collaborative activity.

This paper presents a system based on a collaborative tool for high school education. This system allows work collaboration through forums, chats and an online editor with a set of monitoring indicators. Once the interaction is carried out in the collaborative work, the system provides statistical graphs based on the interactions. Thanks to this information, the teacher can visualize the students' level of participation in the collaborative work.

The proposed system was evaluated for its effectiveness in visualizing collaborative work participation. For this, the precision, recall and F-measure metrics were used.

This article is organized as follows: Sect. 2 describes the most relevant works on monitoring tools. Section 3 presents the architecture of the proposed system. The evaluation and results are described in Sect. 4. Finally, conclusions and future work are shown in the last section of the article.

2   Related Work

In the educational field, online platforms facilitate teaching and learning activities, and the analysis of online participation of students is increasingly important so that teachers can effectively monitor and manage the progress and performance of their students.

The authors [6] present a tool for visual analysis of data that explores the behavior and discovers possible relationships between students and also graphically shows class performance.

In the same way in [7], they present a study where a prototype was developed for the integration of a dashboard for learning analytics whose objective was to improve the ecosystem of students with learning services, showing different graphics related to cognitive computing of student activities. Visualization tools allow educational supervision and follow-up in which information is graphically presented to students who participated in a group activity based on interaction indicators during their online work [8].

In addition, the interaction among the students provides essential information that describes their behavior when using the e-learning platforms. The evaluation of the level of knowledge can be completed with indicators related to the dimension of the interaction [9]. In the literature, there is also the development of systems for monitoring and evaluation of the collaborative learning process, such as the one presented in the article "Software Tool to Support the Improvement of the Collaborative Learning Process" [10], which main objective is to support the improvement of the collaborative learning process in each of its phases, through the integration of monitoring and evaluation.

Implementing this online platform in educational institutions has improved the teaching and learning processes because they contain relevant information about the participants' interactions, and they can be visualized by mirroring tools [11], which helps increase student participation and facilitates the evaluation of online courses.

The main objective of this project is to present a collaborative application for tracking interactions of built-in tools such as chat, forum and text editor, evaluating its effectiveness in visualizing collaborative work using the metrics precision, recall and F-measure.

3   Collaborative Architecture System

This section describes the main components of the collaborative system based on the monitoring indicators that are proposed in this work. The hardware used for this tool corresponds to a VPS server with a CPU with 4 cores, 8 gb of AM, 200 gb HDD and the software used for the development of the tool was MySQL, HTML, JavaScript, Ajax. As shown in Fig. 1, the system architecture comprises two main modules: (1) the indicator display module and (2) the collaborative tools module. Also, users can be observed while interacting with the applications.

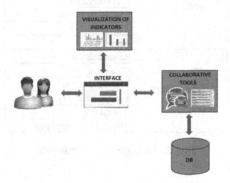

Fig. 1. The architecture of the collaborative system

3.1   Collaborative Tools Module

Collaborative tools incorporate three modules: (a) chat, (b) forum and (c) online editor. The chat and forum are tools designed for the collaborative system, and the online editor used the Etherpad application [12] to facilitate the collaboration of an online editor with chat included.

Indicators based on "keywords" were implemented in the collaborative tools for their work monitoring to start a contribution in a dialogue [13], with this representation, the student can choose from a list of keywords and phrases the one that best represents the intention of their collaboration and then complete their contribution by entering the desired text [14].

To define the sentences in participation, it was taken as a base, the classification of the individual dimension of collaborative work proposed by Zangara [15], which, as shown in Fig. 2, is organized into three main types of messages: (a) organization, (b) content and (c) affectivity. Organizational messages (meta-cognitive function) are related to work planning and organization of activities, content messages (cognitive function) are associated with the context of collaborative work content, and affectivity messages (affective function) are related to motivation, solidarity, understanding, and help.

The initial keywords that the participants select in their interactions are stored in the knowledge base; initially, they were entered manually, and later the keywords are added automatically when they are repetitive. In addition, the system allows the user to

INDICATORS	KEYWORDS
ORGANIZATION	Let's get organized
	The slogan is related to
	Let's try
	I think that
	I would explain it like this
	Please explain
	Let's plan
	The activities
CONTENT	According to the author
	The concept of
	It is concluded
	The development
	The content
	Introduction
AFFECTIVITY	Congratulations
	Thank you
	Very kind of you
	I am proud of you
	We made it
	We are on the right path

Fig. 2. Indicators keywords [15]

add, edit and modify the keywords. For its implementation in the chat and forum tool interfaces, it was incorporated in a menu view with specific buttons for each indicator and with the option to open a keyword to complete the participation in a free text area. To provide students with a visualization of the different indicators, it was decided to group them by keywords in drop-down lists by indicator.

In the chat and forum tool, each student is identified by their name and surname, and their participation comprises the selected keyword and the free text they have entered.

Fig. 3. Chat with indicators (Spanish content)

All interactions carried out by students and teachers are stored, identifying both the user who issues it and the group to which he is part of. An example of a chat interface is shown in Fig. 3.

In addition, Fig. 4 shows the Etherpad application (collaborative online text editor), this tool contains a chat that appears in the lower right part.

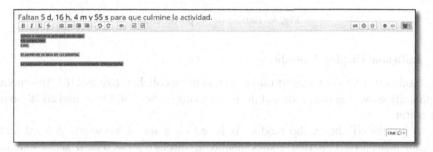

Fig. 4. Etherpad (Spanish content)

An algorithm was developed to extract the keywords from the text entered in the conversation, and finally, it classifies it by indicator. The algorithm is based on two procedures:

- Figure 5 describes the procedure that performs the storage of all the messages sent by the students of the different groups, presenting the following structure with the fields: num, padid, datepub, txtchat y autorid.

```
Procedimiento NewTableChat()
Select cast(substring_index(substring_index(`base_name`.`store`.`key`,':',-(1)),':',1) as unsigned) AS
`num`,substring_index(substring_index(`base_name`.`store`.`key`,':',2),':',-(1)) AS
`padid`,from_unixtime(round((substring_index(substring_index(`base_name`.`store`.`value`,'"time"',':',-(1)),'}',1) /
1000),0)) AS `datepub`,substring_index(substr(`base_name`.`store`.`value`,10),'"',"userId":'",1) AS
`txtchat`,substring_index(substring_index(`base_name`.`store`.`value`,'userId":'",-(1)),'"',"time',1) AS `autorid` from
`base_name`.`store` where (`base_name`.`store`.`key` like '%chat%') order by
substring_index(substring_index(`base_name`.`store`.`key`,':',2),':',-
(1)),cast(substring_index(substring_index(`base_name`.`store`.`key`,':',-(1)),':',1) as unsigned)
```

Fig. 5. Extract of the procedure1

- Figure 6 shows the second procedure that performs the query in the database with respect to each type of keyword that has been registered to be compared with the registered messages and to obtain the number of messages that have used at least one keyword as shown in the following algorithm called FindKeyWord.

```
Procedimiento FindKeyWord()
$group[]= #group to find
foreach($db->query('select upper(keyword) as keyword, type_kw from indicators WHERE type_kw =
"PARAMETER"') as $row) {
$keyword = $row['keyword'];
        foreach($db->query('select * from NewTable where padid ="'.$padid2[0].'gr'.$group[$x].'"    and
upper(txtchat) like _utf8 "%'.$keyword.'%" COLLATE utf8_general_ci ') as $row2) {
        $counter = $counter + 1;
        }
}
```

Fig. 6. Extract of the procedure 2

3.2 Indicator Display Module

This module displays the monitoring indicators in the collaborative tool [8]. This module graphically shows the interaction of the participants in the chat, forum and collaborative text editor.

As mentioned above, the module is based on a set of keywords defined in the tracking indicators. This tool allows displaying through a dashboard and a graphical representation, the indicators that participate in the follow-up of the collaborative work.

The algorithmic rules used by the module were established from the keywords selected in the interaction during the collaborative work process. In this way, each keyword is classified in the corresponding indicator, to later visualize them graphically. Figure 7 represents the process.

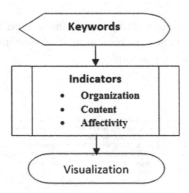

Fig. 7. Workflow

In the teacher's application, it will allow the monitoring of the entire class of a particular subject, they will also be able to select and supervise a particular student. And in the student application, it will allow students to monitor their participation in the collaborative activity, promoting self-assessment of the learning process.

The application offers a web interface that shows the interactions graphically in three tools: chat, forum and the collaborative text editor (it incorporates a chat). The follow-up of the activities is shown for each group of students with an indicator of the interaction carried out in the collaborative work.

In Fig. 8, a dynamic graph of the students' contribution to the collaborative chat activity is presented. This shows the number of messages sent by each student.

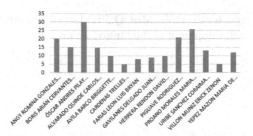

Fig. 8. Number of messages sent in the chat

Figure 9 shows the number of messages sent in the chat by each student considering the keywords grouped in each of the message categories (organization, content and affectivity).

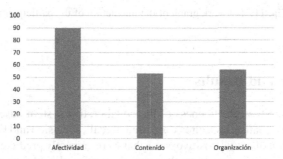

Fig. 9. Chat contributions by type of message

In the case of the forum, the progress of the activity will be displayed graphically in a similar way to the chat. On the other hand, in the Etherpad tool, the progress of the activities can be visualized graphically, one concerning the built-in chat and the other about collaborative writing. The forum and Etherpad charts are based on the indicators described.

Fig. 10 shows a graph that allows visualizing the number of contributions of the students in the collaborative activities, considering the three tools.

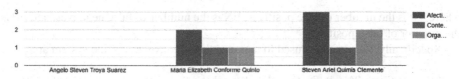

Fig. 10. Number of contributions by student

Figure 11 shows the analysis of group work in the collaborative activity in the collaborative editor through a network graph that reflects each group's composition and interaction. The graph shows each member with their initials and the interactions carried out by each stage, for example, MECQ:59 (Maria Elizabeth Accord Quinto) with 59 interactions for the development of the "Introduction".

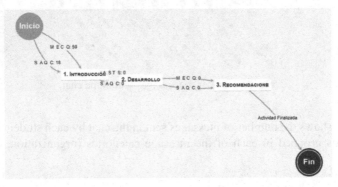

Fig. 11. Network graph of the interaction of the participants

4 Evaluation and Results

In order to evaluate the effectiveness of the collaborative system based on monitoring indicators, three evaluation measures were used: Recall, Precision and F-measure. Recall (1) is the proportion of actual positive cases that were correctly predicted as such. On the other hand, Precision (2) represents the proportion of predicted positive cases that are true positives. Finally, F-measure (3) is a single weighted value of precision and recall [16].

$$Recall = \frac{TP}{TP + FN} \tag{1}$$

$$Precision = \frac{TP}{TP + FP} \tag{2}$$

$$\text{F} - \text{measure} = 2 * \frac{Precision * Recall}{Precision + Recall} \tag{3}$$

where TP is the number of true positives, FN is the number of false negatives, and FP is the number of false positives.

Specifically, the variables used to measure the effectiveness of the system are:

- True positives. The indicators that have been correctly identified in the system interaction.
- False positives. Indicators that were correctly identified but are not indicator keywords in the system.
- False negatives. Indicators that were not identified as errors, but are correct keywords by indicator.

The experiments were carried out in the virtual classroom with the address http://62.171.142.126/index.php (Fig. 12), on the administrator host a collaborative indicator detection system was installed. This system supervises all the interactions of the chat, forum and online editor tools presented through the collaborative system in graphic form.

The collaborative system extracts data through data mining and text mining for the case of the online editor to display the statistical graphs, however, due to the complexity of synchronous tools such as chat and online editor, some of the data displayed could get lost when making the graphic representation. To improve the algorithms of the system, the evaluation of the indicators was carried out as it is an essential point in the follow-up of collaborative work. Once all the failures were detected, they were evaluated with the metrics described above to measure the system's effectiveness.

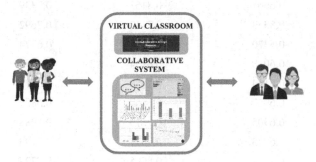

Fig. 12. Collaborative system evaluation

The effectiveness of the system proposed in the present work was evaluated considering a population of 160 students corresponding to 56% male (90) while 44% female (70), from the third year of Hideyo Noguchi Highschool in the city of Guayaquil. 20 groups were participating and using the system indicators interchangeably, generating a total of 1,376 interactions.

As seen in Table 1, there is a variety of results in the groups due to the different interactions that the students presented within the collaborative tool. In addition, the ages of the students, regardless of gender, ranged between 16 and 17 years and their mechanism of writing and expression vary in the use of keywords in the system.

However, in the first column (Precision), the results are mostly higher than 50%, except for group 6, which presents 28.6% use of the indicators in the collaborative tool and with a value (Recall) that represents 71.4%, which are the responses that have been quickly and correctly identified. The average result obtained from the 20 groups provides essential information regarding the functioning of the collaborative activity monitoring system using the different indicators proposed. In the column Precision, the result is 63.25% referring to the use of the indicators, in the column Recall the result is 75.27% which refers to the proper identification of the indicators and demonstrating the importance of relating the two previous metrics, column F-measure provides a value of 67,94%.

Table 1. Evaluation of system results

Test	Precision	Recall	F-measure
1	0,7143	0,8333	0,7692
2	0,6000	0,8000	0,6667
3	0,6000	0,8000	0,7273
4	0,3000	0,8000	0,4598
5	0,5000	0,7500	0,6000
6	0,2857	0,7143	0,4082
7	0,6364	0,6364	0,6364
8	0,6667	0,8163	0,7339
9	0,8333	0,7143	0,7692
10	0,5370	0,7838	0,6374
11	0,6038	0,6154	0,6095
12	0,6154	0,7059	0,6575
13	0,6957	0,6667	0,6809
14	0,6905	0,7073	0,6988
15	0,6923	0,7377	0,7143
16	0,7391	0,8095	0,7727
17	0,8182	0,8571	0,8372
18	0,6744	0,7436	0,7073
19	0,6596	0,7209	0,6889
20	0,7872	0,8409	0,8132
AVG	0,6325	0,7527	0,6794

5 Conclusions and Future Work

This work presents the analysis of a collaborative system based on monitoring indicators that provides teachers and students with visualization [17] of the collaborative monitoring indicators based on the mirroring strategy [18].

The general operation of this system is based on taking the interactions carried out by teachers and students through the forum and chat of the collaborative platform. Furthermore, this solution was established based on the experience of experts in the online educational area.

The system was evaluated to measure its efficiency and effectiveness in terms of displaying the indicators in graphic mode. The results obtained are encouraging because the values fitted the tests carried out.

Despite all the advantages and characteristics offered by the collaborative system, it presents some limitations that must be addressed in future works. For example, the online editor module corresponds to an open-source tool and was integrated into the system using the Etherpad application, therefore it consumes hardware resources through a VPS (Virtual Private Server), and also implies an additional monetary cost. Therefore, it is important to explore other tools or APIs [19] that can be easily integrated into the collaborative system.

On the other hand, the interactions were carried out in an environment related to a collaborative system, however, to obtain a broad perspective of monitoring collaborative activities, the indicators could be implemented through an LMS.

Finally, the presented system focuses its work locally, limiting its evaluations to a particular academic scenario, for this reason it is important to carry out new experiences in the follow-up of collaborative activities based on Artificial Intelligence [20] that contribute to the management and visualization so that the teacher can make timely decisions in the training process of the students.

References

1. Kaendler, C., Wiedmann, M., Leuders, T., Rummel, N., Spada, H.: Monitoring student interaction during collaborative learning: design and evaluation of a training program for pre-service teachers. Psychol. Learn. Teach. **15**(1), 44–64 (2016). https://doi.org/10.1177/1475725716638010

2. Al-Samarraie, H., Saeed, N.: A systematic review of cloud computing tools for collaborative learning: opportunities and challenges to the blended-learning environment. Comput. Educ. **124**, 77–91 (2018). https://doi.org/10.1016/J.COMPEDU.2018.05.016

3. Mangaroska, K., Sharma, K., Giannakos, M., Trætteberg, H., Dillenbourg, P.: Gaze insights into debugging behavior using learner-centred analysis. In: ACM International Conference Proceeding Series, pp. 350–359 (2018). https://doi.org/10.1145/3170358.3170386

4. Dimitracopoulou, A: Computer based interaction analysis supporting self-regulation: achievements and prospects of an emerging research field. Technol. Instr. Cogn. Learn. **6**(4), 291–314 (2009)

5. Mangaroska, K., Giannakos, M.: Learning analytics for learning design: towards evidence-driven decisions to enhance learning. In: Lavoué, É., Drachsler, H., Verbert, K., Broisin, J., Pérez-Sanagustín, M. (eds.) EC-TEL 2017. LNCS, vol. 10474, pp. 428–433. Springer, Cham (2017). https://doi.org/10.1007/978-3-319-66610-5_38

6. Goulden, M.C., et al.: CCVis: visual analytics of student online learning behaviors using course clickstream data. Electron. Imaging **31**(1), 681-1–681-12 (2019). https://doi.org/10.2352/ISSN.2470-1173.2019.1.VDA-681

7. Aljohani, N.R., Daud, A., Abbasi, R.A., Alowibdi, J.S., Basheri, M., Aslam, M.A.: An integrated framework for course adapted student learning analytics dashboard. Comput. Hum. Behav. **92**, 679–690 (2019). https://doi.org/10.1016/J.CHB.2018.03.035

8. Vásquez-Bermúdez, M., Sanz, C., Zangara, M.A., Hidalgo, J.: Visualization tools for collaborative systems: a systematic review. In: Valencia-García, R., Bucaram-Leverone, M., Del Cioppo-Morstadt, J., Vera-Lucio, N., Jácome-Murillo, E. (eds.) CITI 2021. CCIS, vol. 1460, pp. 107–122. Springer, Cham (2021). https://doi.org/10.1007/978-3-030-88262-4_8

9. Brahim, B., Lotfi, A.: A traces based system helping to assess knowledge level in e-learning system. J. King Saud Univ. Comput. Inf. Sci. **32**(8), 977–986 (2020). https://doi.org/10.1016/j.jksuci.2018.10.008

10. Agredo Delgado, V., Ruiz, P.H., Collazos, C.A., Fardoun, H.M., Noaman, A.Y.: Software tool to support the improvement of the collaborative learning process. In: Solano, A., Ordoñez, H. (eds.) CCC 2017. CCIS, vol. 735, pp. 442–454. Springer, Cham (2017). https://doi.org/10.1007/978-3-319-66562-7_32

11. Vásquez-Bermúdez, M., Sanz, C., Zangara, M.A., Hidalgo, J.: Mirroring tools and interaction indicators in collaborative work: a systematic review. In: Valencia-García, R., Alcaraz-Marmol, G., Del Cioppo-Morstadt, J., Vera-Lucio, N., Bucaram-Leverone, M. (eds.) CITI 2020. CCIS, vol. 1309, pp. 179–192. Springer, Cham (2020). https://doi.org/10.1007/978-3-030-62015-8_14

12. Etherpad. https://etherpad.org/. Accessed 22 Jan 2022

13. Lazonder, A.W., Wilhelm, P., Ootes, S.A.W.: Using sentence openers to foster student interaction in computer-mediated learning environments. Comput. Educ. **41**(3), 291–308 (2003). https://doi.org/10.1016/S0360-1315(03)00050-2

14. Yanacón-Atía, D., Costaguta, R., De Los, M., Menini, A.: Indicadores colaborativos individuales y grupales para Moodle Individual and group collaborative indicators for Moodle. Available: www.revistacampusvirtuales.es (2018). Accessed 02 Mar 2021

15. Zangara, M.A., Sanz, C.: Trabajo colaborativo mediado por tecnología informática en espacios educativos. Metodología de seguimiento y su validación Collaborative work mediated by computer technology in educational spaces. Monitoring methodology and its validation Esta obra se distribuye bajo Licencia Creative Commons CC-BY-NC 4.0 Resumen. Rev. Iberoam. Tecnol. en Educ. y Educ. en Tecnol. **25**, 8–20 (2020). https://doi.org/10.24215/18509959.25.e01

16. Powers, D.M.W.: Evaluation: from precision, recall and F-measure to ROC, informedness, markedness and correlation. Available: https://arxiv.org/abs/2010.16061v1 (2020). Accessed: 13 Feb 2022

17. Calvani, A., Fini, A., Molino, M., Ranieri, M.: Visualizing and monitoring effective interactions in online collaborative groups. Br. J. Educ. Technol. **41**(2), 213–226 (2010). https://doi.org/10.1111/J.1467-8535.2008.00911.X

18. Zangara, A., Sanz, C.: Visualización del proceso colaborativo como metaconocimiento. Descripción de una estrategia de mirroring y sus resultados (2017)

19. Cho, B., Ng, A., Sun, C.: CoVim: incorporating real-time collaboration capabilities into comprehensive text editors. In: Proc. 2017 IEEE 21st Int. Conf. Comput. Support. Coop. Work Des. CSCWD 2017, pp. 192–197 (2017). https://doi.org/10.1109/CSCWD.2017.8066693

20. Chen, X., Zou, D., Xie, H., Cheng, G., Liu, C.: Two decades of artificial intelligence in education: contributors, collaborations, research topics, challenges, and future directions. Educ. Technol. Soc. **25**(1) (2022)

IoT Monitoring for Real-Time Control of Industrial Processes

Manuel Ayala-Chauvin[1]([⊠]) [iD], Pedro Escudero[2] [iD], Patricio Lara-Alvarez[2] [iD],
and Carles Domènech-Mestres[3] [iD]

[1] Centro de Investigaciones de Ciencias Humanas y de la Educación (CICHE), Universidad
Indoamérica, Ambato 180103, Ecuador
mayala5@indoamerica.edu.ec

[2] Carrera de Ingeniería Industrial, Facultad de Ingeniería y Tecnologías de la Información y la
Comunicación, Universidad Indoamérica, Ambato 180103, Ecuador
pescudero2@indoamerica.edu.ec, patolara@uti.edu.ec

[3] Centro de Diseño de Equipos Industriales, Universitat Politècnica de Catalunya-Barcelona
Tech, 08034 Barcelona, Spain
domenech@cdei.upc.edu

Abstract. Today's industries require monitoring and control of all manufacturing processes. Computer integrated manufacturing (CIM) systems provide a framework for integrating production systems. In this regard, the Internet of things (IoT) has rapidly evolved to digitize and interconnect devices in industrial processes. However, to achieve the integration of a complete system implies high costs in software and hardware, which limits its penetration in medium and low size industries. For this reason, this project proposes the creation of a low-cost IoT platform whose objective is to monitor and analyze both physical and electrical parameters of an industrial process in real-time. To achieve this objective, the software and hardware specifications were defined and characterized, the conceptual design and detail of the prototype were made, and finally, the materialization was carried out. The platform was structured in two parts, a web video supervision module with a continuous monitoring camera ESP32-CAM and an interface that integrates the sensors that measure the physical and electrical variables of the environment. The experimental results show the effectiveness of the proposed system in a practical machining application on a CNC machine. With the data coming from the sensors, a database was generated to analyze and create temperature versus cutting speed control models to monitor the manufacturing process. Tests were performed on several materials, and the mathematical model of the system behavior was determined for each material in order to monitor and visualize the performance in the machining process. Finally, the cost of the project complies with the specifications proposed.

Keywords: IoT monitoring · Real-time control · Industrial process

R. Valencia-García et al. (Eds.): CITI 2022, CCIS 1658, pp. 203–213, 2022.
https://doi.org/10.1007/978-3-031-19961-5_15

1   Introduction

1.1   Background

In the last decade, a challenge for researchers has been to unify industrial systems under a common infrastructure based on the Internet of Things (IoT) [1]. This infrastructure provides control options for the systems and real-time information that optimizes production times [2]. In recent years a wide range of industrial applications based on IoT has been developed and implemented [3]. In this sense, the ease of integrating wireless, mobile devices, and low-cost sensors has helped the development of the IoT-based industrial ecosystem [4].

Industrial environments are becoming more competitive, so it is necessary to make an innovative, technical, organizational, and financial effort to ensure viability. In this sense, the Flexible Manufacturing Systems (FMS) is a domain that has progressed and offers the ability to make all systems communicate through the Industrial Internet of Things (IIoT) [5, 6].

Data is a critical factor in integrated IIoT solutions. In this regard, the new machinery can integrate and manage data streams within the cloud-based Internet of Things (IoT) platform. Therefore, high-performance processing will be significant in manufacturing processes [7].

Bernardos et al. showed that industrial automation and manufacturing, the Industrial Internet of Things (IIoT), is the next step of the industrial revolution where precision machining takes prominence as the requirements and demand for high-quality products and manufacturing tolerances with shorter lead times increase. Therefore, developing innovative approaches and methodologies makes IIoT a suitable platform [8].

Today, industries and individuals have made the Internet of Things (IoT) an integral part of everyday life. This platform enables devices and sensors to be detected, connected and controlled remotely at a meager cost. Many sensors, such as temperature, pressure, vibration, sound, and light, can be used in industrial processes and the residential environment with robustness [9].

Several researchers have investigated the effect of digitization on production processes and the possibilities of optimizing them, with IoT being considered the most widely used tool among other technologies [10]. However, the high cost of their implementation limits their widespread application in small and medium-sized enterprises [11].

The IoT's technical challenges after its implementation are yet to be determined, including modeling and data analysis of the systems to optimize processes. For this, it is necessary to generate the operating curves of the processes, model them and monitor them in real-time to make decisions [12]. In addition, research problems and challenges are discussed, considering trends in 5G communications and edge computing [13].

1.2   Related Works

One of the challenges facing the manufacturing industry is to improve productivity and process efficiency. Reducing downtime due to machine failure is a significant objective. Royandi et al. have developed an IoT system using open source platforms such as the

Arduino microcontroller [14]. Siddhartha et al.'s work has developed a similar platform where he presents a multi-sensor-based availability and condition monitoring system implemented on a CNC machine [15]. Kovalev et al. have progressed with augmented reality applications in manufacturing processes [16]. However, modeling the machine in operation under load to determine the operating curve has not been performed. This model will allow real-time control of the physical variables of the manufacturing process.

In this paper, we present the implementation of a low-cost IoT platform to monitor and analyze an industrial process's physical and electrical parameters in real-time. Through an analytical study of the operating curve. For this purpose, we started with an analysis of requirements to design a versatile system able to be easily mounted on any equipment. A compact system was implemented, including external terminals to connect sensors (Temperature, Humidity, Fume) and video. Tests of connectivity and the limits of detection of sensors were performed to characterize the system. The system was evaluated by monitoring the work of a computer numerical control (CNC) while mechanizing materials of different types.

2   Method

Within the framework of this research, the software and hardware specifications were defined and characterized, the conceptual design was carried out, and then the prototype was implemented in detail. The data obtained by the sensors and the camera are displayed through the Blynk platform [17], which facilitates monitoring and portable control. Finally, the modeling of the system was performed, where an appropriate mathematical model was found that expresses the relationship between the cutting speed and the temperature of the work cabin. Figure 1 shows the flowchart method.

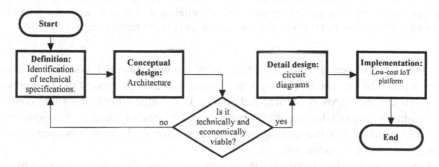

Fig. 1. Flowchart method.

The principle of the solution has been generated in conceptual design, considering requirements and specifications, including mechanical, electrical, and electronic schematics. The specifications have been determined based on the real needs of a manufacturing company. In addition, an application has been created to monitor the machining process variables in real-time and store these data in a database.

2.1 Architecture

The platform was structured in two parts, a web video supervision module with an Arduino ESP32-CAM [18]; continuous monitoring camera, and an interface that integrates the sensors that measure the physical and electrical variables of the environment, as seen in Fig. 2.

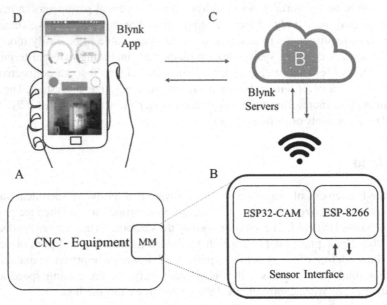

Fig. 2. Diagram of architecture, A) CNC where is mounted the monitoring system, B) Monitoring system modular structure and information flow, C) wireless data flow between the monitoring system and Blynk servers, D) Blynk app for portable and remote monitoring.

For the experimental validation of the proposed work, the IoT system was implemented in a CNC machine. This system was encapsulated to prevent electromagnetic compatibility and exposure to heat and smoke. In addition, shock-absorbing contacts were installed to avoid damage due to continuous vibrations typical of the operation of the CNC machine. The monitoring and data acquisition (IoT) system is open-sourced through the use of RStudio Software.

Figure 3 shows the electronic circuit that constitutes the sensor interface by and Arduino ESP-8266 [19], the video streaming module ESP32 CAM, and the ports that connect sensors, led indicators, power feeding, and programming jumpers.

The ESP32-CAM allows the streaming in real-time by a small VGA camera. An FTDI programmer is necessary to upload the code to this module. The ESP-8266 module controls the data from the sensors of temperature (DHT11 dual sensor temperature and humidity) [20], and fume (MQ2 gas sensor for smoke, butane, propane, methane, alcohol, hydrogen, and carbon monoxide concentrations until 10000 ppm.) [21].

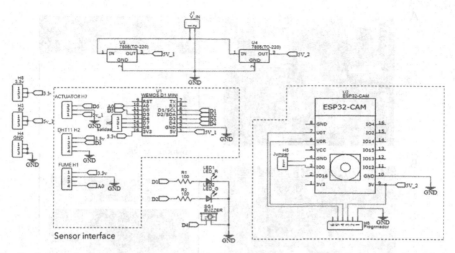

Fig. 3. Schematic electronic circuit that includes the sensor interface and streaming in real-time by a small camera.

Both modules are programmed by basic Arduino code and by the simple configuration of the local wireless network SSID and password, and the Blynk application interface visualizes the data in a user terminal.

Figure 4A shows the initial prototype that includes the sensor interface, the camera module, and ports for individual sensor connection and power feeding. All the elements are mounted in a handmade single-face PCB. The system was encapsulated in a 5 mm thick polymeric case. The structure helps to isolate the system from possible flying residues when the CNC is under operation. The system encapsulated was mounted on the lateral side of CNC, as shown in Fig. 4B, and the temperature and fume sensors were mounted close to the milling rotor to monitor the mechanization process.

As shown in Fig. 4C, the Blynk application was configured in a standard smartphone, previously signed up with a username and password in the app, and for Blynk cloud on the website. The user dashboard was created by adding widgets for each sensor and for the camera streaming. For the sensors, two gauges were added, one for monitoring temperature and the other one for fume. The data from humidity was shown by a value display widget. The widgets were set to display data for one-second intervals. For the camera was added a video streaming element and configured with the IP address assigned for the local network. Additionally, two LEDs were added to indicate the low and high levels of fume in the CNC camera; values previously established with the results of the CNC operation tests.

A flowchart was defined in order to control the operation process of the system Fig. 5, being able to manage the connectivity, and the individual process when the system starts. The connectivity includes the connection to the Blynk server and the user application.

Blynk server was configured to monitor the physical variables for each second, and the data from sensors was captured in working periods of one minute. Continuous experimental tests were performed in order to evaluate the sensors' reading, including variations in temperature, humidity, and fume. The variations were added to the standard

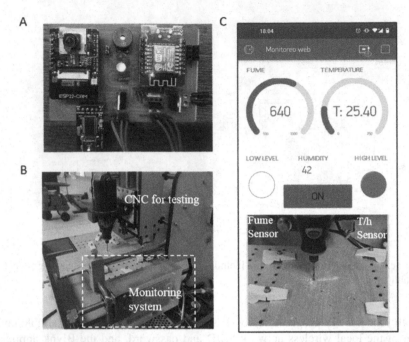

Fig. 4. System prototype, A) System mounted in the PCB, B) System mounted in a testing CNC, C) Blynk interface design for the variable monitoring.

material mechanization in the CNC while working with wood, copper, and carbon steel. These variations include the sensor exposition to external fume, water vapor, and hot wind.

These experiments serve us to define the limits of detection prior to activating the alarms, evaluate the detection range of sensors, and define the strategic position to install in the CNC.

No finite element method (FEM) simulations of gasses diffusion were done in this work. The data analyzed was totally experimental.

3　Results

The effectiveness of the proposed system has been demonstrated in a practical machining application on a CNC machine. With the data from the sensors, a database was generated. The analysis of the data series allowed to generate models that express the relationship between shear rate and temperature. Tests were carried out on various materials, and the mathematical model of the system's behavior was determined. This allowed monitoring and visualizing the operation in the machining process in real-time. In addition, the control adjusts the model curve with the real data; this allows alarms to be generated when values are outside the operating range.

10 tests were performed for each cutting speed and type of material, for a total of 100 samples per model. Abrasions of 0.2 mm were made in 10 probes with dimensions

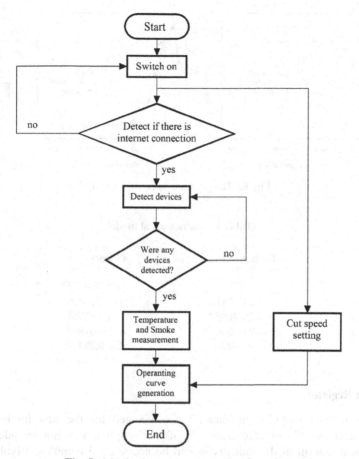

Fig. 5. Monitoring system operation flow chart

of 50 × 50 mm. The cutting conditions were: Cutting speed Vc = 0 to 1500 m/min; Feed rate, Va = 1000 mm/min; cutting depth, ap = 0.2 mm and cutting width, ae = 1 mm.

Figure 6 shows the results of the experiments with carbon steel and copper. Table 1 shows the analytical study of the operating curve for each material.

The curve fitting of the system was performed with two materials. It was determined the appropriate model that expresses the relationship between the cutting speed and the temperature inside the work cabin. The curve fitting refers to finding an appropriate mathematical model that describes the relationship between a dependent variable *y*, which represents the temperature, and the independent variable *x*, which represents the shear rate. These results correspond to analyzes carried out in the literature on temperature variations at different cutting speeds for ferrous and non-ferrous materials [22]. This fitting was achieved by estimating the values of its parameters using nonlinear regression. These experimental results contribute to condition of the system in order to generate alarm signals in the case of anomalous events of the system in regular operation.

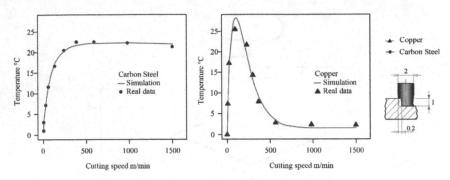

Fig. 6. Temperature vs cutting speed.

Table 1. Mathematical model

	Carbon steel	Copper
Formula	$y \approx a - b^{-cx^d}$	$y \approx (a + bx)^{-cx} + d$
Parameters	a = 27.17416 b = 29.76957 c = 0.09206 d = 0.44889	a = 1.16599 b = 0.82798 c = 0.01898 d = 0.88170

3.1 Cost Register

The costs register included in Table 2 was planned for the first implementation of the system as a Proof of concept (Blynk subscription was not included). For a final implementation in the industry would be necessary a complete Blynk package subscription.

Table 2. Manufacturing costs

Element	Total cost
Camera	$7.50
Structural components	$10.00
Electronic components	$40.00
Human labor	$40.00
Blynk basic platform subscription	$00.00
Total	$97.50

The manufacturing costs approximately 100,00 dollars for the first monitoring system prototype. The costs for elements were considered from the local final public price for each individual element.

4 Discussion

The information captured by the Blynk server was corroborated with the information visualized for the Blynk application and the real process in the CNC. The time of response also helps us to define whether to call real-time monitoring or fast monitoring. The IoT facilitates the monitoring in real-time, but this concept includes the management of short times close to one second of latency. For control of industrial equipment that needs response times of less than one second would be difficult to take actions before a failure or stoppage event, even if the actions are automatic. For monitoring, the management of these times lapses is enough to make a decision such as stop or continue the equipment process; that is why we also considered a real-time monitoring system for this work. Similar implementations were reported as real-time monitoring using cloud-based platforms [15, 23–25].

The fume sensor mounted close to the rotor tool was established prior analyzed the propagation of the fume Fig. 4C. Materials such as acrylic, methacrylate, Teflon produces minimum fume while mechanization. Compared with wood or metallic derivatives, the tool heat increases the fume while working, especially when drilling wood continuously. The temperature sensor was mounted as proximate as possible to the cutting tool to monitor the temperature of the CNC cabin and the tool temperature. Most of the cutting tools break when the temperature is high. The application detects when the tool temperatures rise the limits and activate the alarms to stop the system while the cutting tool is cooled.

The evaluation performed in our system was experimental in a controlled laboratory environment. The evaluation in an industrial environment would include monitoring for long hours of equipment working. The Blynk server allows us to perform this type of tracking by the server storage capacity. It also depends on the subscription type; perhaps it would be needed the support of the storage in the cloud or external physical storage. In this work was used a basic free Blynk plan with data available only for one week. However, this was enough to evaluate most of the conditions of the monitoring system.

Even the Arduino technology allows us the plug-and-play of sensors, for our implementation is recommendable to stop the system because the sensors are installed in the mobile part of the CNC. Nevertheless, the plug-and-play allows installation in fixed parts without losing connection with the Blynk server.

The monitoring system allows the migration to other equipment without the need for extra adaptations. The IoT system needs to install the sensors in a strategic position and place the system in a secure equipment place. This portability characteristic allows using the monitor system in different equipment to be used as a portable tester system.

5 Conclusions

This paper presents a practical approach to integrating the IoT systems to monitor industrial equipment. The proposed systems allow the advantages of a versatile system able to be adapted to a variety of industrial equipment. The system allows the integration of sensors to monitor the working process with the advantages of IoT systems.

The project's cost complies with the exposed specifications, and the approach proposed in the platform can be used in future installations of companies that need to control industrial processes. Finally, being a flexible system, it is replicable, and in the future, active control functions in the architecture can be implemented into the preventive maintenance system to avoid stoppages due to failures. Specific functionalities can also be added with more sensors and updating the control code without the need for significant modifications. The system also facilitates the plug-and-play of sensors, which means that sensing elements can be updated without needing to reboot the system, allowing high availability of the system.

6 Future Scope

Several improvements could be made to the monitoring system. These improvements includes but no limited to.

- A detailed analysis of the data acquired by sensors could be used to train mathematical models, in order to implement predictive controls in the equipment.
- A best montage of sensors on the equipment could help to alert also possible errors in the mechanization process (proof movements, alignment displacements, cutting tool breaking…).
- Add a thermal camera to monitor the heat of cutting tools helps to control working process to avoid equipment stops for tool braked.

The system modification could have minimal affectation in the final cost of the system, keeping the low-cost and system performance.

References

1. Rudra, B., Verma, A., Verma, S., Shrestha, B.: Futuristic Research Trends and Applications of Internet of Things. CRC Press, Boca Raton (2022)
2. Madakam, S., Lake, V., Lake, V., Lake, V.: Internet of Things (IoT): a literature review. J. Comput. Commun. **3**, 164 (2015). https://doi.org/10.4236/jcc.2015.35021
3. Xu, L.D., He, W., Li, S.: Internet of Things in industries: a survey. IEEE Trans. Ind. Inf. **10**, 2233–2243 (2014). https://doi.org/10.1109/TII.2014.2300753
4. Varela-Aldás, J., Pilla, J., Andaluz, V.H., Palacios-Navarro, G.: Commercial entry control using robotic mechanism and mobile application for COVID-19 pandemic. In: Gervasi, O., et al. (eds.) Computational Science and Its Applications, vol. 12957, pp. 3–14. Springer, Cham (2021). https://doi.org/10.1007/978-3-030-87013-3_1
5. Cronin, C., Conway, A., Walsh, J.: Flexible manufacturing systems using IIoT in the automotive sector. Procedia Manuf. **38**, 1652–1659 (2019). https://doi.org/10.1016/j.promfg.2020.01.119
6. Jaidka, H., Sharma, N., Singh, R.: Evolution of IoT to IIoT: applications and challenges (2020). https://papers.ssrn.com/abstract=3603739, https://doi.org/10.2139/ssrn.3603739
7. Haghnegahdar, L., Joshi, S.S., Dahotre, N.B.: From IoT-based cloud manufacturing approach to intelligent additive manufacturing: industrial Internet of Things—an overview. Int. J. Adv. Manuf. Technol. **119**, 1461–1478 (2021). https://doi.org/10.1007/s00170-021-08436-x
8. Benardos, P.G., Vosniakos, G.C.: Internet of Things and industrial applications for precision machining. Solid State Phenom. **261**, 440–447 (2017). https://doi.org/10.4028/www.scientific.net/SSP.261.440

9. Rahmani, A.M., Bayramov, S., Kiani Kalejahi, B.: Internet of Things applications: opportunities and threats. Wireless Pers. Commun. **122**(1), 451–476 (2021). https://doi.org/10.1007/s11277-021-08907-0

10. Salih, K.O.M., Rashid, T.A., Radovanovic, D., Bacanin, N.: A comprehensive survey on the Internet of Things with the industrial marketplace. Sensors **22**, 730 (2022). https://doi.org/10.3390/s22030730

11. Xing, K., Liu, X., Liu, Z., Mayer, J.R.R., Achiche, S.: Low-cost precision monitoring system of machine tools for SMEs. Procedia CIRP **96**, 347–352 (2021). https://doi.org/10.1016/j.procir.2021.01.098

12. Kalsoom, T., et al.: Impact of IoT on manufacturing industry 4.0: a new triangular systematic review. Sustainability **13**, 12506 (2021). https://doi.org/10.3390/su132212506

13. Mao, W., Zhao, Z., Chang, Z., Min, G., Gao, W.: Energy-efficient industrial Internet of Things: overview and open issues. IEEE Trans. Ind. Inf. **17**, 7225–7237 (2021). https://doi.org/10.1109/TII.2021.3067026

14. Royandi, M.A., Hung, J.-P.: Design of an affordable IoT-based monitoring system for versatile application in machine tool. In: 2021 17th International Conference on Quality in Research (QIR): International Symposium on Electrical and Computer Engineering, pp. 76–80 (2021). https://doi.org/10.1109/QIR54354.2021.9716199

15. Siddhartha, B., Chavan, A.P., HD, G.K., Subramanya, K.N.: IoT enabled real-time availability and condition monitoring of CNC machines. In: 2020 IEEE International Conference on Internet of Things and Intelligence System (IoTaIS), pp. 78–84 (2021). https://doi.org/10.1109/IoTaIS50849.2021.9359698

16. Kovalev, I., Nezhmetdinov, R., Kvashnin, D.: Development of a mobile application for training operators to work with machine tools with CNC systems using augmented reality. In: 2021 International Russian Automation Conference (RusAutoCon), pp. 863–867 (2021). https://doi.org/10.1109/RusAutoCon52004.2021.9537320

17. Blynk group: Blynk IoT platform: for businesses and developers. https://blynk.io/. Accessed 10 Aug 2022

18. ESP32-CAM Video Streaming and Face Recognition with Arduino IDE|Random Nerd Tutorials. https://randomnerdtutorials.com/esp32-cam-video-streaming-face-recognition-arduino-ide/. Accessed 10 Aug 2022

19. Arduino ESP8266: ESP8266 Arduino Core's documentation. https://arduino-esp8266.readthedocs.io/en/latest/. Accessed 10 Aug 2022

20. DHT11-Datasheet: Digital-output relative humidity & temperature sensor/module – DHT (2022). https://image.dfrobot.com/image/data/KIT0003/DHT11%20datasheet.pdf

21. Hanwei Electronics group: MQ-2 Gas Sensor (2022). https://www.mouser.com/datasheet/2/321/605-00008-MQ-2-Datasheet-370464.pdf

22. Zhu, K.: Modeling of the machining process. In: Zhu, K. (ed.) Smart Machining Systems: Modelling, Monitoring and Informatics, pp. 19–70. Springer, Cham (2022). https://doi.org/10.1007/978-3-030-87878-8_2

23. Saez, M., Maturana, F.P., Barton, K., Tilbury, D.M.: Real-time manufacturing machine and system performance monitoring using Internet of Things. IEEE Trans. Autom. Sci. Eng. **15**, 1735–1748 (2018). https://doi.org/10.1109/TASE.2017.2784826

24. Raju, H.S., Shenoy, S.: Real-time remote monitoring and operation of industrial devices using IoT and cloud. In: 2016 2nd International Conference on Contemporary Computing and Informatics (IC3I), pp. 324–329 (2016). https://doi.org/10.1109/IC3I.2016.7917983

25. Gan, S., Li, K., Wang, Y., Cameron, C.: IoT based energy consumption monitoring platform for industrial processes. In: 2018 UKACC 12th International Conference on Control (CONTROL). pp. 236–240 (2018). https://doi.org/10.1109/CONTROL.2018.8516828

Metric Identification Evaluating Security Information: A Systematic Literature Review

Daisy Imbaquingo-Esparza[1,2](✉), Javier Díaz[1], Silvia Arciniega[2], José Jácome[2], and MacArthur Ortega-Bustamante[1,2]

[1] Universidad Nacional de La Plata, Buenos Aires, Argentina
daisy.imbaquingoe@info.unlp.edu.ar
[2] Universidad Técnica del Norte, Ibarra, Ecuador

Abstract. Metrics for the evaluation of information security basically contribute to risk reduction within organizations dealing with the manipulation of information. However, in information security metric approach, generally there is not a standard classified appreciation regarding essential metrics within the required scope to do this activity in risk reduction and asset protection. Therefore, this research is a Systematic Literature Review (SLR) regarding the evaluation of information security. In this study, 50 bibliographical data-base extracted articles such as ScienceDirect, Scopus, IEEE, ACM Digital Library, Hindawi, MDPI and Springer were gathered and analyzed. Scientific documents answered the proposed research question whereas results identified several information security metric classifications such as integrity, vulnerability, authorization and confidentiality.

Keywords: Information security · Metrics · Security · Cyber-security

1 Introduction

As time goes by, information security has become crucial within the financial system scope, the industry circle and the general public since "financial losses not only pose a risk, but also legal recovery and reputation" (Diesch et al. 2020). A clear example is that: "At present, totally rely on information such as financial data so that Banks remain the market and remain competitive as well." (Diesch et al. 2020). The question about information security is raised, which is at the same time, based on a highly efficient authorization/authentication system in order to have access to databases from a particular organization containing personal, sensible and valuable information for commercial interests (Ma 2021).

On the other hand, "The Internet of things (IoT), information security is regarded as not only to cryptography, secure communication, privacy guarantee, but also to security professional's protective behavior." (Ma 2021). As a consequence, security trained professionals should take into account different situations that may risk privacy like security gaps among others, so that they are capable of providing optimum system security services. Information security from an organization depends more and more on attitudes and activities performed by they own IT security experts who should be sufficiently

R. Valencia-García et al. (Eds.): CITI 2022, CCIS 1658, pp. 214–231, 2022.
https://doi.org/10.1007/978-3-031-19961-5_16

trained to gather, analyze and use data, in addition to acting responsibly by protecting user data which they have access to and committing themselves to safeguarding it in a reliable way. According to some studies, one of the main reasons for security failures is the fact that, security professionals are the most vulnerable link in the security chain. For instance, between March and October 2016 an IT expert from Zhaopin, a well- known Internet Company in China sold more than 155.000 personal information elements within the organization, including home addresses, workplaces and salaries to a technological company based in Beijing. Such act had serious consequences for the organization, economic losses and damage to the company reputation and charges for privacy infringement. Therefore, it would be beneficial for organizations to focus on the emergence of information security behavior as well as organization's members behavior influencing availability, confidentiality and information security integrity (Ma 2021).

To avoid these situations, there are information security programs (InfoSec) helping to slowly evolve technical and human protection aspects, detection, mitigation and recovery from security threats. InfoSec refers to information about practice and organizational strategies able to safeguard information files from a company such as client data, product and sales information (Hassandoust et al. 2021).

As for information security evaluation metrics, they have been classified according to: Authorization. - allowing exclusive access information sources of an organization to authorized consumers. Integrity. - referring to real and accurate information, not modified, making sure that data has not been manipulated or altered by third parties. Confidentiality. - ensures that information is highly safeguarded to prevent it from being disclosed, stolen or sabotaged. Vulnerability. - It may be a failure jeopardizing information; will be explained throughout this study.

The rest of the article is organized as follows: Sect. 2 contains materials and methods describing research design and how it was achieved. Section 3 details results and discussion where the investigation question was answered. Lastly, Sect. 4 conclusions are drawn.

2 Materials y Methods

Descriptive type research aiming to identify information security evaluation metrics. Seven bibliographical databases used: *IEEE Xplore, Springer, ScienceDirect, ACM Digital Library, Hindawi, MDPI and Scopus*. Documents based on the following acceptability parameters were selected: Scientific articles or Q1, Q2 y Q3 quartile reviews published between 2016–2021 (5 last years).

Applied methodology for conducting the research was a revision process presented in Fig. 1 showing 4 phases: (I) Research questions (II) Document search (III) Article selection (IV) Extracting relevant information. Each phase explained as follows:

2.1 Research Question

To conduct this research, a research question was raised (PI) as shown in Table 1, considered a guide for the Literature Systematic Review.

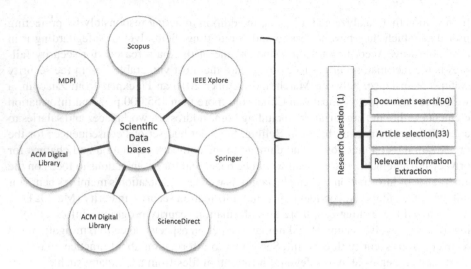

Fig. 1. Search diagram

Table 1. Research questions

N°	Research question	Motivation
PI1	What metrics are made to evaluate information security?	Identify metrics to evaluate Information security

2.2 Document Search

Chains are used to perform document search in bibliographical databases, the selected ones were: (metrics AND security AND evaluation AND information AND OR cybersecurity). Some auxiliary words like computer, network and Key Performance Indicator (KPI), were also used to obtain a higher number of articles from databases.

Table 2 shows search chains and combinations used, considering that each bibliographical data base has varied search criteria. A total of 50 articles were found, 19 are from *ScienceDirect*, 12 from *Scopus*, 11 from *IEEE Xplore*, 5 from *Springer*, 1 from *ACM Digital Library*, 1 from *Hindawi* and1 *MDPI*.

2.3 Article Selection

Two stages for article selection were considered. Phase one- Inclusion and exclusion criteria were taken into account. Inclusion criteria considered by authors: Scientific articles, literature reviews and other indexed articles, relevant for the study. Every article is related to IT, engineering and IT security disciplines published in English for the last 5 years. (2016–2021) Exclusion criteria considered by the authors: (i) Duplicate work (ii) thesis (iii) studies published in other knowledge areas. As for the second phase, metrics classification criteria were considered according to metric type corresponding

Table 2. Metrics AND to AND evaluate AND information AND security

Chain	Artícles
(Metrics AND to AND evaluate AND information AND security)	23
(Cybersecurity AND metrics)	10
(Metrics AND of AND computer AND network AND security)	2
(Evaluation AND metrics AND in AND cybersecurity)	1
(KPI AND cyber AND security)	2
Information AND security AND and AND metrics)	7
(Information AND security)	3
(Computer AND network AND security)	2
TOTAL	**50**

to research approach. "Which metrics are used to evaluate information security? (PI1)". Table 3 shows research documents were ordered by publication year and were initially analyzed by title, abstract and key words.

Table 3. Article selection

Bibliographical databases	Phase I	Phase II
IEEE Xplore	11	7
Springer	5	2
ScienceDirect	19	14
Scopus	12	7
Hindawi	1	1
ACM Digital Library	1	1
MDPI	1	1
Total	50	33

2.4 Data Mining

Table 4 shows 33 selected articles, reviewed and selected by the research team for its respective classification according to research question. More than One-metric articles were grouped into one category with the aim of facilitating result reading.

Article data were obtained considering metrics used for the evaluation of information security in project implementation, services or simulations. 33 articles were categorized corresponding to the research question specifying metrics used and results to evaluate information security.

Table 4. 33 Final scientific articles selected

Code	Title	Bibliographical data bases	Year	Country
A1	"Model-Based Quantitative Network Security Metrics: A Survey"	IEEE Xplore	2017	United States
A2	"Dynamic Security Metrics for Measuring the Effectiveness of Moving Target Defense Techniques"	ScienceDirect	2018	United Kingdom
A3	"A conceptual framework for resilience: fundamental definitions, strategies and metrics"	Springer	2021	United States
A4	"Detection DDoS Attacks and Flash Events using Information Theory Metrics - An Empirical Investigation"	ScienceDirect	2017	The Netherlands
A5	"Technical Privacy Metrics: A Systematic Survey"	ACM Digital Library	2018	United States
A6	"An Approach for Internal Network Security Metric Based on Attack Probability"	Hindawi	2018	Egypt
A7	"IoT Cybersecurity Risk Modeling for SCADA Systems"	IEEE Xplore	2018	United States
A8	"A selective ensemble model for cognitive cybersecurity analysis"	ScienceDirect	2021	United States
A9	"HARMer: Cyber-Attacks Automation and Evaluation"	IEEE Xplore	2020	United States
A10	"Cyberphysical Security and Dependability Analysis of Digital Control Systems in Nuclear Power Plants"	IEEE Xplore	2016	United States
A11	"General Confidentiality and Utility Metrics for Privacy-Preserving Data Publishing Based on the Permutation Model"	IEEE Xplore	2020	United States

(*continued*)

Table 4. (*continued*)

Code	Title	Bibliographical data bases	Year	Country
A12	"Cyber security risk assessment for seaports: A case study of a container port"	ScienceDirect	2021	United Kingdom
A13	"An Integrated Cyber Security Risk Management Approach for a Cyber Physical System"	MDPI	2018	Rumania
A14	"A comprehensive model of information security factors for decision-makers"	ScienceDirect	2020	United Kingdom
A15	"Information security policy non-compliance: Can capitulation theory explain user behaviours?"	ScienceDirect	2021	United Kingdom
A16	"Learning to upgrade internet information security and protection strategy in big data era"	ScienceDirect	2020	The Netherlands
A17	"A neo-institutional perspective on the establishment of information security knowledge sharing practices"	ScienceDirect	2021	The Netherlands
A18	"Is professionals' information security behaviours in Chinese IT organizations for information security protection"	ScienceDirect	2021	United Kingdom
A19	"Towards quantification and evaluation of security of Cloud Service Providers"	ScienceDirect	2017	United Kingdom
A20	"Lightweight method of shuffling overlapped data-blocks for data integrity and security in WSNs"	ScienceDirect	2021	The Netherlands
A21	"Evaluating the Observability of Network Security Monitoring Strategies With TOMATO"	IEEE Xplore	2019	United States

(*continued*)

Table 4. (*continued*)

Code	Title	Bibliographical data bases	Year	Country
A22	"Random Forest Bagging and X-Means Clustered Antipattern Detection from SQL Query Log for Accessing Secure Mobile Data"	Scopus	2021	Egypt
A23	"On the improvement of the isolation forest algorithm for outlier detection with streaming data"	Scopus	2021	Switzerland
A24	"Secrecy performance analysis of amplify-and-forward cooperative network with relay selection in the presence of multiple eavesdroppers"	Scopus	2021	The Netherlands
A25	"A novel technique for speech encryption based on k-means clustering and quantum chaotic map"	Scopus	2021	Indonesia
A26	"D-FAC: A novel ϕ-Divergence based distributed DDoS defense system"	Scopus	2021	Saudi Arabia
A27	"Fast Policy Interpretation and Dynamic Conflict Resolution for Blockchain-Based IoT System"	Scopus	2021	Egypt
A28	"Novel security models, metrics and security assessment for maritime vessel networks"	Science Direct	2021	The Netherlands
A29	"Side-channel leakage assessment metrics and methodologies at design cycle: A case study for a cryptosystem"	Science Direct	2021	United Kingdom
A30	"Contextualizing and aligning security metrics and business objectives: A GQM-based methodology"	Science Direct	2021	United Kingdom
A31	"A Systematic Approach to Threat Modeling and Security Analysis for Software Defined Networking"	IEEE Xplore	2019	United States

(*continued*)

Table 4. (*continued*)

Code	Title	Bibliographical data bases	Year	Country
A32	"False data injection attack (FDIA): an overview and new metrics for fair evaluation of its countermeasure"	Springer	2020	United Kingdom
A33	"Physical layer security over fading wiretap channels through classic coded transmissions with finite block length and discrete modulation"	Scopus	2019	The Netherlands

3 Results and Discussion

For article classification, evaluating controls for security compliance requirements, particularly authorization, integrity, confidentiality and vulnerability (Gómez Enciso and Porras Flores 2018).

Table 5 shows results obtained are revealed for each article so that the research question proposed in this study is answered.

Table 5. Article classification according to metric

Classificatory	Article
Authorization	A2, A14, A18, A22, A27, A30
Integrity	A1, A5, A12, A13, A19, A21, A23, A25, A31
Confidentiality	A10, A11, A15, A16, A17, A20, A24, A33
Vulnerability	A3, A4, A6, A7, A8, A9, A26, A28, A29, A32

Table 6 shows in detail all metrics to evaluate information found in selected documents.

Authorization:
Security key indicators: --MSF have a direct impact on the organization security status. Therefore, the rectangle that includes MSF: "Physical security"; "vulnerability"; "access control"; "awareness"; "infrastructure" is Security Key Indicators. Due to a direct connection to the information security concept these factors are considered real information security status of an organization. Security management should implement countermeasures to actively improve these crucial factors because of its direct impact. (Diesch et al. 2020).

Table 6. Summary of metrics for each article

Classificatory	Metrics	Articles
Authorization	Effort attack-metrics/defense-effort metrics	A2
	Physical security vulnerability, access control, awareness and infrastructure	A14
	PMT takes into account coping assessments and threats, TPB, authorization, authentication	A18
	Anti-pattern detection, time complexity and computational charge	A22
	General performance metric--FPICR, resolution rate metric, interpretation performance and overhead blockchain metric to evaluate CPU overload	A27
	Authorized personnel metric and process effectiveness metric	A30
Integrity	Process security metric, software security metric, network metric, organization metric, compliance metric and efficacy metric	A1
	Privacy and entropy metrics	A5
	KPIs (Key Performance Indicators): confidentiality, integrity, availability, utility, security, authenticity, flexibility	A12
	KPIs: Confidentiality, high availability, integrity, resilience, authenticity, non-repudiation and maintainability	A13
	Implementation, effectiveness and impact metrics	A19
	Efficiency, observation and attack metrics	A21
	Performance rating and receptor metrics or F1 integrity in data transmission	A23
	Signal to noise ratio, segment signal-to noise ratio, pondered frequency signal-to noise, correlation coefficient and logarithmic plausibility relationship	A25
	Attack-impact metric	A31
Confidentiality	Reliability, maintainability and availability metrics (mean time resolution known as MTTR and mean time failure also called MTTF)	A10
	Reliability metrics (higher canonical correlation, reliability metrics from all canonical correlations and reliability and no-mapping confidentiality)	A11
	Confidentiality, reliability compound and mean variance extracted	A15
	Reliability and data validation	A16
	Memetic influence, validity and reliability	A17
	Integrity and reliability	A20

(*continued*)

Table 6. (*continued*)

Classificatory	Metrics	Articles
	Probability of capacity of secret other than zero, probability of secret interruption and mean-low secret capacity different parameters	A24
	Information theoretical metrics, secret, reliability and security metrics	A33
Vulnerability	Operative changes metrics, quantifying failure metrics and to quantify failure sequence	A3
	GE and GID Metrics	A4
	Internal Network Security metrics based on attack probability	A6
	CVSS (Common vulnerability scoring system)	A7
	Vulnerability-seriousness metrics (such as reliability impact) or threat-profile metrics (for example service denial)	A8
	CVSS (Common Vulnerability Scoring System)	
	NAS (Number of attack scenarios) vulnerability seriousness percentage level, return to attack (ROA) based on CVSS	A9
	System security evaluating metric is divergence/closest presence point router computing (PoP)	A26
	Vulnerability level metrics, nodule level, network level and threat risk metrics	A28
	SVF metric (vulnerability factor), MTD metric (extensively used to assess hardness) SAVAT metric (instruction level metric) T-value metric (assessed through T testing)	A29
	Vulnerability identification metric, Impact identification, data allocation metric (Dlm)	A32

Attack stress metrics: Static networks allow attackers to discover vulnerabilities and plan its attack indefinitely. In order to raise attack stress, attack surface may continuously change. Defense effort metrics—There are associated cost with technique-implementation MTD in the network (Hong et al. 2018).

The aim is to motivate SI professionals to protect information security from potential risks based on theoretical frameworks—Protection Motivation theory (PMT) which take into account coping assessment (self-sufficiency and response cost), threat evaluation (susceptibility and threat seriousness) and the Theory of Planned Behavior (TPB) which components include information security attitudes and subjective norms significatively influencing information protecting behavior.

Information security is based on highly efficient authorization and authentication systems in order to have database access in an organization containing personal and sensible information from a commercial point of view. It would be beneficial if organizations focused on information vulnerability related to employee's behavior and attitudes who possess integrity over information security (Ma 2021).

Metrics impact on commercial objectives is explicitly traced via ascendant feedback mechanism allowing for growth increase where metric- feedback has an impact on commercial objectives and vice-versa. Thus, ensuring that a metric only allows only-access to authorized personnel to personal records and a metric to determine process, implementing training on new contracts in terms of successful finalization. (Philippou et al. 2020).

Random Forest Bagging X-means SQL Query Clustering (RFBXSQLQC) is a technique used by some metrics such as: Anti-pattern accuracy detection, time complexity, false-positive rate and computation load. Regarding the number of queries, the application of such technique overcame existing algorithms by 19% regarding patter detection minimizing Mobil data security issues (Dhanaraj et al. 2021).

Blockchain-based IoT System, (BC-IoT) having new features, help protect against security risks up to a degree. The lack of security management based on (PbSM) policies makes it difficult for BC-IoT to confront DDoS attacks *on'off and Parity Wallet*. For this reason, developing an efficient PbSM in the BC-IoT system should be under the following metrics: FPICR general performance, resolution rate, blockchain and overhead interpretation performance and CPU overload evaluation (Fang et al. 2021).

Integrity:
Key Performance Indicators (KPIs) used to evaluate information security corresponding to CPS (Cyber-Physical System) from maritime ports of the Mármara region (Turkey) were: confidentiality, integrity, availability, utility, security, authenticity and flexibility so that infrastructure, IT, communication and machinery—among others is adequately targeted to guarantee confidentiality, integrity and availability (security information pillars) through proactive solutions to deflect catastrophic incidents causing operation ruptures, human injuries, illegal traffic, load theft, system damage and environmental pollution (Gunes et al. 2021).

Confidentiality, high availability, integrity, resilience, authenticity, non-repudiation and maintainability were KPIs used to perform cyber-security evaluation of a CPS (Cyber-Physical System) corresponding to an intelligent network to efficiently manage risks. Therefore, security issues were analyzed, critical assets, potential threats and vulnerabilities in cascade identified that may turn into a major issue if not timely addressed. (Kure et al. 2018).

Security services evaluation—in the cloud should be based on standard vocabulary and effective metrics which lack in the current cloud. Three security valuation metric types were identified according to their roles: implementation metrics which pretend to measure progress in program implementation, controls, polices and information security procedures. Most metrics of this kind measure progress in percentages in adequate security mechanism- deployment. Effectiveness metrics pretend to monitor security processes and controls as long as correctly implemented and work accordingly, they help measure performance and implemented techniques and procedures security levels. Impact metrics are intended to articulate user security service failure. Furthermore, organizations' missions express the effects of security mechanisms implementation regarding the performance of the application in the cloud. For instance, processing overload (Halabi and Bellaiche 2017).

Security metrics may be applied for comparison of several security mechanisms or to indicate the level of security an organization requirements compliance such as: Process security metrics quantifying security levels of a product through an associated development process evaluation, since process security metrics measure security indirectly. Software security metrics evaluate source code defects, wrong software configuration as well as other software-related vulnerabilities. Network metrics evaluate partial or complete network security—N SM considering rising vulnerabilities from application-interaction executed among several hosts.

Organization metrics: This category include metrics evaluating physical and personal security. Compliance metrics intend to measure how well security requirements of an objective are fulfilled. Efficacy metrics measure how well implemented counter measures may protect, detect and even respond to security breaches (Ramos et al. 2017).

Privacy metric can be interpreted as an effective anonymity set or the right amount of information bits an adversary needs for user identification. Uncertainty metrics suppose that an adversary is unsure of its estimation, unable to violate privacy as efficiently as someone who is sure of what he is doing. Entropy metric—It does not matter how an adversary performs his attack, the attack may be based for example, in Bayesian inferences, random guessing, previous ideas or a combination of methods. Positive Information Dissemination metric. – Quantifies the level of adversary possibility indicating the best improvement in every secret (Wagner and Eckhoff 2018).

Security evaluations are performed by 3 methods. First, Network centrality measure to consider the importance each nodule constitutes in the threat model. The second is security evaluation using a vulnerability score system. System security is evaluated using known vulnerabilities. Finally, attack impact metrics are used to evaluate security which shows a system's integral security (Eom et al. 2019).

For information security evaluations in a network, an evaluation observation tool and threat monitoring TOMATO. It evaluates a system's behavior efficiency through a set of monitoring senses in a way that observability metrics are generated, as a result from security monitoring data gathered by a network. Graphic system inputs, known attack techniques and real time date are necessary for this process. (Halvorsen et al. 2019).

In order to improve the isolation forest algorithm for atypical value detection with data transmission, a *PCB-iForest* algorithm was developed making use of the receiver function score metric or F1 to detect malicious activity reliably. Evaluation criteria use true and false positive parameters which, in the same way allow for data transmission integrity evaluation. Average execution time measures were performed by OD algorithm which is the metric representing computational performance (Heigl et al. 2021).

Multi-media content transmission is a process in which information confidentiality and integrity should be assured. In voice encryption technique through binary codification representation (BiRS) several metrics determining encryption quality and data encryption have been used. For analyses results the following measures have been used:

signal-to-noise ratio, segmentary signal-to-noise ratio, pondered in frequency signal-to-noise ratio, correlation coefficient and plausibility logarithmic relationship (Khaleel and Abduljaleel 2021).

Confidentiality
Demonstrating reliability in a cyber-physical and cybernetic nuclear plants, has been done through reliability metrics (a system's probability to provide continuous services during a specific time interval), maintainability (probability that a failed system is reinstated in an operative state within a specific inactive period). Availability - a fraction of time the system provides services during an observation period, measured through a mean resolution time known as MTTR and failure mean time also called MTTF) (Cho et al. 2016).

Three confidentiality metrics are present when quantifying confidentiality and data utility by statistical disclosure control methods (SDC) based on permutation as follows: The largest canonical correlation confidentiality metric, confidentiality metric of all canonical correlations and no-mapping confidentiality metric, all of them use rank-based correlation Spearman with the aim of leading anonymity. Similarly, a limited-utility metric has been provided which may be used to evaluate compensation between utility and confidentiality. (Domingo-Ferrer et al. 2020).

Average variance extracted (AVE) measures captured variance by the construct in comparison to variance quantity due to measurement error. Reliability was evaluated using Cronbach Alfa as well as composite reliability (ρc). The study was performed with employees of a certain company. Employee information security self-efficacy may be evaluated applying questionnaires, training and may reinforced with awards like completion certificates, improvement recognition and possibly departments classified by having the least number of security warnings (McLeod and Dolezel 2021).

Depending on different factors, an Internet information security research was performed, suggesting an evaluation algorithm based on the analysis of gray clusters carrying out internet information security influencing factors. Indicators or factors test data reliability and validity. Therefore, a confirmatory analysis method is used for data processing to guarantee the above-mentioned standards. In order to accurately analyze internet security information, the use of KPCA—pre presented algorithm is key, which not only preserves performance capacity, but also improves later classification capacity suitable for intrusion detection and internet security classifying of information (Guo and Wang 2020).

Research model suggests that memetic influence may be considered determinant to set up ISKS practices—Information security knowledge exchange. Organizations my restrict other organizations' security policies in two ways: complying with successful security controls by other organizations within the industry; or by minimizing security solution-search costs and reduce risks by no being the first to invent security policies. InfoSec policy compliance was defined (Information security programs) as the measure employees adhere and recommend most in terms of InfoSec policies, considering validity and reliability (Hassandoust et al. 2021).

Integrity and confidentiality are crucial security requirements for information protection, attack resources and malicious behavior when it comes to metrics. Integrity means scopes that take into account modifying information external interaction issues. These modifications may be intentioned or involuntary such as injection attacks or message alterations. Confidentiality analyzes techniques to prevent secret or private information dissemination. Such mechanisms are classified in two categories: symmetrical and asymmetrical cryptographical algorithms (Alcaraz Velasco et al. 2021).

Three performance metrics were used to improve security from the physical layer to checking amplification in wireless cooperative network: other than zero secret probability capacity. Secret interruption probability and mean-low secret capacity under different parameters. Results were obtained from Monte-Carlo simulations in order to verify mathematical expressions validity. (Torabi et al. 2021).

Vulnerability

A vulnerability-exploits risk supervision analysis was performed through control system data acquisition (SCADA) belonging to the Industrial Internet of things (IIoT) of critical infrastructure using statistical methods. Risk metrics were evaluated by common vulnerability scoring system (CVSS) created by *First.org* reaffirming that these metrics are no correlated with exploits with all software vulnerabilities. The study main contribution is that CVSS metrics may be used to determine exploit risks for SCADA systems software sub-class (Falco et al. 2018).

For a cybersecurity frame to have research momentum, it should integrate natural language processes, data mining and automatic learning, considering a model channeling machine learning selective sets producing classifiers according to cybersecurity sets of metrics issues entered, like seriousness vulnerability i.e., confidentiality impact, threat metrics i.e., service denied and so on. Classifiers are trained using historical data correlating new vulnerability instances in distinct patterns. Furthermore, differentiation among validation for binary classification tasks, multiple- task classification metrics, multiple-label classification metrics as well as CVSS (Common Vulnerability Scoring System) used to back quantitative vulnerability evaluations and seriousness in both, academic research and industrial domain (Jiang and Atif 2021).

To evaluate security posture from automatization framework to model attack threats and strategies based on the representation of Hierarchical Attack Representation Model –HARM—the following metrics were used: Number of Attack Scenarios (NAS) which indicate the total number of possible attacks with known modules, vulnerability seriousness percentage degree identifying possible attacks found in network hosts critical nature, (ROA) which determines benefit obtained by the attacker when taking advantage of vulnerabilities based on CVSS (Common Vulnerability Scoring System and lastly, impact attack which measures potential damage caused by the attacker when seizing a vulnerability (Enoch et al. 2020).

Resilience metrics for operative changes. They help designers and interested parties in decision-making processes to understand a system's resilience state. Capacity quantifying metrics for failure prevention are related to reduced possibility failure resilience robustness—intended to measure system capacity to prevent disruptive consequences as changes are produced. Failure consequence quantifying metrics –they quantify reduced consequence of goal failure and graceful degradation with resilience vison intended to measure system capacity to contain or reduce negative consequences caused by the occurrence of a change (Andersson et al. 2021).

GE and GID metrics have proven to be efficient in FE legitimate traffic detection from HR-DDoS attacks or similar aspects. Likewise, it has been observed that GE and GID metrics can obtain greater information distance between legitimate traffic vs malicious and vs FE Traffic α increasing order compared to other detection metrics (Behal and Kumar 2017).

A network security metric provides quantifiable evidence to help security professionals protect IT networks. Therefore, an internal network security method metric is proposed, based on attack probability that solves the security existing metric issue based on an attack graphic because of camouflage characteristics and internal attack complexity (Shan et al. 2018).

Well defined security metrics are adopted with the proposed model to evaluate possible attacks or threats and compare cybersecurity efficacy and defense strategies based on varied network attack scenarios so that network security and defense mechanisms are evaluated. Well defined metrics include: attack success probability, system risk and metric specific risk. Security metrics are calculated using MV-HARM in three levels: Nodule, attack route level and network level. Nodule and level metrics are calculated from the bottom layer while attack route and network level are determined by the model top layer. As an example, network level metrics are calculated based on attack routes, nodules and vulnerability metrics (Enoch et al. 2021).

MTD metric is widely used to evaluate hardness. The implementation against lateral channel attack is a minimum follow up for dissemination. SVF metric stimulates the lateral channel, design vulnerability at architectonic level before proceeding to RTL design. SAVAT is a metric intended to solve one of SVF inconveniences helping IT architects to understand which architecture and micro-architectonic characteristic are the main filtration. T value is a metric evaluated during "T testing" with a lateral channel evaluation methodology (Bokharaie and Jahanian 2020).

Vulnerability identification metrics refer to vulnerabilities through which the attacker gets access to a system or network to inject false data. Impact identification metric refers to the FDIA countermeasure capacity to identify or estimate with the most accuracy possible, impact caused by cyber-delinquency. Data imputation metric is one of the expected characteristics from FDIA counter measurements. Statistically, imputation is the process of replacing missing data with a substitute value (Ahmed and Pathan 2020).

Information theoretical security robust metrics—Secret metrics based on practice error rate such as secret capacity metrics. Curiosity metrics are also used as interleaved codification technique for telephone hearing channel exploring interference. Error rate is used as reliability and security metric throughout the call as security breach to study instances (Baldi et al. 2019).

Distributed defense system based on anomalies D-FAC is oriented to detect different types of attacks DDoS and its mitigation. The metric that evaluates system security is router divergence/computation closest point of presence (PoP). This metric is calculated by distributing memory computational overload from all entry presence points -- PoP and a central coordinator is sent to add a detection metric. Evaluation metric is produced in PoP where a web server is connected since the attack traffic is focalized at that point (Behal et al. 2021).

4   Conclusions

Analyzed articles show diverse results as far as evaluation metrics, since there is no one single classification or universal definition describing this type of information. However, there are articles in which authors coincide with some metrics description applied to information security information. Such metrics are vital contributing to significative assets for optimum information management in organizations that work with data groups. Thus, an organization will be considered reliable and reputable knowing that sensible personal information, is highly safeguarded.

After analyzing results and identifying different security metrics creation purpose in each studied article, it was concluded that the importance of analyzing and evaluating security within organizations where a great amount of data is safeguarded. Moreover, the impact generated as vulnerabilities are identified to perform a correct audit follow-up and risk assessment, in turn creating future useful metrics for pertinent decision-making with the aim of keeping efficient security within an organization.

Common metrics in the 33 scientific articles in line with their classification: authorization—Attack stress, Defense effort, Access control, Infrastructure, Vulnerability and computational load. Integrity—Authenticity, flexibility, utility, availability, resilience, non-repudiation, maintainability, information transmission integrity, observation, efficiency, attack impact. Confidentiality—resolution mean time, failure mean time, canonical correlation, mean variance, memetic influence, other than zero capacity, secret interruption. Vulnerability—Failure quantification, common risk score system vulnerability, PoP router divergence/computation, vulnerability factor, data imputation, instruction level.

References

Ahmed, M., Pathan, A.S.K.: False data injection attack (FDIA): an overview and new metrics for fair evaluation of its countermeasure. Complex Adapt. Syst. Model. **8**(1), 1–14 (2020). https://doi.org/10.1186/S40294-020-00070-W/FIGURES/7

Alcaraz Velasco, F., Palomares, J.M., Olivares, J.: Lightweight method of shuffling overlapped data-blocks for data integrity and security in WSNs. Comput. Netw. **199**, 108470 (2021). https://doi.org/10.1016/J.COMNET.2021.108470

Andersson, J., Grassi, V., Mirandola, R., Perez-Palacin, D.: A conceptual framework for resilience: fundamental definitions, strategies and metrics. Computing **103**(4), 559–588 (2021). https://doi.org/10.1007/S00607-020-00874-X/FIGURES/10

Baldi, M., Maturo, N., Ricciutelli, G., Chiaraluce, F.: Physical layer security over fading wiretap channels through classic coded transmissions with finite block length and discrete modulation. Phys. Commun. **37**, 100829 (2019). https://doi.org/10.1016/J.PHYCOM.2019.100829

Behal, S., Kumar, K.: Detection of DDoS attacks and flash events using information theory metrics–an empirical investigation. Comput. Commun. **103**, 18–28 (2017). https://doi.org/10.1016/J.COMCOM.2017.02.003

Behal, S., Kumar, K., Sachdeva, M.: D-FAC: a novel φ-divergence based distributed DDoS defense system. J. King Saud Univ. – Comput. Inf. Sci. **33**(3), 291–303 (2021). https://doi.org/10.1016/J.JKSUCI.2018.03.005

Bokharaie, V.S., Jahanian, A.: Side-channel leakage assessment metrics and methodologies at design cycle: a case study for a cryptosystem. J. Inf. Secur. Appl. **54**, 102561 (2020). https://doi.org/10.1016/J.JISA.2020.102561

Cho, C.S., Chung, W.H., Kuo, S.Y.: Cyberphysical security and dependability analysis of digital control systems in nuclear power plants. IEEE Trans. Syst. Man Cybern. Syst. **46**(3), 356–369 (2016). https://doi.org/10.1109/TSMC.2015.2452897

Dhanaraj, R.K., Ramakrishnan, V., Poongodi, M., Krishnasamy, L., Hamdi, M., Kotecha, K., Vijayakumar, V.: Random forest bagging and x-means clustered antipattern detection from SQL query log for accessing secure mobile data. Wirel. Commun. Mob. Comput. **2021** (2021). https://doi.org/10.1155/2021/2730246

Diesch, R., Pfaff, M., Krcmar, H.: A comprehensive model of information security factors for decision-makers. Comput. Secur. **92**, 101747 (2020). https://doi.org/10.1016/J.COSE.2020.101747

Domingo-Ferrer, J., Muralidhar, K., Bras-Amoros, M.: General confidentiality and utility metrics for privacy-preserving data publishing based on the permutation model. IEEE Trans. Dependable Secure Comput. **18**, 2506–2517 (2020). https://doi.org/10.1109/TDSC.2020.2968027

Enoch, S.Y., Huang, Z., Moon, C.Y., Lee, D., Ahn, M.K., Kim, D.S.: HARMer: cyber-attacks automation and evaluation. IEEE Access **8**, 129397–129414 (2020). https://doi.org/10.1109/ACCESS.2020.3009748

Enoch, S.Y., Lee, J.S., Kim, D.S.: Novel security models, metrics and security assessment for maritime vessel networks. Comput. Netw. **189**, 107934 (2021). https://doi.org/10.1016/J.COMNET.2021.107934

Eom, T., Hong, J.B., An, S., Park, J.S., Kim, D.S.: A systematic approach to threat modeling and security analysis for software defined networking. IEEE Access. **7**, 137432–137445 (2019). https://doi.org/10.1109/ACCESS.2019.2940039

Falco, G., Caldera, C., Shrobe, H.: IIoT cybersecurity risk modeling for SCADA systems. IEEE Internet Things J. **5**(6), 4486–4495 (2018). https://doi.org/10.1109/JIOT.2018.2822842

Fang, Y., Jian, Z., Jin, Z., Xie, X., Lu, Y., Li, T. : Fast policy interpretation and dynamic conflict resolution for blockchain-based IoT system. Wirel. Commun. Mob. Comput. **2021** (2021). https://doi.org/10.1155/2021/9968743

Gómez Enciso, E., Porras Flores, E.E.: Modelo de evaluación de seguridad para transmitir datos usando web services. Ind. Data **21**(1), 123 (2018). https://doi.org/10.15381/IDATA.V21I1.14927

Gunes, B., Kayisoglu, G., Bolat, P.: Cyber security risk assessment for seaports: a case study of a container port. Comput. Secur. **103**, 102196 (2021). https://doi.org/10.1016/J.COSE.2021.102196

Guo, J., Wang, L.: Learning to upgrade internet information security and protection strategy in big data era. Comput. Commun. **160**, 150–157 (2020). https://doi.org/10.1016/J.COMCOM.2020.05.043

Halabi, T., Bellaiche, M.: Towards quantification and evaluation of security of cloud service providers. J. Inf. Secur. Appl. **33**, 55–65 (2017). https://doi.org/10.1016/J.JISA.2017.01.007

Halvorsen, J., Waite, J., Hahn, A.: Evaluating the observability of network security monitoring strategies with tomato. IEEE Access **7**, 108304–108315 (2019). https://doi.org/10.1109/ACCESS.2019.2933415

Hassandoust, F., Subasinghage, M., Johnston, A.C.: A neo-institutional perspective on the establishment of information security knowledge sharing practices. Inf. Manag. **59**(1), 103574 (2021). https://doi.org/10.1016/J.IM.2021.103574

Heigl, M., Anand, K.A., Urmann, A., Fiala, D., Schramm, M., Hable, R.: On the improvement of the isolation forest algorithm for outlier detection with streaming data. Electronics (Switzerland) **10**(13) (2021). https://doi.org/10.3390/ELECTRONICS10131534

Hong, J.B., Enoch, S.Y., Kim, D.S., Nhlabatsi, A., Fetais, N., Khan, K.M.: Dynamic security metrics for measuring the effectiveness of moving target defense techniques. Comput. Secur. **79**, 33–52 (2018). https://doi.org/10.1016/J.COSE.2018.08.003

Jiang, Y., Atif, Y.: A selective ensemble model for cognitive cybersecurity analysis. J. Netw. Comput. Appl. **193**, 103210 (2021). https://doi.org/10.1016/J.JNCA.2021.103210

Khaleel, A.H., Abduljaleel, I.Q.: A novel technique for speech encryption based on k- means clustering and quantum chaotic map. Bull. Electr. Eng. Inf. **10**(1), 160–170 (2021). https://doi.org/10.11591/EEI.V10I1.2405

Kure, H.I., Islam, S., Razzaque, M.A.: An integrated cyber security risk management approach for a cyber-physical system. Appl. Sci. **8**(6), 898 (2018). https://doi.org/10.3390/APP8060898

Ma, X.: IS professionals' information security behaviors in Chinese IT organizations for information security protection. Inf. Process. Manag. **59**(1), 102744 (2021). https://doi.org/10.1016/J.IPM.2021.102744

McLeod, A., Dolezel, D.: Information security policy non-compliance: can capitulation theory explain user behaviors? Comput. Secur. **112**, 102526 (2021). https://doi.org/10.1016/J.COSE.2021.102526

Philippou, E., Frey, S., Rashid, A.: Contextualising and aligning security metrics and business objectives: a GQM-based methodology. Comput. Secur. **88**, 101634 (2020). https://doi.org/10.1016/J.COSE.2019.101634

Ramos, A., Lazar, M., Filho, R.H., Rodrigues, J.J.P.C.: Model-based quantitative network security metrics: a survey. IEEE Commun. Surv. Tutor. **19**(4), 2704–2734 (2017). https://doi.org/10.1109/COMST.2017.2745505

Shan, C., Jiang, B., Xue, J., Guan, F., Xiao, N.: An approach for internal network security metric based on attack probability. Secur. Commun. Netw. **2018** (2018). https://doi.org/10.1155/2018/3652170

Torabi, M., Parkouk, S., Shokrollahi, S.: Secrecy performance analysis of amplify-and-forward cooperative network with relay selection in the presence of multiple eavesdroppers. Wirel. Netw. **27**(4), 2977–2990 (2021). https://doi.org/10.1007/s11276-021-02611-4

Wagner, I., Eckhoff, D.: Technical privacy metrics. ACM Comput. Surv. (CSUR) **51**(3) (2018). https://doi.org/10.1145/3168389

Apps and User Interfaces

Evaluation of User Interface (UI) and User Experience (UX) for Web Services of a Weather Data Monitoring Platform

Maritza Aguirre-Munizaga(✉) ⓘ, Vanessa Vergara-Lozano ⓘ, Katty Lagos-Ortiz ⓘ, and Ahmed El Salous ⓘ

Facultad de Ciencias Agrarias "Dr. Jacobo Bucaram Ortiz", Universidad Agraria del Ecuador, 25 de Julio Avenue, Guayaquil, Ecuador

{maguirre,vvergara,klagos,eelsalous}@uagraria.edu.ec

Abstract. The user experience UX is a factor that has gained prominence in organisations that present their products on the web. This leads to evaluating the importance of identifying Internet users' expectations and needs and emphasising these factors when designing a web portal. On the other hand, the user interface UI allows to offer a visual, simple and friendly environment, to interact with the applications and experience the usability of the web website the present work, the evaluation of the interface and user experience of an environmental data monitoring platform was carried out, emphasising the use of a survey applied to external beneficiaries allowing the assessment of different parameters corresponding to a user-centred design approach such as usability, functionality, performance, portability and reliability; obtaining data on the positioning of the website as well as the Pearson correlation between the variables generated and the version of the platform. This research uses as a case study the data generated by google analytics and google data search console tools, with which the information of the sessions in the "Platform for monitoring atmospheric data in real-time from the network of weather stations of the Agrarian University of Ecuador, Guayaquil and Milagro headquarters" was obtained.

Keywords: Google analytics · Google data studio · Meteorology · User interface · User experience

1 Introduction

The design of user-centred products and services has been generated since the 1980s [2]. Several companies have adopted this method to create products focusing on identified customer needs. In this area, the technology applied to the design of applications also participates in implementing this paradigm.

Within the software development methodology, one of the essential interactions is the design since its objective is to generate more familiar and practical aspects in visualising the graphic interfaces structured for the user [23]. In office automation, tools are used to evaluate the acceptance by the users of the website. These tools are applied in several areas for validation of the characteristics and quality standards of software.

Research studies on user experience for various interactive software systems are widely available [5]. However, there is not much information on evaluations applied in the environmental field. In this context, this research identified parameters of the project design process, which allowed a survey and a usability study to relate user experience and interface factors in a multiplatform website.

Platforms of this type are used in areas such as climate change analysis, as cited in the study by Overeem, Robinson, Leijnse, Steeneveld, Horn, & Uijlenhoet [17]. Agriculture has also taken advantage of the publication of information in open access platforms, according to Van Etten [6], without leaving aside public health, as indicated by Brabham, Ribisl, Kirchner, & Bernhardt [4], among others.

This research aims to generate indicators that allow evaluating the experience of a user when using an environmental data platform, it is expected that the identified parameters will be a reference framework for future research. The evaluation methodology focused on choosing a sample of beneficiaries, that took a survey in order to validate the aspects of functionality and design. Also, accesses were monitored through Google analytics and these accesses were related to the sociodemographic study of the beneficiaries of the project, including parameters that helped to detect the response efficiency of the designed website compared to other sites that perform the same function.

When measuring effectiveness, it is necessary to define what success and failure mean for the user in a given task, which is the reason why we focus on the task of monitoring environmental data, these environmental activities are used by experts in various areas for purposes research and consulting. In this case, the gmetrix tool was used to validate the performance of each of the platforms that would be used, in order to define the effectiveness comparison within the monitoring task, in which the following metrics were identified: category, performance, structure, total blocking, cumulative layout shift and content loaded time.

The results of this article show the importance of the collection of quantitative data and allow the application of longitudinal research in the context of the evaluation of a software product, the same that was generated in the Agrarian University of Ecuador, as part of a research project. It is important to highlight that this evaluation allowed to get better insights of the transition phase of the project, which was generated with the Rational Unified Process methodology.

Since 1992, the mission of the Universidad Agraria del Ecuador has been to train agricultural and environmental professionals at the highest level. For this reason, the institution created a research project to implement a platform based on the open data policy and access to information. Thus provide access service to historical atmospheric data from the stations installed on its premises for use in various studies of the University community, external researchers and private enterprise, respecting the Organic Law of Transparency and Access to Public Information in Ecuador.

2   Related Works

Web platforms are a direct communication mechanism with users; thanks to them, we can know if the user is satisfied with the usability and the ease of performing processes.

Nowadays, multiple techniques allow us to evaluate web pages to improve the quality of the information presented and the visibility and navigation of websites [18].

Reis and Ferreira [21] proposed a framework for evaluating a cyberlearning platform using evaluation techniques with cognitive walkthroughs and heuristic evaluation surveys. Their purpose was to improve practice and emphasise the importance of assessing learning environments using UI/UX evaluations.

We compared three different areas in a proposal presented to evaluate the understanding and production capacity of an interface on the Internet, operating system and content [8]. In the design research, content and design production, the highest percentage of people evaluated did not understand the UI/UX, so they concluded that designs today must be created focusing on the user and the site's usability.

Some platforms implement UI/UX authoring tools, such as [7], which propose an adaptive user interface methodology based on the use of contextual and environmental factors. Statistical methods were used to evaluate the effectiveness of the tool. The results showed that the method outperforms existing approaches in user interface adaptation.

This work evaluates a weather data monitoring platform's user experience and interface, which will help the user or researcher obtain environmental data quickly and efficiently.

Several Ecuadorian institutions have weather stations in different parts of the country dedicated to monitoring these parameters to obtain real-time information for meteorological surveillance systems and warning systems. Higher education institutions such as the Pontificia Universidad Católica del Ecuador through the School of Geography have a conventional weather station located in Nayón, which according to the University, has instruments to measure different elements and meteorological parameters such: as temperature, the humidity of the atmosphere, evaporation, precipitation, sunshine, wind speed and direction [20].

The National Polytechnic School manages the Quito Astronomical Observatory (OAQ), a scientific institution located in La Alameda Park, which was created in 1873 to build a lasting monument to Ecuadorian science [12]. Currently, they have the Davis weather station. Through their web page, it is possible to consult statistical data in the form of graphs, with data such as temperature, humidity, rainfall, and UV index [15].

Also, the Universidad de las Américas at the Granados campus in Quito uses a weather station to study climate, phenomena and climatic changes. These results are helpful for livestock, fisheries and agriculture and are linked with INAMHI, to which it reports the data.

As analysed at the national level, INAMHI has the most significant number of meteorological stations. However, historical data is available at a determined cost for private and public institutions, and access to the information is possible once a written request has been made. The other institutions possess the knowledge and are used privately for research [25]. This process makes obtaining meteorological information for outsiders cumbersome and bureaucratic. They make it challenging to access the data, and users have an unpleasant experience navigating these websites.

Environmental data represent a valuable resource for researchers; however, there are not enough records in many countries, and they are unreliable. The institutions' platforms often only allow viewing the data but not downloading them, complicating the user experience, and presenting difficulties in obtaining the data.

3 Methodology

This article aims to highlight the results of the evaluations carried out on the website as part of the assessment of the performance of the technological tool designed at the Agrarian University of Ecuador [1]. It focuses on what the user feels while using each of the options available on the platform and the tool's intuitiveness, interactivity, reliability and usability [10].

We carried out three methodologies for the evaluation of this site. Firstly, using the survey as a method of data collection [9] to know the user's opinion. While using the platform and thus validating the intuitiveness, interactivity, reliability and usability of the information that the designed website environment has, for this purpose, we used a sample of 80 users of the website through simple random sampling. When obtaining the data from the surveys, the normality between the variables will be analysed through the Shapiro-Wilk Test. Additionally, we weighted the analysed variables to know the user's satisfaction and correlations between variables. The users gave the score for the variables analysed on a scale of 1 to 5, where one strongly disagrees, and five strongly agree. The questions were grouped according to the variables studied and averaged to determine the score for each variable.

The second tool used is the analysis of interaction indicators within the website through the use of Google Analytics, which has been used in conjunction with Google Data Studio and Google Search Console, providing critical data to monitor different aspects of the web performance environment [24]. In the case of Google tools, it is worth mentioning that a summary of the most critical metrics and notifications is used. The performance that the designed site maintains in Google Search, the index coverage and mobile usability metrics will complement the assessment of the level of user satisfaction (UX) and the interface (UI) usability.

Google Analytics provides time-based series data, which generates statistics about website visits [19]; it is a free service supported by Google. Knowing how visitors found the site and how they interact with it is possible. In turn, the metrics calculated by google analytics allow us to evaluate the usability of websites and find potential problem areas.

On the other hand, Google Search Console [26] has been used to monitor, maintain and solve visibility problems in google searches. It has been possible to use this tool to crawl the website, solve indexing problems, consult website traffic data, and receive alerts when spam problems are detected. The search console also provides data to monitor the performance of web platforms and improve their search rankings [13]. With this tool, it has been possible to analyse the performance of the environmental data platform to know its status and usefulness for the user.

In addition, the Data Studio tool allowed us to compare, filter and organise the data necessary for generating reports through interactive and customisable control panels and link them with external sources.

Finally, the third methodology of analysis is to make a comparative table of the performance of web platforms that present meteorological data in various institutions in the country. Several metrics were evaluated using a website analysis application for performance, total block time, cumulative design scrolling, and DOM content loading time, as described in Table 1.

Table 1. Metrics and description

Metrics	Description
Category	This rating best reflects the overall experience of your website, as it represents both your front-end structure and the actual performance experienced by the user
Performance	It is related to the browser and hardware specifications that load correctly on the end-user; among these, we have a speed index and time to interact
Total Blocking Time	Measures the total amount of time your web page was blocked, preventing the user from interacting with it; a good user experience should maintain a range of 150ms or less
Cumulative Layout Shift	Cumulative Layout Shift (CLS) is a performance metric introduced in 2020 by Lighthouse to measure the perceived visual stability of a page load. Measures the unexpected change of web elements while the page is rendering
DOM Content Loaded Time	It is the way the browser internally structures the HTML so that it can render it

Source: https://gtmetrix.com/

4   Results

Once the project's website has been socialization through various media, the interface and user experience in the use of the information generated on the website will be validated through surveys and indicators from Google Analytics.

From the survey applied to a sample of 80 users (website visitors), information was obtained on the analysed variables such as intuitiveness, interactivity, reliability and usability through a questionnaire. First, the Shapiro/Wilk test was applied, getting values of $W = 0.91417$, p-value $= 0.1811$; with which we do not have enough statistical evidence to reject the hypothesis of normality, that is to say, that the sample of our data tends to a normal distribution, something that is very important when analysing a statistical model. The sample data analysis shows that the most frequent ages of the application users are between 20 and 35 years old, as shown in Fig. 1.

The average obtained from the scores given by users to each of the questions, which were then grouped by the variables analysed, is shown in Fig. 2, where it can be identified that all variables have a score higher than 4, i.e. users have a marked tendency to agree and strongly agree with the web tool.

The areas that use this tool the most are IT, Environment, Industry and Education, as shown in Table 2, representing 81% of the users consulted.

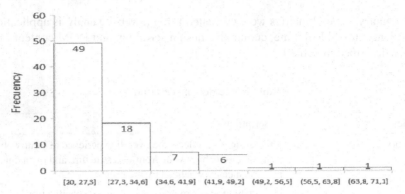

Fig. 1. Frequency by age

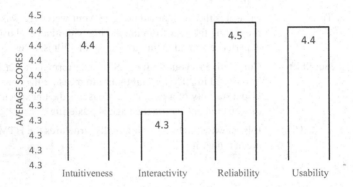

Fig. 2. Scores of variables analysed.

Table 2. Areas using the tool

Areas	Usuarios	%
TI	38	48%
Environment	11	14%
Industry	10	13%
Education	6	8%
Others	15	19%
Total	80	100%

Of these areas that use the tool, the use given to the meteorological information obtained from the platform was consulted, and it was found that 65% of the users use the meteorological information for me-environmental and agricultural studies, as shown in Table 2 (Table 3).

Table 3. Uses of meteorological information.

Use the meteorological information	Users	%
Environmental studies	27	34%
Agricultural studies	25	31%
Making predictions	20	25%
Unknown utility	8	10%
Total	80	100%

To determine the relationship between the performance the user estimates the tool has. With the number of variables, a correlational analysis was performed between these two variables through the Pearson coefficient giving an $r = 0.743$, which means that there is a direct relationship, i.e..The more meteorological variables the user uses, the higher the score he provides to the application. Additionally, multivariate variance analysis took into account the career to which the respondent is linked, age and whether the user qualifies as necessary the website designed. In this case, the variables' residuals obtained in the MANOVA analysis are plotted. In Fig. 3 we can identify a dependent behaviour between the study variables.

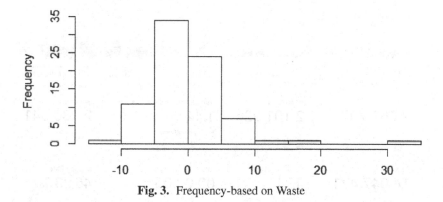

Fig. 3. Frequency-based on Waste

Additionally, the performance of the web tool was validated through Google Analytics indicators. From what could be analysed based on the developed interface, there is a marked tendency to the highest rating, so it is established that most users strongly agree with the intuitiveness of the site, as shown in Fig. 4.

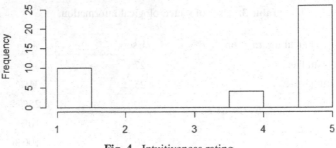

Fig. 4. Intuitiveness rating

In Fig. 5 shows the trend analysis of the last three years through the Google data studio tool; a graph highlights the number of users visiting the platform and the number of sessions per user. Data Studio relies on the usual combination of charts and graphs to convey meaning; the tool enhances these with features that include the ability to integrate multiple sources into a single report.

These data are related to the indicators analyzed by establishing a trend based on the experience of old users so that new users can visit the website.

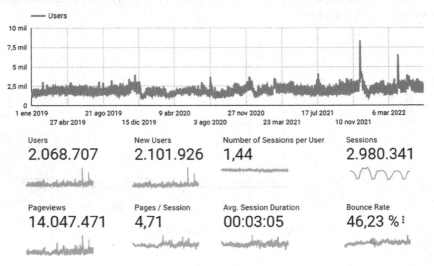

Fig. 5. Sessions by users

Human-computer interaction (HCI) [11] is a predominant theme in the scientific and business universe, considering that digital systems intended for various purposes are globally accessible and considerably impact people's daily lives. Nowadays, desktop applications are no longer generated since the solutions must be multiplatform, respecting portability and reliability [16]. However, there are countless challenges to be faced in terms of user interface (UI) and user experience (UX) so that the user's needs and satisfaction continue to be met. A commonly used evaluation strategy is the assessment of metrics that correspond to the performance of websites. This parameter is one of the most important in validating the functionality and permanence that a user tends to identify when using a tool. The increase in the size and complexity of web pages has challenged the efficiency of HTTP [3], evidencing that the end user's product must comply with performance characteristics that can be generated in an automated manner.

Table 4 shows the scores obtained from four websites that generate information related to the case study. The website of the Ecuadorian Civilian Space Agency is the one that reflects the highest score in the Cumulative Layout Shift (CLS) metric. It quantifies the perceived visual stability of the Oceanographic and Antarctic Institute of the Navy. The Universidad Técnica Particular de Loja presents one of the weakest categories and the lowest performance percentage. The Loja Technical University platform offers the highest performance and the optimal structure, which indicates how well the page is built about performance. Finally, the National Institute of Meteorology and Hydrology obtained a Regular rating in the category and has the highest response time compared to the other sites evaluated. With the above, we can deduce that the site maintained at the Agrarian University of Ecuador generates the highest ratings and performance rates at the National Level.

Table 4. Performance comparison of WEB platforms

WebSites		Category	Performance	Structure	Total blocking time (150 ms or less)	Cumulative layout shift (0,1 or less)	DOM Content loaded time
Institución	Verified link						
Ecuadorian Civilian Space Agency	http:// gye. exa.ec/	B	86%	83%	0 ms	0.26 s	1.2 s
Oceanographic and Antarctic Institute of the Navy	https:// www.ino car.mil. ec/web/ index. php/pro ductos/ estaci ones-met eorolo gicas	B	87%	77%	0	0.01 s	1.5 s
Particular Technical University of Loja	https:// vincul acion. utpl.edu. ec/es/obs ervato rios/ clima	F	30%	59%	1.8 s	0.15 s	1.2 s

(*continued*)

Table 4. (*continued*)

WebSites		Category	Performance	Structure	Total blocking time (150 ms or less)	Cumulative layout shift (0,1 or less)	DOM Content loaded time
Institución	Verified link						
	http://meteorologia uae.uag raria. edu.ec/	B	90%	86%	0 ms	0 s	1.2 s
Agrarian University of Ecuador	http:// 186.42. 174.236/ Inamhi Emas/	C	78%	66%	8 ms	0.01 s	1.6 s

Source: https://gtmetrix.com/

The results were analyzed using Google Analytics, search console and data studio tools. They are related as follows through analytics and search console to monitor historically the parameters that helped to inspect and analyze the website traffic for the surveys applied to users, unlike Google data studio that was used to generate reports and reportage of the data collected.

Online data publishing is already a valuable tool to engage the public. Suppose proper validation and quality control procedures are adopted and implemented. In that case, it has much potential to provide a valuable source of high temporal and spatial resolution and real-time data, especially in regions where few observations currently exist, adding value to science, technology and society [14]. That is why this work evaluates the implemented web application in the interface and user experience in terms of the presentation and collection of atmospheric data through weather stations located in Guayaquil and Milagro at the Agrarian University of Ecuador. Web applications facilitate the use of massive data of important atmospheric variables and provide several statistical applications that help researchers in the meteorological area and sectors that use this input to conduct new research directly affected by these variables.

5   Conclusions

This article aims to compare performance metrics through the Gmetrix tool and to deepen the quality of experience (QoE) of a user using Lighthouse [22]. This open-source auditing tool (and various metrics) allowed us to quantify the results corresponding to 5 websites that generate information related to meteorology. We show through a case study the importance of meteorological data in various aspects. Such indicators of global patterns help in sectors like agriculture, science and research. We verify this through statistical information and descriptive statistics, using data collection tools and web environment performance tools. We can conclude that our data comply with the principle of normality and that the device is used by users between 30 and 40 years of age; the tool is very intuitive to use, and finally, the trend is growing by the number of visits to the site.

The above corroborates that the use of these platforms, which are free of charge, is beneficial in the field of science. In the future, we hope to carry out a complementary study among different types of users within the web platform, focusing on agriculture and the industrial and research sectors.

This research proposes a frame of reference for future evaluations of websites related to the meteorology area to date. Few references compare the aspects that should be identified in validating the user experience.

Additionally, it should be noted that Google nowadays, free of charge, keep available to web admins a large number of metrics related to web traffic and other aspects of the presentation of software products that are presented to the end user.

References

1. Aguirre-Munizaga, M., et al.: Analysis of atmospheric monitoring data through micro-meteorological stations, as a crowdsourcing tool for technology integration. In: Rocha, Á., Serrhini, M. (eds.) Information Systems and Technologies to Support Learning. SIST, vol. 111, pp. 181–187. Springer, Cham (2019). https://doi.org/10.1007/978-3-030-03577-8_21
2. Baur, F.: User Experience BT - Bürokommunikation/Office Communications (1984)
3. Biswal, P., Gnawali, O.: Does QUIC make the web faster? In: 2016 IEEE Global Communication Conference GLOBECOM 2016 - Proceedings (2016). https://doi.org/10.1109/GLOCOM.2016.7841749
4. Brabham, D.C., et al.: Crowdsourcing applications for public health. Am. J. Prev. Med. 46(2), 179–187 (2014). https://doi.org/10.1016/j.amepre.2013.10.016
5. Brown, A.R.: Experience design and interactive software in music education research. Vis. Res. Music Educ. 20, 1–38 (2012)
6. Van Etten, J.: Crowdsourcing Crop improvement in Sub-Saharan Africa: a proposal for a scalable and inclusive approach to food security. IDS Bull. 42(4), 102–110 (2011). https://doi.org/10.1111/j.1759-5436.2011.00240.x
7. Hussain, J., et al.: Model-based adaptive user interface based on context and user experience evaluation. J. Multimodal User Interfaces 12(1), 1–16 (2018). https://doi.org/10.1007/s12193-018-0258-2
8. JOO, H.S.: A Study on UI/UX and Understanding of Computer Major Students. Int. J. Adv. smart Converg. 6, 4, 26–32 (2017). https://doi.org/10.7236/IJASC.2017.6.4.4
9. Kashyap, N., Pati, U.C.: Multi channel data acquisition and data logging system for meteorology application. In: 2015 International Conference on Smart Technologies and Management for Computing, Communication, Controls, Energy and Materials, ICSTM 2015 – Proceedings, pp. 220–225 (2015). Institute of Electrical and Electronics Engineers Inc. (2015). https://doi.org/10.1109/ICSTM.2015.7225418
10. Kim, K.S., et al.: Requirement analysis for agricultural meteorology information service systems based on the fourth industrial revolution technologies. Korean J. Agric. For. Meteorol. 21(3), 175–186 (2019). https://doi.org/10.5532/KJAFM.2019.21.3.175
11. Liu, Y., et al.: Research on interface design of meteorological cloud radars based on cognitive load theory. In: Proceedings of 2020 IEEE 3rd International Conference on Safety Produce Informatization, IICSPI 2020, pp, 88–92 (2020). https://doi.org/10.1109/IICSPI51290.2020.9332415

12. Lopez, E.: The Quito Astronomical Instruments Heritage. Eff. Teach. Learn. Astron. 25th Meeting IAU Special Session, 4, 24–25 July 2003, Sydney, Aust. Meet. Abstr. id. 40. 4, (2003)
13. Montti, R.: A Complete Google Search Console Guide for SEO Pros
14. Muller, C.L., et al.: Crowdsourcing for climate and atmospheric sciences: current status and future potential (2015)https://doi.org/10.1002/joc.4210
15. Munoz, A.G., et al.: An environmental watch system for the Andean countries: El Observatorio Andino. Bull. Am. Meteorol. Soc. **91**(12), 1645–1652 (2010). https://doi.org/10.1175/2010BAMS2958.1
16. Noguera-Arnaldos, J.Á., Rodriguez-García, M.Á., Ochoa, J.L., Paredes-Valverde, M.A., Alcaraz-Mármol, G., Valencia-García, R.: Ontology-driven instant messaging-based dialogue system for device control. In: Ciuciu, I., et al. (eds.) On the Move to Meaningful Internet Systems: OTM 2015 Workshops. LNCS, vol. 9416, pp. 299–308. Springer, Cham (2015). https://doi.org/10.1007/978-3-319-26138-6_33
17. Overeem, A., et al.: Crowdsourcing urban air temperatures from smartphone battery temperatures. Geophys. Res. Lett. **40**(15), 4081–4085 (2013). https://doi.org/10.1002/grl.50786
18. Paredes-Valverde, M.A., et al.: A systematic review of tools, languages, and methodologies for mashup development. Softw. Pract. Exp. **45**(3), 365–397 (2015). https://doi.org/10.1002/SPE.2233
19. Plaza, B.: Google analytics for measuring website performance. Tour. Manag. **32**(3), 477–481 (2011). https://doi.org/10.1016/J.TOURMAN.2010.03.015
20. PUCE: Estación Meteorológica Nayón. https://www.puce.edu.ec/portal/choosePage?sp=page94n&LanguageISOCtxParam=es&link=ln759n&kcond311n.att31n=720&miu4.icp1=326. Accessed 01 Jan 2019
21. Reis, C., Ferreira, A.: The relevance of UI/UX design in human-computer interaction of educational games and therapeutic practices BT. In: Martins, N., Brandão, D. (eds.) Advances in Design and Digital Communication II, vol. 19, pp. 159–169. Springer, Cham (2022). https://doi.org/10.1007/978-3-030-89735-2_14
22. Saif, D., et al.: An early benchmark of quality of experience between HTTP/2 and HTTP/3 using lighthouse. In: IEEE International Conference on Communications (2021). https://doi.org/10.1109/ICC42927.2021.9500258
23. Sarferaz, S.: User experience BT - compendium on enterprise resource planning: market, functional and conceptual view based on SAP S/4HANA (2022). https://doi.org/10.1007/978-3-030-93856-7_30
24. Snipes, G.: Product review Google data studio. J. Librariansh. Sch. Commun. 6, General Issue, eP2214 (2018). https://doi.org/10.7710/2162-3309.2214
25. Trapasso, L.M.: Meteorological data acquisition in Ecuador, South America: problems and solutions. GeoJournal **12**(1), 89–94 (1986). https://doi.org/10.1007/BF00213025
26. Google Search Console

Comparison of Free Android Mobile 3D Modeling Tools for AR Apps

Carpio A. Pineda-Manosalvas[1]([✉]) [ID], Fausto A. Salazar-Fierro[1,2] [ID],
Nancy N. Cervantes-Rodríguez[1] [ID], and Ana T. DelaCruz-M[1] [ID]

[1] Faculty of Engineering in Applied Sciences, Universidad Técnica del Norte, Ibarra, Ecuador
{capineda,fasalazar,nncervantes,atdelacruzm}@utn.edu.ec
[2] Facultad de Ingeniería de Sistemas e Informática, Universidad Nacional Mayor De San Marcos, Lima, Perú
fausto.salazar@unmsm.edu.pe

Abstract. User expectations regarding the functionality of mobile devices have led to the development of applications with digital representations very close to reality that require the least amount of resources. Until recently, three-dimensional modeling required the compulsory participation of an expert in the field, increasing two valuable resources: time and money. Augmented reality offers the possibility of recreating reality on your smartphones through 3D objects. Currently there are applications that generate three-dimensional objects using photogrammetry. The objective of this work was to compare free Android mobile applications, to identify one that generates a good enough result to be used in augmented reality. The investigation corresponds to the quantitative model with experimental design, the tests were carried out in: 3D Escáner Live, 3DScanLink and Qlone; the results were tested on a prototype AR app. For the analysis, the quantitative evaluation methodology of textured models was used with the metrics: density, in which the 3D Escáner Live app generated a higher value in two of its three objects, with an equivalent to 66.67%; as well as in the difference of forms and comparison of contours where it obtained the highest percentage with 90.23%; and in the variation of the curvature in which it reached an average of 62.61% similarity in contours and edges; while in the number of textures over the number of visible points, all the applications obtained 100%. In conclusion, 3D Escáner Live is the one that generates a 3D model of better quality.

Keywords: Modeling tools · Modeling 3D · AR Apps · Comparison tools

1 Introduction

Currently, many technologies allow visualizing virtual and real environments with superimposed information, these applications are called virtual reality (VR) and augmented reality (AR) [1]; its accelerated development is mainly due to the increasingly demanding requirements of mobile device users as well as the increase in tools for these devices [2], their use is popular, since they introduce information: new, interesting and attractive

© The Author(s), under exclusive license to Springer Nature Switzerland AG 2022
R. Valencia-García et al. (Eds.): CITI 2022, CCIS 1658, pp. 247–259, 2022.
https://doi.org/10.1007/978-3-031-19961-5_18

in all fields, although it is more evident in medicine, manufacturing, tourism and culture in general [3].

One of the elements that has made it possible for a mobile device to become the indispensable daily tool of the human being due to its innumerable benefits, is the camera, which provides increasingly better resolution at a very low cost with the application of algorithms due to use of the built-in GPU [2]. And in this research, it constitutes the accessory that makes possible the creation of 3D objects through photogrammetry, free of charge and with the possibility of being used by any user who requires this type of resource for their projects.

Photogrammetry in the last decade made possible the flexible modeling of 3D objects, limiting itself to the reconstruction of visible surfaces of an image and providing information on the area to be viewed [4]. Photogrammetry or 3D scanning allows an object to be reproduced visually with reliability of size and shape [5]. Among virtual objects, gamification is especially important because it provides additional information and active participation [6].

The most widely used model is the central projection model for photogrammetry, which consists of a geometric process that transforms a 3D entity into a 2D reality. This means that when you have an object with a flat projection center oriented in some way with regarding to object, by connecting the object points by a series of straight lines intersecting the projection plane, a new digitally visible reality is obtained [7].

In the market there is proprietary software that applies photogrammetry to model 3D objects such as RealityCapture, Photoscan and 3DF Zephyr, Autodesk Recap, and also free software such as VisualSfM7, Regard3D8 and The Meshroom that allow genera-ting 3D models in a certain period of time according to the selected application [8].

The applications of photogrammetry are wide and varied, being a 3D information reconstruction technique [9] that is emerging as an area mapping alternative [10], that provide details that are not explicitly described in any explanation and has been applied in areas such as education in the playful process, nutrition, sexual prevention, educational and commercial video games for both mobile devices and desktop computers, reconstruction of different environments such as museums, cities, pieces and archaeological sites [6, 11–13].

2   Material and Methods

The research was carried out framed in the quantitative paradigm with an experimental design. For the selection of the mobile applications that were part of the comparison, a directed search was carried out on the Google Play digital platform that distributes applications for mobile devices that work with the Android operating system through the Play Store; the strings used in the process were: "3D scanner application", "3D scanner" and "3D object scanner application". As a result of this first action and after reviewing the information provided in "about this app", ten were identified that met the following conditions: generate a 3D model, make use of images or captures through the camera to generate the model 3D, scan real objects into 3D models and export an.obj file. The selected apps are presented in Table 1.

Table 1. Downloaded mobile applications.

Application	Cost	Extra HW	Early access	Version	Download size	Points
SCANN3D	Yes	No	No	3.1.0-10024	20 MB	2,0
ARitize360	Yes	No	No	0.1	95 MB	2,9
Qlone	Single Payment	No	No	3.13.0	50 MB	2,6
3DScanLink	No	No	No	1.0.14	32 MB	2,4
Unlimited 3D Scanner	Yes	No	No	1.0	45 MB	1,5
Gespodo Footscan 3D	Yes	No	No	1.5.6	19 MB	3,2
MOD 3d Scanner App	Yes	No	Yes	0.2	124 MB	–
Handy Scan	No	Yes	No	2.1.3	25 MB	2,9
Pix4DCatch: 3D scanner	Yes	No	No	1.1.3	10 MB	2,6
3D Escáner Live	NO	No	Yes	2021-Q2-08	16 MB	–

The ten applications use photogrammetry as a capture technique, so they were installed on a Huawei mobile device, model P20 Lite ANE-LX3 with Android version 9 operating system, 4.0 GB of RAM, 32 GB internal memory and rear dual camera (16 + 2 mega-pixels), with 1080p video capture at 30 frames per second.

Once the applications were installed, the scanning conditions were established: a Rubik's cube (5.7 cm per side) was selected as the test object; a coffee-colored table without any design was chosen as a surface, additionally a solid vertical background was added to generate greater color contrast with respect to the object. To ensure that all the captures are made in the same place, marks were made on a 26 cm diameter circumference drawn on the table and the center was marked as the point where the object was located. The cell phone was placed on a tripod in order to eliminate the possibility of movement during the captures, in addition to setting the distance and angle.

Next, a study of the characteristics of the ten installed applications was carried out, to identify those that fit the project considering its free nature and that do not require any additional hardware, for which the following apps were discarded from the experiment: ARitize360, Unlimited 3D Scanner, Gespodo Footscan 3D, MOD 3D Scanner App, Pix4DCatch: 3D Scanner, SCANN3D, since each scan has a cost or subscription, although they do offer the trial version for two or three objects. The Handy Scan was also not selected since for its use it requires the Revopoint POP 3D scanner, with which the captures are made, which represents an additional cost not considered for the purposes of this investigation. According to the above, the experiment was carried out in the three remaining applications: 3D Escáner Live, 3DScanLink and Qlone.

2.1 3D Escáner Live

This app is one of the early access applications, that is, it has not yet been released to the market in its final version. It offers important functionalities such as facial and open space scanning and uses photogrammetry as a technique. Figure 1 shows the capture process: the first step was to load the app and select the online photogrammetry option to proceed with capturing the images at the previously established distance and angle. The photographs were taken according to the app's own guide that appears on the screen; once the shots required by the application are completed, it starts processing the data, to finally present the generated 3D object.

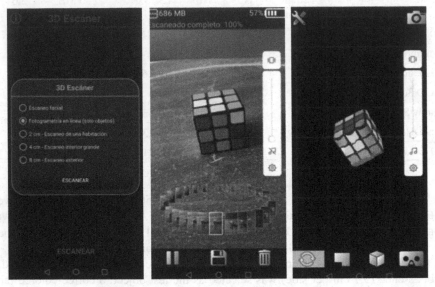

Fig. 1. Capture process with 3D Escáner Live app

2.2 3DScanLink

This app has two capture modes: 1. Laser and 2. Photography, being the second alternative for which it was selected. The process is similar to the one described in the previous application, except that there is no position guide for the photographs, so the same locations from the previous experiment were used. At the end, the photographs are uploaded to the cloud to be processed and project the generated 3D object. Figure 2 shows the executed process.

2.3 Qlone

Is an application that requires a template that is available for download in the same app and on which the object to be scanned is located, which represents a limitation regarding the size of the bodies to be captured since they must necessarily reach inside the matrix. Additionally, the same app creates a sphere on the mobile screen within which the object must be centered. The capture process ends when the entire capsule appears colored. Figure 3 shows the capsule of the test object and the result obtained.

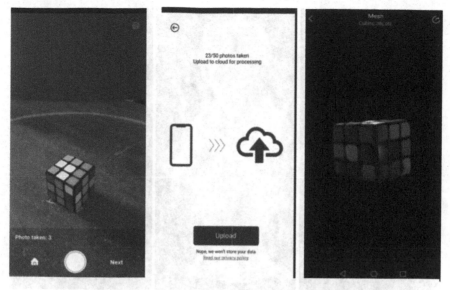

Fig. 2. Capture process with 3DScanLink

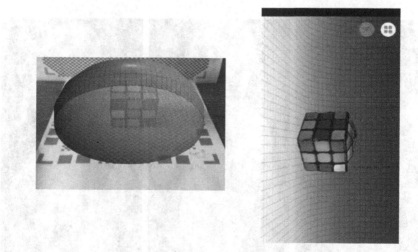

Fig. 3. Capture process in the Qlone app

To carry out tests regarding the size variable, a ceramic human figure (child) was chosen, available in various sizes and with a predominant cream color. The measurements of each object are presented in Table 2.

All the captures were made through the rear camera of the smartphone described above and through the viewer of each app. The accuracy of each of the application viewers is presented in the metric results section when comparing the obtained object versus the

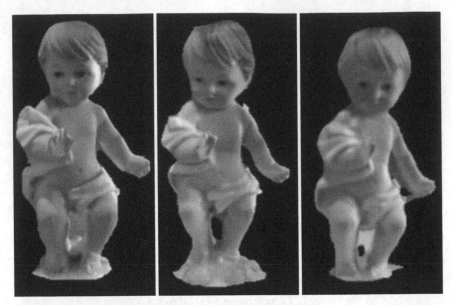

Fig. 4. Results obtained with the 3D Escáner Live app

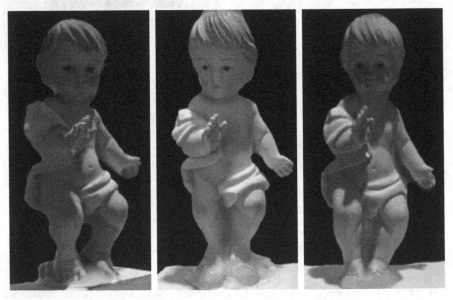

Fig. 5. Results obtained with the 3DScanLink app.

real object. The 3D objects obtained with the 3D Escáner Live app are presented in Fig. 4 according to the order presented in Table 2.

With the 3DScanLink application, the three-dimensional objects shown in Fig. 5 corresponding respectively to the order of Table 2 were obtained.

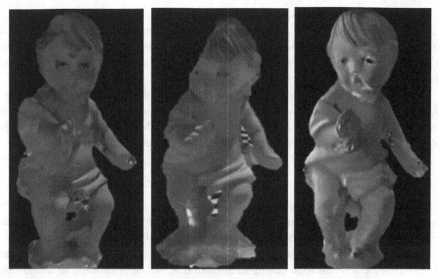

Fig. 6. Results obtained with the Qlone app

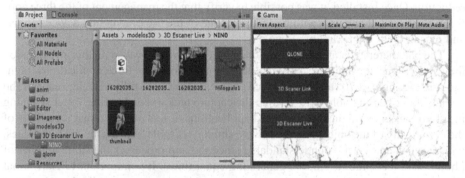

Fig. 7. Screenshot of the Assets folder

Table 2. Measurements of the test objects

Description	Height (cm)	Wide (cm)
Boy 1	19	11
Boy 2	15	8
Boy 3	9	6

Finally, the scan was performed with the Qlone tool and the results obtained are presented in Fig. 6.

The next step was the creation of a prototype augmented reality application using the Vuforia software development kit – Unity version 2018.4.36f1. The objective of the app was to verify that the 3D objects created digitally in the selected apps can be used for AR solutions. The application had three action buttons: Btn3DEscanerLive, Btn3DScannerLink and BtnQlone. Pressing one of the buttons brings up the corresponding 3D object, which was previously loaded as a Unity asset. The Assets folder is seen in Fig. 7.

In the prototype app, the ImageTarget resource was used as a marker for the recognition of RA objects, so when the application is executed on the mobile device, the camera is activated, it recognizes the image, and it searches the database for the object that matches the detected characteristics and finally presents it on the screen.

3 Results

According to the results obtained on the Glassdoor platform, in Latin America the monthly salary of a 3D designer varies between $400 to $600 and the time required depends on the degree of knowledge, experience and of course the characteristics of the object to be modeled, a fact that is mentioned since The intention of this research is to minimize costs and time during the creation of AR applications, so a mid-range cell phone with basic features that supports AR was used and only applications that do not require payment for use were selected, with which intend to demonstrate cost reduction. Once installed, it was possible to verify that the management of the three apps is intuitive, so that any user with basic knowledge of the use of a mobile device can use and master them in maximum of one day.

The parameters: distance and angle of capture can vary, however, in this investigation they were set as constants to apply the same conditions in the three applications, highlighting the angle of 70° and the distance of 16 cm allowed to fully visualize each of the objects described in Table 2. Regarding the capture and processing time, after scanning the study objects with the three selected applications, it was observed that regardless of the complexity of the object, the times were similar, so Table 3 shows the median values, which, when analyzed, is understandable since the app processes the same number of photos with the same resolution, generating equal times. It is important to clarify that the capture time is subjective to the person executing the process, while the processing depends exclusively on the app. Finally, the number of captures (23), in 3D Scanner Live is set by the app, so in the 3D Scan Link app it was set to the same number. The case of the Qlone app is different since the shots depend on the size of the capsule generated by the application.

Adding the capture and processing times, it is evident that the app that requires less time is 3D Escáner Live with 16 min, so if time is the most critical aspect, this is the tool to choose. The Qlone app differs in just 2 min from the chosen app, so if it is a question of few objects it is a minimal difference, but in a greater number the time would increase in the total sum. In addition, it should be considered that the Qlone application has a restriction regarding size, since the object to be scanned must be a maximum of the dimensions of the required template, in addition to the number of photos that are necessary for the generation of the digital 3D object they represent 12.34 times more photos compared to the other applications.

In order to compare the scans of objects with more complex shapes, a second experiment was carried out, in which the human figure was used in three different sizes. For

Table 3. Test results with the object: Rubik's cube

	3D Escáner Live	3DScanLink	Qlone
Capture time	12 min	10 min	8 min
Processing time	4 min	15 min	10 min
Capture angle	70°	70°	70°
Distance	16 cm	16 cm	16 cm
Number of photos	23	23	284

the analysis of results, the methodology of quantitative evaluation of textured models was used, which quantitatively evaluates the reconstruction of textured models from the application of a texture mapping method through various metrics that establish the relationship and correspondence between 3D information and texture. The metrics presented are applied to a single range image or to a fully reconstructed textured model [14]. Each metric: density; number of textures over number of visible points; Variation of model curvature with texture edges; and, difference of shapes and comparison of contours with distance measurement, was adapted for this study according to its own characteristics. To obtain the values of the metrics, the 3D Object Converter program was used, which generated the values that allowed the comparison of the 3D objects analyzed to be quantified.

The metrics mentioned are not related to each other; thus, the density measures the level of detail in the texture of the object and the number of textures on visible points indicates if there are spaces that have not been covered with the texture, in these two metrics the information is retrieved from the 3D object by means of of a viewer, ie it is compared with the.obj file. The difference in shapes and comparison of contours with distance measurement, on the other hand, are carried out by comparing 2D images of the objects obtained with respect to the 2D image captured of the original object.

Regarding the density (number of pixels in the polygon), a metric that determines the level of detail that the texture possesses on the digital model, the results presented in Table 4 were obtained with the three objects and in the three applications.

Table 4. Density metric results.

	Small	Medium	Large
3D Escáner Live	6,62	7,043	7,31
3DScanLink	4,87	6,95	12, 66
Qlone	0,23	0,29	3,1

According to the values obtained, the 3D Escáner Live app, both in the small and medium sized objects, contain the highest number of pixels, which is directly related to the texturing detail and therefore to the quality of the model. In the case of the largest object, the highest density was achieved with the 3DScanLink app; however, it must be taken into account that, due to its dimensions, it exceeded the capture area, so the value includes a surplus area that corresponds to the environment.

The next parameter considered was the number of textures over the number of visible points (number of polygons), which quantifies the points projected on the image. In this aspect, it is emphasized that the 3D model always generates a value of 100% for the texture map in the three applications, however, this scan includes not only the object but also the scenery. Therefore, it is important that there is a high contrast between the object and the surface on which it rests. The results are presented in Table 5.

Table 5. Results of the metric number of textured over number of visible points.

Application	Small		Medium		Large	
	Polygon	Polygon UV	Polygon	Polygon UV	Polygon	Polygon UV
3D Escáner Live	44802	44802	72268	72268	104336	104336
3DScanLink	204055	204055	221482	221482	369648	369648
Qlone	56376	56376	87840	87840	143472	143472

According to the values obtained, it is observed that the 3DScanLink application is the one that captures the most points for the texture parameter. In the case of this experiment, both the number of polygons of the object and the number of polygons covered by the texture (UV texture) are equal, so the capture is made of the entire surface.

The next metric analyzed was the difference in shapes and the comparison of contours with distance measurement, for which the Python programming language was used with the OpenCv, Structural_similarity & Numpy libraries that measure the similarity of the three-dimensional digital object created by each application relative to the physical object. The results are presented in Table 6.

Table 6. Results of the metric difference of shapes and comparison of contours

	Small (%)	Medium (%)	Large (%)
3D Escáner Live	90.17	90.41	90.10
3DScanLink	90.64	90.83	88.26
Qlone	90.04	88.62	89.94

This metric measures the number of textures over the number of visible points, which quantifies the points projected on the image and, as shown in Table 6, the 3DScanLink application generates the highest percentage of similarity of contours with respect to the physical object in the small and medium objects, while in the largest object it is the 3D Escáner Live app that has the highest value.

Finally, the variation of the curvature of the model with the texture edges was compared with the distance measurement, which differs from the previous parameter, since it analyzes the level of detail considering all the internal curves and external edges, obtaining the percentages of similarity that are presented in Table 7.

Table 7. Curvature variation metric results.

	Small (%)	Medium (%)	Large (%)
3D Escáner Live	63.23	66.36	58.25
3DScanLink	59.64	63.13	54.73
Qlone	58.05	58.64	58.01

When analyzing the values obtained, it is observed that, although in the analysis of external edges, it was the 3DScanLink app that obtained the highest percentage of similarity, in the metric that makes a comparison of all the internal and external curvatures, it is the app 3D Escáner Live the one with the highest values in all three object sizes.

After verifying all the metrics considered for the comparison, it is observed that the 3D Escáner Live application generates the highest density, as well as the best results in terms of shape comparison with an average of 90.23% and curvatures (detail of the 3D model) with an average of 62.61%, so it is concluded that it would be the best alternative, if it is about choosing a totally free tool that generates models that can be used by an RA app. At least until the date on which the investigation was carried out.

4   Discussion

When reviewing specialized bibliography on this subject, an article was found on recommendations for the digitization of objects, describing some specifications that have been accepted by other investigations [15, 16], in which easily accessible, economical and transportable equipment was used. In this work, suggestions were also considered to achieve the best quality of the final products.

Unlike the investigation by [15], in the present investigation we worked exclusively with daylight and with dimming to eliminate the brightness on the most prominent edges. In the same way, instead of using a professional camera, the one included in the mobile device was used, generating images with a resolution of 16 Mp.

Regarding the photogrammetry technique, it coincides with what was expressed by [17], that is, it is projected as a promising alternative due to its effectiveness, ease of use and low cost.

Regarding the use of mobile applications for photogrammetry and modeling of 3D objects, in the research carried out by [18], a search was also made for apps for smartphones that allow facial scanning, both for iOS and Android, in the mentioned investigation 6 eligible mobile applications were found: Bellus 3D, Heges, Scandy Pro, Capture, Trnio, 3D scanner Pro. It differs from this work, in that it was limited to tools under the Android operating system, free and for any type of object, although an object with a human face (greater complexity than another object) was chosen, to ensure that it can be used in any modeling. As these are different tools, it is not possible to make a comparison between the results obtained; however, it can be concluded that in both cases it was possible to identify mobile applications that generate good quality 3D objects for their respective objectives.

5   Conclusions

For the experiment of this research, the distance and capture angle parameters were previously set and kept constant. Regarding the capture and processing time, it is observed that they remain constant without the complexity of the object influencing this value.

At the end of the experiment in the three applications, it is evident that the 3D Escáner Live app is the one that requires less time (capture + processing) to obtain the resulting digital 3D object, therefore, if time is the most critical aspect, this It is the tool of choice.

The metrics used in the experiment are defined in the quantitative evaluation methodology of textured models: density; number of textures over number of visible points; variation of model curvature with texture edges; and, difference of shapes and comparison of contours with distance measurement. In this way, the reconstruction of textured models is quantitatively evaluated from the application of a mapping method, making the results visible in numerical terms.

The three selected applications return objects that are recognized by an augmented reality app; however, according to the values obtained, it is observed that the 3D Escáner Live app is the one that generates the best result in the applied metrics.

The use of tools such as 3D Object Converter is necessary to find the numerical values that allow the comparison to be quantified and objective results to be exposed.

References

1. Barrile, V., Fotia, A., Bilotta, G.: Geomatics and augmented reality experiments for the cultural heritage. Appl. Geomatics **10**(4), 569–578 (2018). https://doi.org/10.1007/s12518-018-0231-5
2. Ch'ng, E., Cai, S., Zhang, T.E., Leow, F.T.: Crowdsourcing 3D cultural heritage: best practice for mass photogrammetry. J. Cult. Herit. Manag. Sustain. Dev. **9**(1), 24–42 (2019)
3. Prokhorov, O.V., Lisovichenko, V.O., Mazorchuk, M.S., Kuzminska, O.H.: Developing a 3D quest game for career guidance to estimate students' digital competences. CEUR Workshop Proc. **2731**, 312–327 (2020)
4. Iglhaut, J., Cabo, C., Puliti, S., Piermattei, L., O'Connor, J., Rosette, J.: Structure from motion photogrammetry in forestry: a review. Curr. For. Rep. **5**(3), 155–168 (2019). https://doi.org/10.1007/s40725-019-00094-3
5. Eve, S.: Losing our senses, an exploration of 3D object scanning. Open Archaeol. **4**(1), 114–122 (2018)
6. Tokarieva, V., Volkova, N.P., Harkusha, I.V., Soloviev, V.N.: Educational digital games: models and implementation. CEUR Workshop Proc. **2433**, 74–89 (2019)
7. Aicardi, I., Chiabrando, F., Lingua, A., Noardo, F.: Recent trends in cultural heritage 3D survey: the photogrammetric computer vision approach (2017)

8. De Paolis, L.T., De Luca, V., Gatto, C., D'Errico, G., Paladini, G.I.: Photogrammetric 3D reconstruction of small objects for a real-time fruition. In: De Paolis, L.T., Bourdot, P. (eds.) Augmented Reality, Virtual Reality, and Computer Graphics. LNCS, vol. 12242, pp. 375–394. Springer, Cham (2020). https://doi.org/10.1007/978-3-030-58465-8_28

9. Lyra, V.G.M., et al.: Development of an efficient 3D reconstruction solution from permissive open-source code. In: Proceedings - 2020 22nd Symposium on Virtual and Augmented Reality, SVR 2020, pp. 232–241 (2020)

10. Aljabar, H., Cahyono, A.B., Hidayat, H.: Application of augmented reality and close range photogrammetry technology for mapping of cultural heritage areas (case study: Ai Renung Site, Sumbawa Regency). IOP Conf. Ser. Earth Environ. Sci. **389**(1) (2019)

11. Templin, T., Popielarczyk, D.: The use of low-cost unmanned aerial vehicles in the process of building models for cultural tourism, 3D web and augmented/mixed reality applications. Sensors (Switzerland) **20**(19), 1–26 (2020)

12. Voinea, G.-D., Girbacia, F., Postelnicu, C.C., Marto, A.: Exploring cultural heritage using augmented reality through Google's project tango and ARCore. In: Duguleană, M., Carrozzino, M., Gams, M., Tanea, I. (eds.) VR Technologies in Cultural Heritage. CCIS, vol. 904, pp. 93–106. Springer, Cham (2019). https://doi.org/10.1007/978-3-030-05819-7_8

13. Maiwald, F., Henze, F., Bruschke, J.N.F.: Geo-information technologies for a multimodal access on historical photographs and maps for research and communication in urban history. ISPRS Ann. Photogramm. Remote Sens. Spat. Inf. Sci. **42**(2/W11), 763–769 (2019)

14. Hernández, J., Prieto, F.: Metodología de evaluación cuantitativa de modelos texturados. Dyna **74**, 115–124 (2007)

15. Bucchi, A., Luengo, J., Fuentes, R., Arellano-Villalon, M., Lorenzo, C.: Recomendaciones para mejorar la calidad de las fotos en fotogrametría de corto alcance, ejemplificado en huesos de las manos de chimpancés y gorilas. Int. J. Morphol. **38**(2), 348–355 (2020)

16. Lauria, G., Sineo, L., Ficarra, S.: A detailed method for creating digital 3D models of human crania: an example of close-range photogrammetry based on the use of Structure-from-Motion (SfM) in virtual anthropology. Archaeol. Anthropol. Sci. **14**(3) (2022). https://doi.org/10.1007/s12520-022-01502-9

17. Novotny, A.C.: Implementing photogrammetry in three bioarchaeological contexts: steps for in-field documentation. Adv. Archaeol. Pract. **7**(1), 87–96 (2019)

18. Dzelzkalēja, L., Knets, J., Rozanovskis, N., Sīlītis, A.: Mobile apps for 3D face scanning. In: Intelligent Systems Conference, IntelliSys 2021, vol. 295, pp. 34–50 (2022)

A Web App for Teaching Specialized English Vocabulary – Case of Study: Computer Sciences

Ricardo Fabrizio Martínez-Valencia⃝, José Antonio Montero-Valverde⁽⊠⁾ ⃝,
Miriam Martínez-Arroyo⃝, and Juan Miguel Hernández-Bravo⃝

IT de Acapulco, Tecnológico Nacional de México, Acapulco, México
{mm20320010,jose.mv,miriam.ma,juan.hb}@acapulco.tecnm.mx

Abstract. In this work, it is presented a technological tool for helping students and professionals from Computer Sciences, to acquire specialized English vocabulary, in order to increase their proficiency both in the language and in the managing of technical information. Three main aspects were considered, first, a reliable source of specialized vocabulary to teach, that contains words that let users to learn useful vocabulary related to their areas; second, an effective-proven methodology for learning the vocabulary in a practical way; and third, a tracking system that allows to know the learning status and the ideal times to practice every word. Combining these factors in a single tool like a web app, it is possible to make users obtain a learning of 36 specialized English words on average per week, traduced on an average learning rate of 65.29% of the words to learn in the same interval, no mattering the English proficiency of the users. Obtained results are promising, and we continue working in its improvement.

Keywords: English vocabulary · Computer sciences · Web app

1 Introduction

English proficiency has proven to be one of the most important aspects of the high level of competitiveness in some countries, being one of the main keys for development of important areas such as economy, innovation and general well-being [12]. In fact, it has been found that places with a high English proficiency, tend to have a better Gross Domestic Product [16], a more competitive labor force [27], increasing of innovation [6], great gender equality [28], environmental care [29], and more freedom [9]. Each of these improvements are part of essential needs in countries to grow in all areas and give to their populations a better life quality.

China, South Korea, and India, have found that investment on scientific production in English, improve their level of innovation and help them to obtain a highly relevant economic growth [31]. In the case of Mexico, its population has a very low English proficiency [7], a problem that has been present for several years, and that affect negatively the growing of innovation and competitiveness [13]. Some actions have been carried out in order to improve this level, for instance, some educational institutions have tried teaching all academic courses totally in English [11]; give specialized training to professors in order to improve their English proficiency and give them enough knowledge to be able to help in a better way to students [24]; and do research to find what are the main causes associated to a low English proficiency in the country, and generation of possible solutions [1]. Despite this, new actions are still required to help solve the deficit, and use of technology is considered as one of the main channels to achieve it [18].

Currently, there are few technological tools for supporting the training of English for academic and professional purposes, and, with the rise of usage of technology for education, and the good results observed [3, 4, 10, 14, 15, 25, 32], it is essential to make use of these resources to help increase the proficiency in English, mainly, in countries where English level is low, such as Mexico.

Given the importance of English proficiency oriented to specialized areas, it was proposed a technological solution for helping students and professionals to increase their knowledge on the subject, and acquire a better understanding of all academic, technical, and scientific information available, in order to help on the development of countries competitiveness.

The solution presented in this work, takes as a case of study to the Computer Sciences area, and follows the design patterns for developing apps for teaching specialized English vocabulary [17]. Unlike other apps, it makes use of a source vocabulary list generated through a scientific methodology [23], which increase the reliability of the content to teach. Also, it is prepared for including vocabulary lists from other areas, converting it in a scalable tool that can serve as a platform for professional training both in academic and work environments in the future.

2 Related Works

Vocabulary teaching has been a subject that generates a great interest, specially, when English language is the target language to learn. Learning a language in classrooms is not enough, and students tend to utilize apps for practicing and improving their knowledge in home. However, with the use of commercial apps, and the restricted privacy of data generated from users, it is not possible to know how much they learn. For this reason, some researches have been carried out, in order to measure, from different perspectives, if users are actually learning the language, or some aspects of it, such as vocabulary and grammar, using different teaching methodologies.

Kohnke et al. [14] developed an app called "Excel@EnglishPolyU", which includes two games for learning vocabulary. The first one is a "hangman" style game, where a grid of letters is given to users, and they have to choose letters one by one until forming the hidden word, having only a limited number of movements. The second one, presents a brief description of every word, which users take as a clue in order to infer which word the app is trying to teach, users write their answer in a field and the app validates if it is correct or not. The app was tested with 51 business undergraduate students ranging from 19 to 23 years age. The process consisted in a pre-test and post-test comparison about their business English vocabulary knowledge before and after using the app. In the pre-test users were asked about their knowledge of 120 words grouped by difficult (30 words for each level: beginner, elementary, intermediate, advanced), through the question "Do you know the word?", with only two possible answers: yes, or, no. From this, it was taken the percentage of students who reported to know all of the words in each level. Then, it was requested to students to use the app for a period of one month. At the end of this period, a post-test was applied, having the same questions and answers, and measuring again the total percentage of students who reported to know all of the words in each level. After this, it was found an increment of 2.67% of students who acquired all beginner level words; 2.13% who learned all elementary words; 4.81% for the intermediate level words; and, 3.52% for the advanced ones.

Chen et al. [4] studied the effects of using mobile game-based apps for teaching English vocabulary. Through the implementation of "PHONE Words", an app that includes three types of games (tic-tac-toe, spelling, and word selection), a group of 10 university students made use of the tool during a period of 4 weeks, measuring their vocabulary knowledge using a TOEIC based exam with 15 words to evaluate, before and after using the app. The obtained results were compared to a similar 10 students' group results who learned the same vocabulary set in the same period, but with an app that does not implement game mechanics. Researchers found that users who used a game-based app, had a better score (14.7 pre-test, 48.9 post-test) than those who used a non-game-based app (14.7 pre-test, 39.3 post-test).

Bueno and Nemeth [3] made a research where 25 university students (native Spanish speakers) with ages from 18 to 61, and B2 English level proficiency, used for 3 weeks the Quizlet app for learning English vocabulary related to work and employment subjects, as well as to science and technology areas, through a flashcard activity. Using a pre-test and post-test conformed by a 14-words evaluation, researchers measured how many words users learned using the app, finding a learning average of 11 words for work and employment vocabulary, and 9 for science and technology areas.

Some other works were analyzed but were not included here because of the lack of similar characteristics to the current work, such as the target population (university students), focused on teaching vocabulary, and the use of an app with game-based activities for learning English words.

3   App Design

It was proposed to create a tool that implemented an effective learning methodology, multiplatform, and with reliable content. For these reasons, it was decided to develop a web application, since it offers the possibility of creating adaptable interfaces to different devices such as smartphones, tablets, and desktop computers, as well as being independent from the operating system, and providing the technological resources for the correct implementation of the chosen teaching methodology.

Before starting to create the tool, the core components were selected: the vocabulary list that contains the words to be taught, the learning activity to be implemented in the app, and the method for controlling when the words have to be practiced.

First, it was made an analysis over the Computer Science related vocabulary lists in English available in literature, being found two candidates that contains, specifically, the content type needed: Computer Science Word List (CSWL) [20], and Computer Science Vocabulary List (CSAVL) [23].

The first one, created in 2013, is compound by 433 family words categorized in 10 subdisciplines, which are determined by the Association for Computing Machinery (ACM) (computer systems organization, computing methodologies, hardware, human-centered computing, information systems, mathematics of computing, networks, security and privacy, software and its engineering, theory of computation).

The second one, from 2021, contains 1,606 words categorized by parts of speech (nouns, adjectives, verbs, adverbs, prepositions), which represent 19.90% of a corpus of approximately 700,000 words extracted from textbooks and journal articles in Computer Sciences (CSWL has a 5.57% coverage for the same corpus).

Given that the goal of the app is being used as a tool for incrementing the vocabulary knowledge in breadth, it took more relevance the number of words that every list offered. Besides, it is also pretended that users can reach a better understanding of academic, scientific, and technical texts in English that they read, so, the list with the highest coverage was preferred over the other. For these reasons, CSAVL was selected as the vocabulary list for conforming the app database.

Both, learning activity and time control method, were selected based on how these could work together. SuperMemo 2 is a spaced repetition methodology that works along with flashcards activity, and that has been demonstrated to be very effective in vocabulary acquisition [30]. Flashcards are used for learning the highest number of possible words in a short time, which perfectly aligned to the purposes of the app.

This way, it was determined to use these three elements as the base components for the app development.

3.1 Database

In order to implement the SuperMemo 2 methodology as the app teaching algorithm, it was necessary to prepare the database that could serve all required information for making the flashcards to work.

First, all words from CSAVL were stored in a CSV (Comma Separated Value) file, specifying in each line, the English word as the first element, and type (part of speech) as the second one.

Next, it was used the Google Cloud Translation (GCT) service to obtain all translations for every word in the list. It was used the expert judgment technique for selecting the best translation in every case, considering context from region and area.

A group of seven experts in Computer Sciences with a high level of English selected the best translations that could be better understood in Mexico, and with a closer meaning to the area. For example, according to GCT the word *computer* had as most popular translation to *ordenador*, and while this is not incorrect, this translation is not usually used in Mexico, instead *computadora* is more frequently used, so in this case experts selected the second translation over the first one.

Once completed this task, the most selected translations were integrated into de CSV file (one translation per word). In cases where two translations had the same number of selections, the most popular word according to GCT was selected. The final CSV file containing 1,606 registers and 3 columns (English word, type, and translation) was uploaded to a database in the MongoDB Atlas platform.

It was also considered to provide a simple usage example for every word inside the flashcards, so, it was necessary to have a set of English example sentences in the database. The source used for acquiring these examples was the OPUS CORPUS API, which allows to search example sentences, according to a word and its context.

Also, it is possible to choose the source corpuses, such as Wikipedia, Wikimedia, and SciELO magazines. For each word, 50 example sentences were obtained and loaded into the database.

```
word: "algorithm"
type: "noun"
translation: "algoritmo"
∨ examples: Array
    0: "nthusiastic evangelist ". == History == The RSA algorithm was publicly…"
    1: "ach processing element can execute its part of the algorithm simultane…"
    2: "ding this problem returns the answer " yes ", the algorithm is said to…"
    3: "n ". In other words, there is a polynomial-time algorithm that transfo…"
    4: "y approach very similar to that used by Huffman's algorithm. No algori…"
    5: "icensing dispute with regard to the use of the RSA algorithm in PGP, t…"
    6: "a premium, one might deliberately choose a slower algorithm in order t…"
    7: "e most powerful optimization is to find a superior algorithm. Although…"
    8: "The origin of this  algorithm  is the type inferencealgorithmfor the s…"
    9: "in the famous Davisson-Germer experiment. Shor's algorithm consists of…"
    10: "encryption is replaced by an MD5-based encryption algorithm. The encry…"
```

Fig. 1. Example document for every word in the database.

Figure 1 shows an example document generated in the database, which contains the information related to each word, and that is used as data source for the flashcards.

3.2 Interfaces

Since the SuperMemo 2 algorithm requires the use of flashcards to generate the necessary information to tracking user practices, it was necessary to develop an interface that would follow the guidelines for this type of activity. This way, a practice round view (Fig. 2) was implemented, it contains simple elements such as:

- Flashcard with the word in English on the front, along with its type and a usage example of the word, and the Spanish translation on the back.
- A text box where the user can, based on the information provided, write the translation, being able to confirm the answer by clicking a confirmation button (arrow button) or by pressing the enter key on keyboard.
- An answer correctness indicator, which let to know whether the translation given by the user is correct (green checkmark) or incorrect (red cross).
- An indicator of remaining time to answer (blue line).
- Indicator of the words to practice in the round (10 words per game round)
- Control buttons for skipping words (in case the user does not know the answer), and for finishing the round.

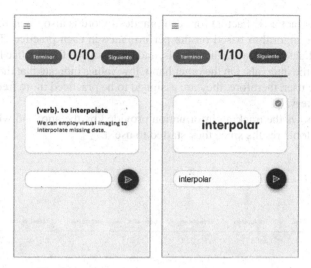

Fig. 2. Flashcard interface. (Color figure online)

Fig. 3. Round results.

After finishing each round, a results view is presented (Fig. 3), which includes the number of correct and incorrect words (and percentage), and the average response time. This information is useful when users want to compare their round results.

Spaced repetition algorithms keep track of the results in every practice, based on this, they are able to determine the ideal reinforcement dates. In the case of the implemented algorithm, in addition to the dates, it also tracks the number of correct and incorrect answers, and based on this information, calculates the effectiveness rate.

An easiness factor (E-Factor) for each practiced word is also tracked. This value is obtained by the algorithm based on the performance in each practice. The higher the value of the E-Factor, the easier the word is, and it is assigned for practice less frequently and at longer time intervals. On the other hand, low values indicate that the word is more difficult for the user, therefore, they are assigned to be practiced more frequently and in shorter time intervals.

Figure 4 shows the tracking information provided by the app, and where users can explore their global results since they started to use it.

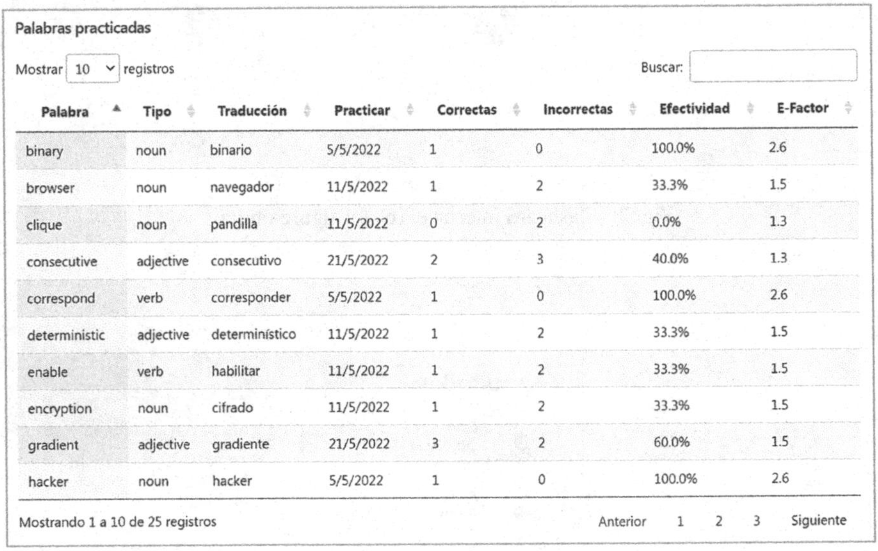

Palabras practicadas							
Mostrar 10 ⌄ registros						Buscar:	
Palabra ▲	Tipo ⇕	Traducción ⇕	Practicar ⇕	Correctas ⇕	Incorrectas ⇕	Efectividad ⇕	E-Factor ⇕
binary	noun	binario	5/5/2022	1	0	100.0%	2.6
browser	noun	navegador	11/5/2022	1	2	33.3%	1.5
clique	noun	pandilla	11/5/2022	0	2	0.0%	1.3
consecutive	adjective	consecutivo	21/5/2022	2	3	40.0%	1.3
correspond	verb	corresponder	5/5/2022	1	0	100.0%	2.6
deterministic	adjective	determinístico	11/5/2022	1	2	33.3%	1.5
enable	verb	habilitar	11/5/2022	1	2	33.3%	1.5
encryption	noun	cifrado	11/5/2022	1	2	33.3%	1.5
gradient	adjective	gradiente	21/5/2022	3	2	60.0%	1.5
hacker	noun	hacker	5/5/2022	1	0	100.0%	2.6
Mostrando 1 a 10 de 25 registros					Anterior 1 2 3 Siguiente		

Fig. 4. Vocabulary tracking

4   Methodology

The methodology approach was specifically shaped in order to focus on vocabulary acquisition, rather than concerning about user experience, user interfaces, behavioral research, pedagogical methodologies exploration, develop of assessment tools, or implementation of trending technologies. Also, it was considered a total focus on specialized vocabulary, principally, because many solutions for learning general vocabulary exist nowadays, coming, not only from a scientific environment, but also from a commercial one; furthermore, the solution is oriented to a Spanish speaking audience by the moment, this because of the problem given in Mexico, but in the future, is considered to include more languages.

Due to the large number of existing academic and professional areas, it was decided to limit the target population to which the tool was going to attend. The area of Computer Science was chosen because it represents one of the most important areas today, not only because of its popularity, but also because of its great influence on the development of innovation and competitiveness of the countries.

In the context of this work, it was decided to do an evaluation throughout the comparison of proficiency in English vocabulary of Computer Science, before and after using the app (pre-test and post-test). To carry out this, the Y/N test [19] was selected as the evaluation instrument, because it allows knowing in breadth the vocabulary knowledge of the users, using a practical word selection activity. This makes possible to find a general idea of the vocabulary knowledge acquired by users in a wide set of words. However, it is important to mention that these results trust on users' asseverations, so, it must be applied a more standardized evaluation for knowing the real proficiency in the future.

The process involved 32 people (7 women and 25 men) with ages ranging from 19 to 65 years. Each one belongs to an academic or professional area related to Computer Sciences, and with different levels of English.

The complete process is divided in four steps (Fig. 5):

1. A 200-word set is generated, conformed by 140 from CSAVL and 60 imaginary words (obtained from thisworddoesnotexist.com).
2. Next, users do a first Y/N test style evaluation (pre-test).
3. Users have to use the app at least 7 days, for 5 min a day.
4. Finally, users have to perform a second evaluation over the same 200-word set generated (post-test).

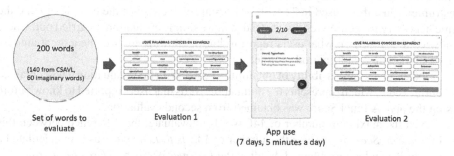

Fig. 5. Procedure to evaluate vocabulary learning.

Figure 6 shows the selection form created for the evaluation. It consists of a group of buttons containing the English words along with the question ¿*Which words do you know in Spanish?*

In order to facilitate the task, the elements were presented in groups of 20 words, giving the option for going back to check previous selected words, and going forward to see next group, this, until reaching the limit of 200 words.

Once having the scores from the pre-test and post-test, a comparison was made in order to find the average number of words that users were able to learn after using the app, as well as the learning rate (number of learned words from those that did not know in the pre-test).

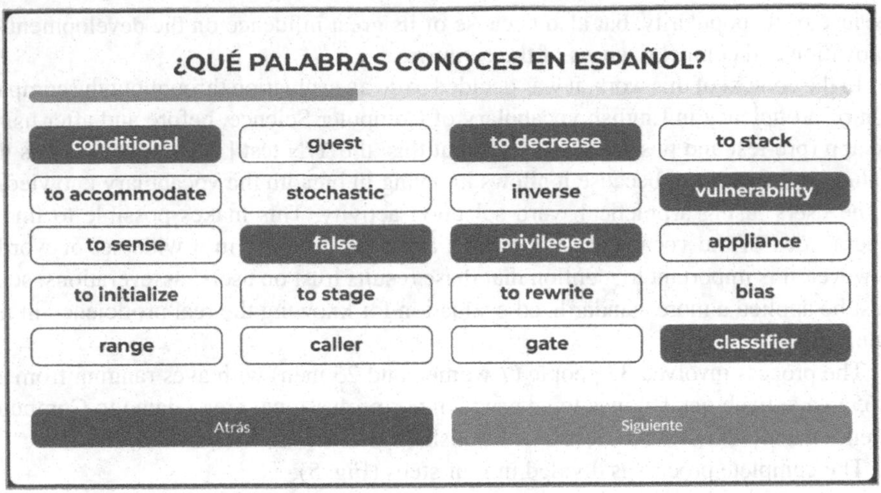

Fig. 6. Selection form used for evaluating the words according to Y/N test.

5 Results

After the two evaluations, it was possible to know how much vocabulary users acquired, this, based on results generated by the Y/N test.

As mentioned before, this test focus on an evaluation in breadth, rather than in depth. This means that vocabulary knowledge is not obtained by applying a standard evaluation instrument (like those used in TOEFL, for instance) because of the complexity and the time necessary for getting results, instead, a more simple evaluation is carried out, where knowledge is based on what users report to know, allowing to evaluate a great amount of vocabulary in a short period of time.

Y/N test gives the possibility of obtaining a score. With first evaluation it was obtained an Initial Score, which represents the number of words that users reported to know before using the app. A Final Score was obtained from second evaluation.

Given the maximum number of 140 words to evaluate, the difference between this and the *Initial Score* represents the number of *Words to Learn*. It was also calculated a *Learning Rate* which is obtained dividing the *Learned Words* by *Words to Learn*.

5.1 Learning

First, a general measurement was obtained based on results of all participants. It was found that users reported to know around 83.58 out of 140 words average in the first evaluation, and this number increased to 120.42 in the second one, having a learning of 36.84 words average in one week, and, given that users had to learn 56.42 words after first evaluation, this represents a learning rate of 65.29% (Fig. 7).

Regarding to English level of users, an expected pattern was found in the knowledge of words after the evaluations, because, as the level of English increases the number of words they report to know also increases. However, the learning rate remains stable among all, ranging between 62.68% and 68.42% (Fig. 8).

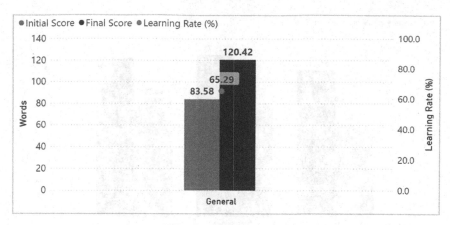

Fig. 7. General results.

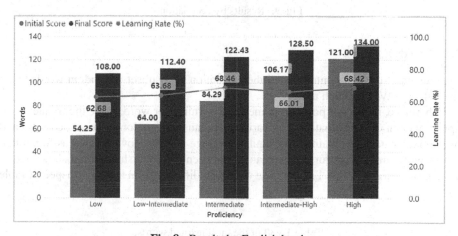

Fig. 8. Results by English level.

The occupation was also taken into account. In this category, it was found that those who are entirely professionals had the greatest learning rate, followed by those who report studying and working, and finally those who only dedicate to studying (Fig. 9).

Also, some other results were obtained from the evaluations. For example, it was observed, that users with an age ranging from 35 to 45 learned more (87.5%), than older than 45 (75%), ranging 25 to 35 (65.7%), and younger than 25 (63%).

Regarding to app usage time, those users who use it 10–20 min a day had a better learning rate (71.01%), than those who used it 5–10 min (61.21%) and 20–30 min (59.46%).

Considering only students, those who are currently studying a Bachelor's learned more (62.74%) than those who study a Master's (58.74%). Among professionals, those with 10–20 years of work experience learned more (81.05%), than users with more than 20 years of experience (75%) and less than 10 (66.35%).

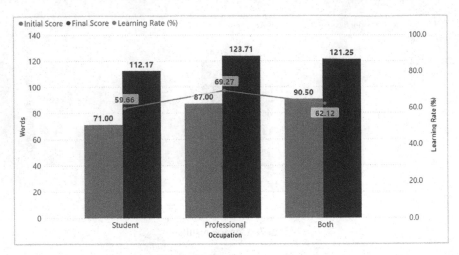

Fig. 9. Results by occupation.

5.2 Words Easiness

The design of the test contemplated the evaluation of a subset of random words taken from the CSAVL, by each user.

Therefore, it was not possible to measure learning per word, since the frequency of appearance in each evaluation was variable (because of randomly generated sets) and not enough data was obtained to calculate average results. However, it was found that words with similarity in form and meaning between the Spanish and English languages were more learned (Table 1) than those with clear differences in these two aspects (Table 2).

Table 1. 30 of the most learned words.

Word	Translation	Word	Translation	Word	Translation
to click	hacer clic	read	leer	to attribute	atribuir
proof	a prueba de	formulation	formulación	duplicate	duplicado
to monitor	monitorear	self	uno mismo	constant	constante
import	importación	primitive	primitivo	robot	robot
malware	malware	invalid	inválido	inverse	inverso
variable	variable	to link	enlazar	null	nulo
to double	duplicar	list	lista	machine	máquina
numerical	numérico	category	categoría	formula	fórmula
base	base	structure	estructura	to color	colorear
virtual	virtual	to check	comprobar	dependency	dependencia

These results coincide with the findings made by some authors [3, 5, 8, 21, 22, 25, 26] who have found that this phenomenon occurs in students of new languages, and where there is a higher learning rate when there are similar words between native and second language.

Table 2. 30 of the least learned words.

Word	Translation	Word	Translation	Word	Translation
strain	tensión	tensor	tensor	to track	rastrear
leakage	fuga	mesh	malla	halt	alto
compound	compuesto	assertion	afirmación	virtue	virtud
taint	mancha	to tune	afinar	nil	nula
appliance	aparato	backward	hacia atrás	strut	puntal
outer	exterior	pairwise	parcs	spam	spam
vertex	vértice	jammer	bloqueador	usage	uso
joint	junta	to bind	enlazar	to crack	romper
to augment	aumentar	to constrain	restringir	to pump	bombear
depth	profundidad	to unroll	desenrollar	assignment	asignación

5.3 Imaginary Words Selection Incidences

No events were observed in which users claimed to know the imaginary words, which coincide with the expected behavior according to educational level of participants, that is, people with higher education tend to be more objective about their skills, while those with lower education tend to overestimate their knowledge, indicating to know more than they really do [2].

6 Conclusions

The goal of this app is to serve as a tool to support the learning of specialized vocabulary, which allows students and professionals, acquire the words that they will mostly find in their academic and professional environments, giving them a best understanding of English texts related to their areas of interest, and this way, helping them to improve their activities.

After the app development and evaluation, favorable results were obtained in terms of its usefulness. This was achieved through the implementation of strategies and teaching resources that have proven to be highly effective in teaching English vocabulary, such as flashcards, spaced repetition algorithms, and reliable vocabulary lists.

With this app, it is possible to learn around 36 new words on average per week (from 140 words), using it around 10 to 20 min a day, which does not require much effort time from users. And, regardless the starting English proficiency before using the app, it was observed that all users obtained almost the same learning rate (between 60% and 70%), which shows that the tool does not favor to any group in particular, and that it offers the same learning opportunities to any person independently of the entry English level.

It is important to mention that, given de length of the vocabulary list used for this particular case of study (1,606 words), users would have to practice around 45 weeks to acquire all words, this is, around 10.3 months on average. This time could differ depending on the user skills, the available time for practicing, and the number of words known before starting to use the app.

It was also found that there are some aspects that influence to have a greater learning rate, such as age and years of professional experience. However, it is important to mention that people that have been doing some specific activities for longer periods, either academically or professionally, have a greater chance of being involved in tasks and projects where English is needed, giving them the possibility of practicing while working. This could be the reason why older and more experienced people got better results.

Regarding to educational level, this time there was only the opportunity to have the participation of bachelor's and master's students, so it was only possible to carry out the comparison between them, obtaining that those of bachelor's level tend to have better learning rate than masters' students. This is possibly due to the fact that English subjects are included in the undergraduate academic programs, or students are required to join extra classes to acquire the language, a situation that does not occur usually at the postgraduate level.

Finally, considering that in the future, new vocabulary lists from other areas will be added to the app, new evaluations have to be done, in order to compare the learning rates among students and professionals with different specializations and technical backgrounds, and this way, find the patterns and correlations among all involved variables and determine the causes of a higher o lower learning using the app.

7 Future Work

One of the concerns in this work was to evaluate in general terms, the usefulness of technology for language learning purposes in specific areas, this time, focusing on English vocabulary learning oriented to Computer Sciences.

The app core components were carefully selected in order to develop a tool that could offer a good learning experience, as well as a good effectiveness for vocabulary retention. Even so, it needs to be improved through addition of new features, resources and methodologies that can make it a more robust tool for new English learners from other areas.

First, although flashcards are a very reliable way of teaching vocabulary, it is not ensured that every user can effectively learn using this method. For this reason, it is planned to implement new teaching activities, in order to offer a greater variety of learning modes to let users choose the kind of activities that fit better to them, including spelling, word associations, word inference (crosswords), word pronunciation, grammar rules, and listening.

Second, new vocabulary lists will be added to the database, in order to cover a wider population and test if the obtained learning rates keep the same in all different professional and academic areas. This is an important point to explore, given that in related researches have not been showed an extensive investigation about it.

Finally, as mentioned before, it was obtained a general overview of user learning experience. The evaluation method used, does not measure in a deep way the amount of vocabulary that users effectively acquire, in the sense that Y/N test trust on users' asseverations of knowing the words, rather than on results from a standardized measuring method. Given this, it is planned to use a new instrument for evaluating the vocabulary knowledge, in order to obtain a more accurate result for comparing against learning rates from similar tools, taking into account as well, the increase of participants and time intervals of the tests.

References

1. Aguilar, N.S., Badillo, B.S.D.S., Jöns, S.: Factores Relacionados con la reprobación en inglés en educación superior. Conciencia Tecnológica (54), 27–32 (2017)
2. Anderson, R.C., Freebody, P.: Reading comprehension and the assessment and acquisition of word knowledge. Center for the Study of Reading Technical Report; no. 249 (1982)
3. Bueno, M. C., Nemeth, K.: Quizlet and podcasts: effects on vocabulary acquisition. Comput. Assist. Lang. Learn. 1–30 (2020)
4. Chen, C.M., Liu, H., Huang, H.B.: Effects of a mobile game-based English vocabulary learning app on learners' perceptions and learning performance: A case study of Taiwanese EFL learners. ReCALL 31(2), 170–188 (2019)
5. Crosson, A.C., McKeown, M.G., Moore, D.W., Ye, F.: Extending the bounds of morphology instruction: teaching Latin roots facilitates academic word learning for English learner adolescents. Read. Writ. 32(3), 689–727 (2019). https://doi.org/10.1007/s11145-018-9885-y
6. Dutta, S., Lanvin, B., Wunsch-Vincent, S.: Global Innovation Index 2020. World Intellectual Property Organization (2020). https://www.globalinnovationindex.org/Home
7. Education First: EF English Proficiency Index. Education First. (2021)
8. Ehsanzadehsorati, S.: A Corpus-driven Approach toward Teaching Vocabulary and Reading to English Language Learners in US-based K-12 Context through a Mobile App (2018)
9. Freedom House: Global Freedom Scores (2020). https://freedomhouse.org/countries/freedomworld/scores
10. Gilbert, R., Matsuno, R., Ushijima, K.: VOCAL: a call multimedia concordance design for vocabulary comprehension in the sciences. In: Proceedings of 2nd International Conference on Information Based Higher Education and Training (2001)
11. González, E.O., García, I.M.: Internacionalización del currículo en México desde la innovación de asignaturas en inglés. Actualidades Investigativas en Educ. 21(2), 197–227 (2021)
12. Instituto Mexicano para la Competitividad: Inglés es Posible. Propuesta de una Agenda Nacional (2015)
13. Instituto Mexicano para la Competitividad: Índice de Competitividad Internacional (2021)
14. Kohnke, L., Zhang, R., Zou, D.: Using mobile vocabulary learning apps as aids to knowledge retention: business vocabulary acquisition. J. Asia TEFL 16(2), 683–690 (2020)
15. Kohnke, L., Zou, D., Zhang, R.: Exploring discipline-specific vocabulary retention in L2 through app design: implications for higher education students. RELC J. 52, 539–556 (2020)
16. Lanvin, B., Monteiro, F.: The Global Talent Competitiveness Index 2020. INSEAD, the Adecco Group, & Tata Communications (2020). https://gtcistudy.com/the-gtci-index

17. Martínez, R.F., Montero, J.A., Martínez, M., Hernández, J.M.: App design for teaching academic English vocabulary using spaced repetition method. J.: Rev. de Tecnol. Comput. 11–20 (2021)
18. Mexicanos Primero: Sorry. El Aprendizaje del Inglés en México. Mexicanos Primero (2015)
19. Meara, P., Buxton, B.: An alternative to multiple choice vocabulary tests. Lang. Test. **4**(2), 142–154 (1987)
20. Minshall, D.E.: A computer science word list. University of Swansea (2013)
21. Nation, I.S.P.: Beginning to learn foreign vocabulary: a review of the research. RELC J. **13**(1), 14–36 (1982). https://doi.org/10.1177/003368828201300102
22. Paiman, N., Thai, Y.N., Yuit, C.M.: Effectiveness of morphemic analysis of Graeco-Latin word parts as a vocabulary learning strategy among ESL learners. 3L: Southeast Asian J. Engl. Lang. Stud. **21**(2) (2015)
23. Roesler, D.: A Computer Science Academic Vocabulary List. Portland State University Library (2020)
24. Sánchez, M.N.: Valoración de la competencia comunicativa del inglés: estudio de caso en la Facultad de Geografía. Rev. RedCA **1**(1), 11–35 (2018)
25. Spiri, J.: Online study of frequency list vocabulary with the WordChamp website. Reflect. Engl. Lang. Teach. **7**(1), 21–36 (2008)
26. Short, D., Echevarria, J.: Teacher skills to support English language learners (2005)
27. United Nations Conference on Trade and Development: UNCTAD Productive Capacities Index – Focus on Landlocked Developing Countries (2020). https://unctad.org/system/files/officialdocument/aldc2020d2_en.pdf
28. United Nations Development Programme: Gender Inequality Index (GII) (2019). http://hdr.undp.org/en/content/gender-inequality-index-gii
29. Wendling, Z.A., Emerson, J.W., de Sherbinin, A., Esty, D.C.: 2020 Environmental Performance Index. Yale Center for Environmental Law & Policy, New Haven, CT (2020). http://epi.yale.edu
30. Wozniak, P.: Application of a computer to improve the results obtained in working with the SuperMemo method (1990)
31. Xie, Y., Zhang, C., Lai, Q.: China's rise as a major contributor to science and technology. Proc. Nat. Acad. Sci. **111**(26) (2014). https://doi.org/10.1073/pnas.1407709111
32. Xodabande, I., Atai, M.R.: Using mobile applications for self-directed learning of academic vocabulary among university students. Open Learn.: J. Open Distance e-Learn. 1–18 (2020)

Author Index

Printed in the United States
by Baker & Taylor Publisher Services